What Israel Means to Me

What Israel Means to Me

ALAN DERSHOWITZ

John Wiley & Sons, Inc.

For general information about our other products and services, please contact our Customer Care Department within the United States at (800) 762-2974, outside the United States at (317) 572-3993 or fax (317) 572-4002.

Wiley also publishes its books in a variety of electronic formats. Some content that appears in print may not be available in electronic books. For more information about Wiley products, visit our web site at www.wiley.com.

Library of Congress Cataloging-in-Publication Data:

What Israel means to me / [edited by] Alan Dershowitz.
　　p. cm.
　ISBN-13 978-0-471-67900-4 (cloth : alk. paper)
　ISBN-10 0-471-67900-3 (cloth : alk. paper)
　1. Israel.　2. Celebrities—Attitudes.　I. Dershowitz, Alan M.
　DS102.4.W45 2006
　956.9405—dc22

　　　　　　　　　　　　　　　　　　2005028991

Printed in the United States of America
10　9　8　7　6　5　4　3　2　1

*Dedicated to the memory of my dear friend
James Oliver Freedman (1935–2006), for whom Israel
and the Jewish people meant so much. He always pursued justice,
wisdom, and righteousness. He was a real mensch.*

Contents

Introduction by Alan Dershowitz, 1

Introduction

by Alan Dershowitz

I t's a tiny country, barely the size of New Jersey. Its population of six million ranks it among the least populated member states of the United Nations. Yet, with the possible exception of the United States —the world's only superpower—the Jewish nation of Israel provokes more passion, receives more media coverage, and engenders more criticism than any other country in the world today. It is fair to say that few people are neutral about Israel. Many love it with the uncritical exuberance of a doting mother toward her child. Many more hate it with what one observer has aptly characterized as an almost "eroticized" passion.

What explains the world's disproportionate love-hate attitude toward Israel?

In one sense, it should come as no surprise that tiny Israel, the Jew among nations, attracts such disproportionate attention from the world. After all, the Jewish people—both before and after the establishment of the state Israel—has always been the focus of disproportionate attention, mostly negative, despite the small number of Jews in the world. Public opinion polls constantly show that non-Jews overestimate—often by a factor of ten—the proportion of Jews in any given country. For example, a recent poll in the United States showed that most respondents believe that Jews constitute twenty percent of Americans, whereas actually we constitute a mere two percent. There's an old joke about a Nazi rally during the 1930s at which Hitler was ranting and raving about the Jews. He ended his speech with a rhetorical question: "Who has caused all of Germany's many problems?"

A member of the audience responded loudly, "The bicycle riders." Taken aback, Hitler asked, "Why the bicycle riders?" to which the man replied, "Why the Jews?"

Recently, in some of the parts of Europe that Hitler controlled during World War II, a public opinion poll asked which country in the world posed the greatest threat to peace today. Fifty-nine percent of the respondents answered: "Israel." Why Israel? Why the Jews? The question may be different, but the answer is not. Until recently, the following chant could be heard on American campuses at anti-Israel rallies (and also at anti-war rallies protesting the U.S. attack against Iraq): "Sharon and Hitler—it's the same, the only difference is the name." Israeli prime ministers are never compared to Mussolini, Pinochet, or even Stalin. It's always Hitler!

This kind of extreme reaction cannot be justified by reference to reality, any more than Hitler's blaming the Jews for all of Germany's woes could be justified by the facts. The explanation lies deep in the history and the psyche of the accusers. This is not to suggest that all criticism of Israel is necessarily motivated by anti-Semitism. It certainly is not. Rational, calibrated, and proportional criticism of specific Israeli policies and actions—such as those contained in some of the essays in this volume—is to be welcomed. Indeed, most Israelis are vociferous critics of at least some of their own government's policies and actions. But when Israel is condemned out of all proportion to its own fault and without comparable criticism of other nations and groups with much greater faults, then the Jewish nation is being subjected to the kind of double standard to which the Jewish people have been subjected throughout history. It is being treated as the Jew among nations.

I am passionate about my defense of Israel, despite my own criticism of many of its policies and actions, because I hate bigotry and double standards. I am passionate about Israel's right to exist, despite my own decision not to make my home in the Jewish state, because I remember the history of anti-Semitism and the Holocaust to which it led. All I ask is that critics of Israel apply a single standard of judgment to all the nations in the world. Judged by any reasonable standard, uniformly applied, Israel rises to the top of any list of nations facing comparable threats, both internal and external.

Yet there are those who would deny Israel's basic right to exist. The very idea of a Jewish nation is anathema to many who would never challenge the right of the many Muslim and Christian countries to exist. If any people in the world has demonstrated why they need a homeland, it is surely the Jewish people, who without a homeland— and an army to protect them—have been so vulnerable to persecution, discrimination, and even genocide. The nations of the world, even our own, shut the gates to Jews during their greatest time of need. Had there been a single nation willing to accept Jewish refugees from Nazi oppression, millions of lives might have been saved. If the Jewish nation of Israel had been in existence, so many lives might not have been snuffed out. Had the British and the Palestinians not closed the door to mandatory Palestine, Hitler might have been satisfied to rid Europe of Jews by emigration rather than by genocide.

A new and different kind of holocaust is not out of the question. With nearly six million Jews now concentrated in tiny Israel, a nuclear bomb could do in a minute what it took Hitler years to do. Had Saddam Hussein's nuclear capacity not been destroyed by the Israeli Air Force in 1981, the scuds he rained down on Tel Aviv during the first Gulf war could have been loaded with nuclear warheads. Today Iran is threatening Israel with nuclear devastation: "In 2001 Hashemi Rafsanjani, the former president of Iran, speculated that in a nuclear exchange with Israel his country might lose 15 million people, which would amount to a small 'sacrifice' from among the billion Muslims worldwide in exchange for the lives of 5 million Israeli Jews. He seemed pleased with his formulation." (Suzanne Fields, "Confronting the New Anti-Semitism," *Washington Times*, July 25, 2004.)

Several years later, Rafsanjani said the following to a crowd at a Friday prayer gathering in Tehran: "If a day comes when the world of Islam is duly equipped with the arms Israel has in possession, the strategy of colonialism would face a stalemate because application of an atomic bomb would not leave anything in Israel but the same thing would just produce damages in the Muslim world. ("Rafsanjani Says Muslims Should Use Weapons against Israel," *Iran Press Services*, accessible at www.iran-pressservice.com/articles_2001/dec_2001/rafsanjani_nuke_threats_141201.htm.)

Even more recently, Hassan Abbassi, a Revolutionary Guards intelligence theoretician teaching at Al-Hussein University, threatened to use Iran's missiles against Jewish and Christian targets: "Our missiles are now ready to strike at their civilization, and as soon as the instructions arrive from Leader [Ali Khamenei], we will launch our missiles at their cities and installations." (Steven Stalinsky, "Iranian Talk of an Attack on America," *New York Sun*, August 18, 2004; *Al-Sharq Al-Awsat* (London), May 28, 2004, MEMRI Special Dispatch Series No. 723.) And now, the president of Iran, Mahmoud Ahmadinejad, has vowed that Israel "must be wiped off the map" and has predicted that it will be "annihilated" with "one storm." (See Nazila Fathi, "Iran's New President Says Israel 'Must Be Wiped Off the Map,'" *New York Times*, October 27, 2005.) These threats must be taken seriously. So too must be the threat posed by Hamas, which despite entering the political fray—and winning—remains a terrorist organization committed to the replacement of Israel with a Muslim theocracy. The alliance between Hamas and Iran, solidified by significant financial support, poses an existential danger to Israel, especially if Iran succeeds in developing nuclear weapons.

Israel's survival as a Jewish democratic nation is among the great moral imperatives of the twenty-first century, for several important reasons: First, the Jewish future will unfold largely, though not exclusively, in Israel. Jewish culture, art, music, literature, and history will center in Israel as American and European Jews assimilate at increasing rates. At the beginning of the Zionist experiment, the great Jewish intellectual and cultural leader Achad Ha'am foresaw the Jewish state as the primary locus of the continuity of the Jewish civilization. This important civilization, as important to world history as any other, nearly came to an end in the 1940s. One important component of it, Yiddish culture, was in fact all but destroyed. On its ashes were built several new strains of Jewish culture, one of which was centered in Israel, where it is thriving.

Another reason Israel's survival is a moral imperative is that the Jewish nation, like the Jewish people, has always represented "the canary in the mine shaft." When the Jewish nation is victimized by bigotry, that bigotry is likely to be a symptom of a more pervasive problem of bigotry that will quickly spread to other people. That is why defending Israel against a double standard is a human rights issue of the greatest significance. That is why I will devote my life to assuring that the Jew among nations does not suffer a fate similar to that suffered by the Jews of Europe. And that is why those who feel as I and so many others do must encourage reasoned, nuanced, constructive, and comparative discussion—including criticism—of Israeli policies and actions. The diverse contributions to this volume are generally in this spirit. The contributors reflect a wide array of attitudes toward the Jewish state, but they all share a commitment to making Israel a better place. There is considerable disagreement about how to achieve that goal, but that should surprise no one familiar with the history of Zionism—and Judaism. We are an argumentative people, and Israel is an argumentative nation. The great writer Amos Oz was once asked what commodity is most prevalent in Israel, and he answered, "Good argument."

These varied reflections on Israel were written over the past three years at different points in Israel's rich history. To read these essays is to engage with their authors. I found myself agreeing with some of each contribution, but not agreeing with all of any. Some made me angry. Some made me sad. Some made me proud. All made me think. That is more than can be said about much of the current academic discussion, if the word "discussion" can even be used to characterize what is going on at most university campuses today with regard to Israel. The lack of nuance in campus discussions, both inside and outside the classroom, is deeply troubling. Name calling, racial epithets, bigoted analogies, and wild exaggerations have become the order of the day. It is understandable that strong feelings will produce strong words, but there is no excuse for the low level of intellectual discourse about the Middle East on most university campuses today.

The contributors to this book express strong feelings as well, and sometimes in strong words, but they are thoughtful words, with powerful arguments. This is not just a "feel-good" book about the Jewish state. It is a collection of deeply felt first-person accounts of a relationship between people and a distant land (at least for those who are not Israeli). The relationships are often complex and multifaceted. Emotions clash with ideologies. Abstract theory clashes with facts on the ground. Hope clashes with despair. But the argument goes on, as does the nation about which so much passion is felt and expressed.

What Israel means to so many is that the arguments will endure forever, along with the imperfect Jewish state of Israel. So read these essays and arguments, with a critical eye. Then ask yourself: What does Israel mean to me? (If the spirit moves you, e-mail a brief response to dersh@law.harvard.edu. We will consider including some in the paperback edition of *What Israel Means to Me*.)

Yosef I. Abramowitz

Yosef I. Abramowitz is the CEO and executive editor of Jewish Family & Life! *an online publisher of Jewish content. He was the recipient of the 2004 Covenant Award, which is given to outstanding Jewish educators.*

With the eyes, judgment, and weight of the world disproportionately focused on a sliver of a country along the eastern Mediterranean, history itself hangs in the balance. Not only the history of the Third Jewish Commonwealth, but of the nations and peoples who point their accusing fingers at Israel without realizing they are peering into a powerful mirror.

Israel is a reminder and symbol of the uncomfortable indispensability of the Jew to history and to the march of human progress. The group-think of intolerant nations, tyrants, cultures, and religions stagnates human progress, for it attempts to homogenize thought itself in the image of the prevailing power. Empires may be built on enforced fictions, but they are never sustained by them.

For four millennia, a dozen great empires across different continents have had one common denominator: hatred of the Jew. The Jew, that is, who would not conform, would not affirm the fiction of ultimate power and authority or divinity to a mere human, even one with many swords and vassals. Israel, in her unwillingness to conform to the desires and undemocratic norms of a billion Muslims in the neighborhood, is yet another Jew in the thorn of a civilization that has not realized the human progress it could have with a trillion petrodollars over fifty-seven years.

If necessity is the mother of invention, then the Jew is the master of innovation. Innovation gushes forward from the uncomfortable margins, from the dissonance of straddling a boundary, from the bridging of worlds and disciplines, from the sheer necessity to stay alive amid challenges and hostilities. All those Nobel Prizes didn't come about necessarily by inherited smarts but by legacies of innovative thinking precisely as a direct consequence of the unconventional social and historical status of the Jew. Thomas Friedman's updated observation of this is that tiny Israel is second only to the United States in new patent registrations.

And so the Jewish state, as the political manifestation of Jewish dreams, is both an imperfect yet bold example of Jewish innovation and an exception. With few natural resources, Israel survives on her brains and the exportable innovations of her people. Caught in the triangle of the Middle East, Europe, and Africa, the narrow land bridge hugging a small coast has also experienced concentrated trading in not just goods but ideas. The burden, the responsibility, and the privilege of being the womb of theology for three great religions is unprecedented. And to host the world headquarters of the peace-loving Bahaiis is not only a historical footnote, but a historic validation.

Tolerant of her own minorities, although not always as fair as she should be, Israel, with immigrants from 170 lands, is nearly as multicultural as the United Nations, yet is only a fraction as hypocritical—and therefore is also a target. For without the disproportional accusations against her, the condemnation of the human condition by Israel's own existence and example would be too overbearing for much of the world. Every time the Jewish state affirms extraordinary values on the international stage, her detractors could not be more infuriated. Thus the airlift of Ethiopian Jews out of famine and civil war, out of the third world and into the first, out of the powerless ancient Jewish history and into powerful modern Jewish history, was vilified.

What Israel means to me is what the idea of the Jew means to history: outcast yet respected, hated and loved, rejected and needed, immoral and moral, hopeless yet hopeful, and yes, ultimately, eternal. Like the God most Jews profess to doubt, thereby only affirming our legacy of wrestling with Ultimate Ideas, Israel is the Jewish state known not for the civility of her political and social culture. Instead, she is known for her impolite boisterousness that is filled with passion, often overflowing, in the pressure cooker of international hostility and enemies who have reintroduced through suicide bombers child sacrifice back and backward into history, to the silent approval of billions and the mild disapproval among so-called civilized nations.

Stiff-necked, yes. Proud, yes. Purposeful, yes. Imperfect, certainly. Consistent with the role of the Jew in history, absolutely. Israel, with her precarious and complicated position in the world, is proof positive that the world is so much still in need of healing. A world in which Jewish blood is still cheaper than other blood is a world in which the ultimate challenge and gift of the Jews—the notion that each person is created in God's image with infinite worth—has not yet been fully accepted, for Jews and therefore for other religious and other minorities to whom history—meaning dominant powers—has not been kind. And a world in which a modern blood libel—the grotesque distortion of Jenin—is broadcast on the BBC and accepted quickly as truth is a world in which truth itself is in question, undermining the sense of security for Jews and other religious groups and minorities to whom history—meaning dominant doctrines and prejudices—has not been kind.

For what we see in the twilight zone of distorted morality and reality when it comes to judging the Jewish state—the hypocrisy and lack of support and double standards and imbalanced reporting and turning-the-other-cheekness to enemies of life and especially of Jewish life—is a tacit nod to a secret desire to have a morally simplistic world. A morally simplistic world is the opposite of a moral world; fundamentalist-style extreme distinctions breed intolerance and violence, and they devalue life. Rather, nonsimplistic morality affirms the reality of subtle, graded, shaded decision making on which all moral individual, communal, national, and global life is based, at least from a Jew's perspective. In the day-to-day security threats, there is probably no other democracy worldwide that wrestles, even imperfectly, with these fine distinctions on a daily basis. A world of simplistic so-called morality is a world in which the Jew is not welcome or safe.

So Israel—as the Jewish state, as the national surrogate for the largely unwilling representatives of the idea of an ethical God, the unrelenting culture of dissent, and the acknowledgment that the positive nexus of values, family, and community can create modern miracles, even against international will—is too powerful a vessel and symbol to coexist with the world and civilization as it is.

For Israel to coexist peacefully in civilization means that mutual responsibility and mutual accountability must be dominant values on the international stage. And that the privileged nations and peoples truly live up to both the horrible scale of hunger and human suffering there is worldwide, in our day, at precisely the time when there are resources and solutions to the most serious threats to humanity. Judaism is about mutual responsibility, in this life and at this time, and the necessary actions that are needed to make miracles happen. Israel, as a collective accomplishment and public face of the Jewish people worldwide, continues to innovate, to lead research in so many arenas of human progress, to welcome in people from the four corners of the earth, to remain a democracy amid persistent military and terror threats, to argue about individual rights, and to publicly wrestle when its own citizen-soldiers and government miss their mark.

Humanity is not living up to our potential or responsibility in the face of the lack of systemic, collective miracles on a planet heavy with over six billion souls. Instead of facing up to this reality, instead of looking into that uncomfortable mirror, Israel is said to be by a majority of Europeans the main obstacle to world peace and by a majority of Muslims to have masterminded the September 11 attacks against the United States.

David Adler

David Adler is an award-winning author of children's books. He has written several books dealing with the Holocaust, including the acclaimed biography of Anne Frank for children, A Picture Book of Anne Frank, *as well as* We Remember the Holocaust *and* One Yellow Daffodil.

I made my first visit to Israel during the summer of 1971, a time of transition for me. In April, I was told my first book, *A Little at a Time*, would be published by Random House. In May, I handed in my graduate thesis, the end for me of decades as a student. In June, I completed another year of teaching math in a tough New York City school, and in July and August, I would take an eight-week trip to Europe and Israel with just a round-trip ticket to Frankfurt on a U.S. Army charter, plans to visit my brother in Germany and Israel, and the intention to take lots of photographs, not of sites but of people, because I felt they would define the character of the places I saw.

My first stop, Frankfurt, has a special significance for me and my family. My mother and grandparents were born there. In the mid-1920s they moved to a suburb of Vienna, and on March 13, 1938—the day German soldiers marched into Austria—they had an overnight guest, a Jewish friend from Munich. The next day my grandfather was off on a business trip and the guest drove him and my uncle to the train station, about ten miles away. There they were, three Jews in a car with German plates, and all along the way their neighbors assumed they were officials of the Anschluss and welcomed them with the Nazi salute, a sad harbinger. Soon, swastikas were everywhere, and my grandparents knew it was time to get out. There were still places to go, still countries that would accept Jewish refugees. Mom and her family went to Holland, then England, Mexico, and the United States.

Once here, Mom met and married my dad, a Baltimore native with roots in Germany and Lithuania. I am the second of their six children, all of us raised in the shadow of the Holocaust, surrounded by people with numbers on their arms and schooled with friends without grandparents, uncles, or aunts. We were trained, before buying any manufactured item, to look first where it was made and to shun anything made in Germany.

In spring 1971, my brother Eddie was about to take our boycott one extreme step further. After college, he volunteered for service in the U.S. Army to fulfill an obligation he felt he owed our country. When he finished basic training in Texas, he was informed he was being sent to Landstuhl, Germany. "I won't go," he told Dad. "I'll ask instead to go to Vietnam." Dad dissuaded him. He told Eddie that just as he felt it was his duty to serve in the U.S. military, it was his duty to serve where the army sent him.

Part of the reason I was traveling that summer was to visit Eddie. I also hoped to see the world.

In early July I landed in Frankfurt, took a train to Kaiserslautern, and from there to Landstuhl. I came with food from home—breads, cakes, frozen kosher chickens, and a salami. There were no cabs at the small train station, so I struggled with my suitcase, shifting it from one shoulder to the other, past German butcher shops, one with a dead pig hanging in the window, up the steep hill to my brother's quarters. That dead pig had a message for me. I didn't belong there, and neither did Eddie.

From Landstuhl, a few days later, I went south to Munich, where I purchased a small map of Europe and planned my travels: train rides to Belgrade and Athens, from there a flight to Israel and a visit with my brother Nathan, who was serving in Sherut L'Am, an Israeli national service program for the poor, then to Paris, Amsterdam, Landstuhl again, and then Frankfurt for my return. While I was still in the train station, I went to the information counter and asked how to get to Dachau, a city just northwest of Munich and the name of the first Nazi concentration camp where one of my mother's uncles had been briefly interned. "Why do you want to go there?" the woman behind the counter asked. When I told her I planned to see what was left of the camp, she said, "Don't bother. There's nothing there, just a memorial."

Nonetheless, the next morning, I went and felt rooted there, unable, or at the very least, unwilling, to leave until late in the afternoon. Among the few visitors that day was a large group of Catholic nuns in their habits and several elderly couples. I went to the small museum, stepped into the one remaining barracks with the number 2831 to the left of the door, and then sat in the grass. I took out my steel pen and sketch pad and tried to draw what I saw and felt.

In Belgrade later that week, I latched onto two other young Americans and together we searched for a place to stay. In the first several hotels we went to, the lobbies were empty, but the rooms, we were told, were all taken. That clearly was not true. Backpack-toting Americans were just not wanted. The Yugoslavian capital was no tourist mecca then, proved by the place we did find, a three-story hotel with large rooms and high ceilings and no other guests.

I was comfortable in Athens and easily lost myself among the many young tourists. But it was at my next stop, Tel Aviv, that I felt welcome and wanted, part of one big extended family. An Egged bus ride soon after I arrived convinced me the feeling was justified. A passenger asked the driver to let her off midway between two scheduled stops. In New York, where I live, such a request would have been either ignored or refused, and not too politely. Instead, the driver asked why she wanted to get off there, and she told him her friend lived on that block. "Which house? Who is it? Maybe I know her," the driver said. The woman answered all his questions, and although he didn't know her friend, he made the unscheduled stop.

I traveled north to Kiryat Shmone and stayed with Nathan there for a few days, then we went together to Jerusalem, to a small family-run hotel. All the rooms were taken, so the owner made a few calls, and when she didn't find a place for us, said, "You'll sleep here." By "here" she meant right there, on a couch in the lobby, a real contrast to my experience in Belgrade. We stayed for two nights. I didn't even know the name of the hotel keeper. Nonetheless, I felt like a visiting relative.

At the Kotel, the Western Wall, a black-coated, bearded man invited me to come home with him for dinner with his family, maybe even for Shabbat. I declined, but he wasn't easily put off; he wrote his name and telephone number on a slip of paper, gave it to me, and told me to call if I changed my mind. I looked at it and was flabbergasted. His name was mine—David Adler. I pulled out my passport and showed it to him, but he wasn't impressed. He didn't care what my name was. He just wanted me to come to dinner.

On my trip that took me to Germany, Yugoslavia, Greece, Israel, France, Holland, back to Germany again, and then home, I took hundreds of photographs of people I met, and I had been right— the people did seem to define the character of the places I visited. When I got home, I looked at the pictures, and those from Israel were different from the others. I felt a real connection to them. The people of Israel felt to me like part of one big family—my family.

Shulamit Aloni

Shulamit Aloni is the founder of the Civil Rights Movement in Israel (Ratz) and was a member of the Knesset, the parliament of Israel, for over twenty years.

My initial, spontaneous, reply is—home. Home in the broadest sense of the term.

The poet Shaul Tchernichovsky wrote, "Man is nothing but the shape of his native landscape." Here in Israel this "shape" encompasses the stories and legends from the old days, and it certainly involves the Hebrew language in its various forms and, of course, the Bible. These are factors that shaped the generation that grew up in Eretz Israel, Mandatory Palestine, before the state of Israel came into being. This was a generation that felt itself free, willing, and able to establish a Jewish state here, a model state, in the spirit of the Zionism advocated and espoused by Herzl, Weizmann, Nordau, A. D. Gordon, and others; a country where the people would return to its land, its roots, to actually work the land; a country that would be based on a bedrock of freedom, justice, and peace in the spirit of the prophets of Israel.

As youngsters we literally walked the length and breadth of the country, clutching both a Bible and a guide to plants. This was not an empty country—there were Arabs living here, it was ruled by the British Mandatory authorities; we knew that things would likely not be easy, and we prepared ourselves and trained for a struggle, including, if need be, an armed struggle when the time came. As things turned out, what was required was even more than we had imagined. But mostly we trained ourselves for work, for building up the country, for enlightened education, science, immigrant absorption—all along the line of Jeremiah's promise to Rachel that her children would "return to their own borders."

We were lucky that in those days publishers were big-hearted, broad-minded, and affluent enough to make a point of translating works of world literature. In the early 1930s, when there were fewer than 300,000 Jews in the country, and those who knew Hebrew were in the minority, Hebrew translations of Spinoza and Descartes, Plato and Aristotle, Rousseau and Mill, in addition to many others, were published, as well as works of fiction by the best Russian, French, and English writers and more. We enjoyed theater, orchestras, and the burgeoning Hebrew literature, and with it Hebrew-language poetry, a Hebrew-language press, high schools, and a university.

Even before a state came into being, we felt ourselves to be native, sovereign beings, sure of ourselves building our homeland, developing our own culture and open to the atmosphere coming to us from different peoples' cultures. We knew the Bible; archeology was an illustrious and much admired professional field. Nor were we afraid to know about Christianity. At the time, one of the things that was taught was Jesus's Sermon on the Mount from the New Testament (today no more). The self-assurance of those who were their own masters in their own country enabled broad-mindedness to flourish and the breezes of culture and science to waft in from the outside world.

As children, thanks to Hayim Nahman Bialik's astuteness and wisdom, we were able to appreciate both the biblical tales and Sefer ha-Aggada, the legends from the Talmud and Midrash.

I am of course talking about the "incubator" in which I grew up, about the way things were for us, for those of us who were educated at the educational institutions for the workers' children in the Hebrew general schools, and youth institutions such as Mikve Israel, Kadoorie, Ben Shemen, Nahalal, Gymnasia Herzliya, the high schools in Jerusalem, and others. These were young people who from an early age belonged to the Zionist youth movements in working Palestine with its labor values, and who when they grew up went to the kibbutzim for training and enlisted in the Haganah at large and the Palmach.

My parents, who were from Poland and whose ancestors were

rabbis, did not cast off their "Jewishness." They were socialist Zionists, atheists; nevertheless Shabbat was Shabbat and the festivals were the festivals and the *zmirot* were *zmirot*, and I am very familiar from home with the entire repertoire known as "Yiddishkeit."

Shabbat and the Jewish festivals have always, right up to the present time, set the rhythm of our lives. Every preschooler can tell the story of each holiday and knows its songs and its heroes. Here the festivals relate to the seasons of the year, to the festivals of those who work the land: sowing, planting, reaping on Pesach, the first fruits on Shavuot, the festival of the giving of the Torah, and bringing in the harvest at Sukkot.

The combination of the historical story with a renewed agricultural way of life has enriched the festivals, making them community and not just family events. The days of awe come, and with them, the autumn. And as the holidays of the year come to an end, with the completion of bringing in the harvest and with Simchat Torah behind us, there comes the anticipation of rain. And by this time, even someone who does not know the prayer will be praying for rain. We are not exactly blessed with rivers and springs; everyone knows that the water that gives life will come from the rain that falls from the heavens and from the dew that gathers on the earth.

Every single boy and girl in Eretz Israel genuinely worries about the level of the Sea of Galilee, whether it is rising or, worryingly, dropping. All of this and more is what makes one's home, is what shaped the pattern of the landscape of one's homeland, its culture, its language, its roots, and its crops. But today this homeland has a state and a society and a government and an army and security services.

Since the War of Independence and the absorption of the vast numbers of immigrants from all four corners of the globe, and especially of the refugees from ravaged Europe, who came bearing with them their unimaginable burdens of suffering and memories—since then we have anticipated and hoped for the realization of our great dream of building a humanistic model, an exemplary society, and more than fifty-seven years have passed. Much has been done and achieved, especially in the early years, but on the other hand much has gone wrong since we became a regional power, and in particular since our major conquest in the 1967 Six-Day War and the years since then.

In September 2004, a Palmach veterans reunion took place at the Mann Auditorium in Tel Aviv. The biggest auditorium in the whole of Israel was absolutely packed, and it was literally standing-room only. This really special get-together, the first large-scale gathering since Yitzhak Rabin's assassination, became a stirring event in which joy and pain were inextricably mingled.

We experienced intense longings, not only for our youth but in particular for the early days of the country, of the state in the making and the state in its infancy—intense longings for what we might have had here today, but do not have.

At the time of the Exodus, when the Children of Israel left Egypt, they were granted freedom but still remained a rabble, a mixed multitude. Slavery had not yet left them. Only after they received a constitution, after the granting of the Torah at Mount Sinai, were they told: "This day you have become a people." (Deuteronomy 27:9)

We knew that we would be absorbing unfortunate people from 102 different countries, with disparate cultures and customs, coming here to their "homeland" after two thousand years of exile, but we failed to prepare a constitution, a common ethical and legal code for all, laying down modes of governance and law, stipulating human rights, a code governing the relations between the citizen and the state and society, and in particular the citizen's responsibility to his country or state. To this day we do not have a constitution; everything is in a constant state of flux, changing in accordance with the needs of the fluctuating coalitions of political parties that care about their own people and their own needs. Democracy here is halt and lame. There is no equality of rights for all of the country's citizens, no equality for women. The population is divided into a dozen religious congregations under the jurisdiction of their clergy from birth to death; when it comes to the laws governing personal status, marriage, and divorce, we have no civil marriage, in order to keep the purity of the Jewish peoplehood.

For about thirty-eight years we have ruled over another people with an iron hand—taking possession of their land, mercilessly uprooting orchards, vineyards, and olive groves; needlessly and maliciously destroying houses and roads; and turning every single town and village into a detention camp. In other words, we destroyed their entire infrastructure. In the occupied territories there are special new roads for the Jewish settlers only, and any Palestinian who drives on such a road has his car confiscated.

It is worth making the point—a regrettable one—that with the notable exception of Levi Eshkol's term of office as prime minister, the state of Israel's strategy has been one of force and of increasingly making a cult out of the Israel Defense Forces; perhaps because the military is the only element that unites the entire people, or perhaps because of the Jewish fear complex. Whatever the reason, this strategy utterly blocks any possibility of taking advantage of any opportunity for building peace that might present itself. To my knowledge, as someone who was a parliamentarian for thirty years and a member of Rabin's cabinet in 1974 and the Rabin-Peres cabinet from 1992 to 1996, there have been such opportunities, which were rejected. And the worst thing of all is that in recent years, all dialogue between us and the Palestinians has ground to a complete halt. After two thousand years the Jews have power, we have the strongest military in the Middle East and one of the strongest in the world, and we are squandering it, acting aggressively, provocatively, in a confrontational way, and humiliating the population, both individuals and the leadership. We are arrogant and self-important, and we are broadening the circle of killing and fear. It must be borne in mind that the Palestinians are not al-Qaida, and Arafat was not Bin Laden. They want a state of their own, too, and self-determination. The terror wreaked by suicide bombers is dreadful and inconceivable, which is why it is so frightening, but it is less dreadful than one-ton bombs being dropped by fighter aircraft onto major concentrations of population. Everyone knows that despair leads to desperate actions, and that far from making people quit, the looting of land and humiliation arouse feelings of revenge. And this is what happens when, for each Israeli who is killed, five and more Palestinians are killed, and they, too, include women and children and old people and handicapped people—not to mention the destruction of houses, industrial plants, vineyards, orchards, and other sources of livelihood.

The strategists of force and the occupation scare the Israeli people by means of the threat that the Palestinians are bent on destroying us, on throwing us into the sea. It is an easy thing to awaken Jewish paranoia and arouse fear and hatred in the midst of a people that lives with the feeling of being history's eternal victim. The upshot is that we are "the ultimate victim" even when we are "victimizing" others. How did Golda Meir put it?—"I'm not willing to forgive them for forcing us to kill them." Here again we are the victims.

She also said that there were no Palestinian people because she too had once been a Palestinian. She also had a passport to the effect. Wonderful. I also have a Palestinian identity document from the British Mandate, but today I am a sovereign Israeli—and what are they, the others living under our humiliating occupation?

Yet it is worthwhile thinking rationally for a moment: we have peace with Egypt and we have peace with Jordan, and Syria and Lebanon are willing to make peace and do not pose a threat to Israel, and Iraq is no longer a threat (if it ever was one), and Iran is a problem for the entire world, and we have the strongest army in the region and deterrent nonconventional arms and an alliance with the strongest country in the world, and the Palestinians have nothing of all of this, so even if we were to assume that they want to throw us into the sea, would they be able to do so? But the brainwashing has succeeded.

The enormous wall, over 190 kilometers (118 miles) long, that is being erected at great expense and mainly on Palestinian land, cutting people off from their land and children from their schools, is intended to separate them from us while basically it is no barrier to hatred, nor to violence. All of this is accompanied by ever-growing "security" budgets, as more and more capital is channeled to the settlers as first priority, neglecting the developing townships in the Negev and the Galilee; and we have changed from a welfare state—a state whose guiding principle was social solidarity—to a brutal, greedy, capitalist society, with one of the biggest gaps in the world between rich and poor—and this in a country most of whose inhabitants are first- and second-generation immigrants who came here without the language, without a profession, and without property.

And here we have another obstacle, which has to deal with religious coercion. Ariel Sharon, the Shinui Party, as well as the Labor Party—all of them pretend to be secular humanist—have become involved in matters of conversion, which is a condition for the granting of full civil rights to those who immigrated under the Law of Return with their family members and who are not halachically Jewish.

In 1492, Isabella and Ferdinand united Spain and ruled that anyone who wished to be Spanish had to be or become Catholic; if not, they would be expelled. Today, over five hundred years later, the Jews in a sovereign, democratic Israel would appear to be doing the same to others—to those who came here to be with us, and for whose coming we prayed.

In those distant days when the Jewish people were living in its land, our rabbis ruled that where a family has assimilated, then it is assimilated, and no inquiries are to be made into it, and no demands are to be made, and all families are "kosher" in the long run and should be accepted in the community without conditions. Nowadays the children of immigrants go to the Hebrew schools, mingling with our children as they assimilate into Israeli lifestyles and culture without the need to convert and adopt a religious lifestyle, but the coalition regime, including the secular people, is giving in to the extreme Orthodox because they want to establish with them their government.

It would appear that in the state of Israel it is not culture that sets the tone, or citizenship, but biology—being born to a Jewish mother— since converting is like being born again, and so conversion is required if the mother is not the daughter of a Jewish mother, and hence the individual's rights are invalidated as a result of this religious coercion that is brought to bear on all members of the family. (Isn't that racism?)

For us today (being honest) it is difficult to talk about "Jewish ethics," about Jewish values of justice and the law, not only because they have been trampled underfoot, but because fewer and fewer citizens of Israel know what democracy and human rights mean. Superstitions, the blatant use of incantations by preachers, pilgrimages to the graves of "saints" (most of which are in fact the graves of Arab sheikhs)—such widespread practices have been turned into a commodity that is erroneously identified and equated with the Jewish religion and tradition.

Yet, despite all of this, I believe that we will manage to shake off these bad things and rid ourselves of these wrongs, that we will stop admiring force and will learn to achieve reconciliation as well. I believe that we will return to the values of freedom, justice, and peace, and that one day in the hopefully not too distant future we will have peace and an enlightened constitution.

In our turbulent history, the Jewish people have experienced many vicissitudes. We have a massive survival instinct, and here in Israel of all places, as a sovereign people in our land, we will certainly not allow the twilight to creep over us. We must hope that the day will come soon when Jerusalem will again become Isaiah's "faithful city," a city ruled by justice. At the same time, we not only are allowed to but owe it to ourselves to become angry at the situation. We must reproclaim publicly our Declaration of Independence, which was an outstanding, seminal document embodying values of enlightenment and democracy. And those who are using the promise that was given Abraham, our forefather, to justify thinking that we are better than others, that we are the chosen people and that greater Israel was given to us and so we have the right to take it by force from the Arabs, should read Genesis 18 again, because Abraham was chosen by his God in order to teach his children and his household after him to do righteousness and justice. In the same chapter, we also read how Abraham opposes divine collective punishment in the case of Sodom and Gomorrah: "Shall not the Judge of all the earth do justly?" and "Wilt Thou indeed sweep away the righteous with the wicked?" And at the same time one should not forget that the Arabs, descended from Ishmael, are also Abraham's children.

We must now act fairly and justly, put an end to collective punishment, refrain from coveting that which is not ours, and remember the words of Hillel the sage: "That which is hateful to you, do not do to your neighbor. That is the whole Torah; the rest is commentary."

A ray of hope for a moral revolution, a change in values, is coming from the large numbers of young people who loathe the occupation, who are revolted by racism, by the hatred of the other, by the acts of humiliation and looting, and by the ignominy and the greed. A fresh and refreshing new wind is beginning to blow, a promising, youthful wind. Not everybody can feel it, and some of those who do are trying to stifle it, to stifle voices so as to prevent them from perturbing the fanatics. Neither the administrative detentions nor the isolating of those who are "breaking the silence" and demanding righteousness, ethics, and integrity, nor arbitrary arrests and imprisonment, can stifle and suppress the "new spirit of the time."

But we feel that the era is ripe for a new zeitgeist—that spirit or mood that can change things and always comes up from the grassroots, from the hands-on activists, from those bordering on the subversive, and yet it infiltrates the mainstream, with more and more people coming to join those who act, who talk, who get together with ever more like-minded individuals, until it becomes all-conquering, common knowledge.

I genuinely believe this is what must happen. I do not wish to leave this world with the feeling that the entire Zionist revolution, all our efforts to gain sovereignty, all my friends and comrades and schoolmates who were killed or wounded and fought for Israel sacrificed themselves for the existence of a violent, occupying, and rapacious state. It's just not fair.

Ben-Gurion spoke of a "treasured people," and the treasure is ethics, knowledge, culture, art, science, literature, openness, and listening to and respecting every single person, man, woman, and child as freeborn human beings, created in the image of God, regardless of their faith, race, religion, and ethnic origins. Change must come about, and what must come, will come.

Robert Alter

*Robert Alter, Ph.D., is a professor of Hebrew and comparative litera-
ture at the University of California, Berkeley. He is the recipient of the
Scholarship Award for Social and Cultural Studies of the National
Foundation for Jewish Culture and has written prizewinning volumes
on literary aspects of the Bible and published widely on the modern
European and American novel and modern Hebrew literature.*

This is, of course, a grim moment for the state of Israel. The
second intifada continues with no end in sight. A substantial
portion of the Palestinian population seems to enthusiastically endorse
the slaughter of Israeli citizens by suicide bombers and to reject any
compromise that would allow the continued existence of a Jewish
state in the Middle East. The countermeasures that the present Israeli
government has taken to suppress terrorism at best put a temporary lid
on it and often appear to provoke further terrorism, while the suffering inflicted on the Palestinian population, whether as a matter of
policy or through "collateral damage" while striking against terrorists,
has gravely compromised Israel in the court of world opinion.

These dire circumstances have led many intellectuals in the West
(and at least a few on the left within Israel itself) to a dismaying readi-
ness to throw out the baby with the bathwater. The fact of the matter
is that you don't have babies without dirty bathwater—especially in
the case of those egregiously unmanageable babies, nation-states.
England, France, and the United States (to mention three countries
where critics of Israel have been especially vocal) have much to answer
for morally in their history as well as in their recent behavior, but
nobody is calling for their abolition as states, and despite a few
extremist critics of George W. Bush, there is no widespread impulse to
equate any of these countries with Nazi Germany. The most shame-

fully hate-driven denials of the legitimacy of the state of Israel are scarcely worth debating, even if they appear in supposedly respectable journals such as the *London Review of Books*. It is more disturbing when an intelligent, otherwise reasonable writer like Tony Judt, himself once a Zionist, proposes in the *New York Review of Books* that Zionism is a retrograde nationalist development in an age when national divisions are disappearing (in what world is this usually well-informed historian living?), and that the only sane solution to the present conflict is to create a binational secular democratic state in all of the territory designated Palestine. This modest proposal, which got no traction when it was first put forth by well-meaning Zionists in the 1930s, of course flatly ignores the fact that under this solution the Jews of Israel (those, that is, who would not immediately flee) would be a minority in an Arab state, at best tolerated, in all likelihood persecuted; that there are no truly democratic states, or secular ones, in the Arab world; and that militant Islamist elements have been increasingly dominant among the prospective Palestinian citizens of this proposed binational state.

Zionism, as is plain to see, is an imperfect solution to the problem of Jewish collective existence, but it is also a necessary one, and the alternatives do not look very good. Historically, there have been two general rationales for the creation of a Jewish state, and even in the present troubled circumstances, they both remain perfectly valid. One rationale is essentially negative: in a world where the status and the physical safety of Jewish minorities in the Diaspora can never be absolutely assured, the Jews require one place of refuge on the face of the earth that can offer the protection of Jewish sovereignty. I am not inclined to knee-jerk evocations of the hobgoblin of anti-Semitism, but it would be Pollyannish not to recognize that there has been a resurgence of it in supposedly enlightened European countries that would scarcely have been imaginable ten or fifteen years ago, and the hostility toward Israel is often an excuse rather than the cause for anti-Semitic feelings and acts. In France, for example, which has the largest Jewish population outside the United States and Israel, emigration to Israel has doubled over the past year (though the absolute numbers remain small). The plain reason is that the Jews of France are beginning to see themselves as an endangered minority, and it is a very good thing that those who feel this way have a Jewish state to which they can go.

The positive rationale for the Jewish state, which I would prefer to emphasize, is that it engages Jewish collective existence in a new and productive relationship with history. The Jews baffle definition because through two millennia in the Diaspora they were both a religion and a people with a national culture. In the sweeping renegotiation of the terms of Jewish existence that has been going on for the past two centuries or more, many have opted to continue to be Jews without being religionists and have found varying ways to do this (Yiddishism, Bundism, and so forth). The Hebrew-speaking community of Jews in the land of Israel, which began a few decades before the state, of course includes religious elements of various stripes—in uneasy and at times highly problematic coexistence with the secular realm—but it constitutes a national culture, not an intrinsically religious one. It has sustained a vibrant literature in the Hebrew language (arguably, the greatest since biblical times); an outpouring of creativity in the other arts, from architecture and painting to theater, music, and dance; vigorous historical research; social thought and analysis; pathbreaking scientific inquiry; and much more.

Critics of the Jewish state sometimes argue that it amounts to a form of self-ghettoization, the Zionists hunkering down behind the walls of a benighted nationalism. Anyone who knows Israeli culture and society intimately will recognize that virtually the opposite is the case. Israel, with all its dilemmas vis-à-vis the Arabs, and with all its internal divisions along religious and ethnic faultlines, is a place where it is comfortable to be a Jew—even in some respects to be a Jew unreflectively—in a Jewish majority culture that participates, as a matter of course, in the larger global culture and its universal values and concerns.

The intensity of traditional Jewish intellectual culture perpetuates itself here, as does the Jewish propensity for vociferous debate. And the grand Zionist project of ingathering of exiles has produced a multiethnic, multifaceted society that makes the sundry Jewish societies of the historical Diaspora look limited and monolithic by comparison. The various groups, of course, sometimes exclude one another, despise one another, exploit one another, as you would expect, but the dynamic of the ensemble holds considerable promise. The Jewish people, which like other peoples needs a land, a language, and national institutions in order to fully realize its existence, is not an ideological construct, as some have claimed, but a long-flickering collective half-life that in Israel has been restored to full life. The actions and policies of the Jewish state, just like those of any other state, are of course subject to criticism, but the attempt of purportedly progressive intellectuals to deny the renewed life of the people should be categorically rejected on both moral and pragmatic grounds.

Christina Applegate and
Nancy Priddy

Christina Applegate is a film, television, and stage actress most known
for her role as Kelly Bundy in the television sitcom Married . . . With
Children. Her mother, Nancy Priddy, is a poet, singer, and songwriter.

In 1996, my mother, Nancy Priddy, and I, along with David
Faustino, my friend and costar of *Married . . . With Children*, and his
mother were guests of the Israeli government. The time there was
much too short, and my mother and I made arrangements to return
for the Y2K millennium celebrations. Unfortunately, my schedule did
not permit me to proceed. My mother, however, and two of our best
friends fulfilled our dream of being at the Western Wall on the stroke
of midnight that New Year's Eve.

On September 9, 2001, my mother, who is a poet and singer-
songwriter, felt compelled to write a poem addressed to this beautiful
land and its people. With your permission, I would like her eloquent
and heartfelt words to also speak for me.

A Postcard from an American Tourist

When I mistily recall,
The coolness of the stone wall . . .
Pressed against my forehead
In that millennium Midnight hour . . .
Savoring the spirit and the Power . . .
The blessed Western Wailing Wall,
    I can only weep,
    I can only weep.

When I still feel the laughter and stinging in my eyes,
From the multitude of tries,
To rinse away the mud,
From head to thighs,
With that strange tingling water,
At the Dead Sea,
    I can only weep,
    I can only weep.

And, sweet sweet Jerusalem,
You are a better mousetrap.
The world would beat a path through your gates,
Your holy winding streets . . .
Sensing God,
Where feet of Prophets and Saints have trod . . .
Those blessed tear-stained streets . . .
    I can only weep,
    I can only weep.

When I touch the gray silver and red threads . . .
Of the sweater,
I so readily purchased at that heady open market,
From the soft-faced lady
Outside that church in Nazareth . . .
    I can only weep,
    I can only weep.

Or taste the wine,
From those Israeli glass goblets
Bargained from the sweet smiling, gently mellow,
Soft-spoken Palestinian fellow . . .
In Jericho. . . . oh, dear friends,
    I can only weep.

Remembering the simple chain link . . .
"Good Fence" at the Lebanese border . . .
And good-naturedly chiding my Israeli guide . . .
(not a small order)
To let me just ask the man in the booth,
"Hey, I'm an American,
I can go inside.

Tell me the truth,
I can go past the gate . . . can't I?
C'mon . . . I can go through?!"

Or chasing like children
Through the then defunct Syrian trenches . . .
The Golan Heights . . .
A mysterious playground of obsolete defenses,
For enraptured childlike visitor's playful curious senses,
    I can only weep.

The photo taken of that gorgeous blue-eyed . . .
Policeman in Bethlehem,
Who so reluctantly . . . embarrassedly . . .
Obliged me . . .
And posed for my disposable Kodak
As I so shamelessly flirted back.

Ah, the bustling Bethlehem!
Amidst its rock concert like atmosphere,
That carnival day . . .
The Y2K
New Year's festivities . . . that night . . .
That festive year . . .
    I could only cheer!
    Now I can only weep.

Dear Palestinian Israel,
Israeli Palestine . . .
Grounds keepers,
Guardians,
Of those sacred hills and pathways,
Those caves and stones,
Those gardens with their ancient olive trees . . .
You alone . . .
A land so full of wisdom and lore,
Of all that's come before . . .
The cradle of our civilization
    Once more . . .

How I long to walk with you,
Through those twisting alleyways,
Filled with the scents of incense and baklava
How I long to laugh with you all again . . .
From atop your camels and your Masada
    Your Roman Aqueduct
    At the sunset on the beach
    But I can only reach out . . . reach out . . .
    And weep.

Giggling teenagers,
In soldiers uniforms.
Sporting rifles that seemed like awkward props,
For some high school play,

A field trip to your Yad Vashem . . . that day,
Exhaling grateful sighs
That you are all home,
You are all safe . . .
As the whole world cries!

How I miss you!
How I love you!
How I long for you,
And the ache in my soul goes far too deep.
But my aching heart . . . it can only weep.
A near-distant dream,
As I awake from a sleep.
    I can only weep, dear friends.
    I can only weep . . . for us all . . .
'Til the madness ends!
    I can only weep,
    I can only weep.

David Arnow

A past president of the New Israel Fund, David Arnow has been involved with NIF for twenty years. He is a psychologist by training and a longtime Jewish communal activist and scholar, and he is the author of Creating Lively Passover Seders: A Sourcebook of Engaging Tales, Texts & Activities *(www.livelyseders.com), published by Jewish Lights.*

Israel as Hope and Responsibility: Building a Just Society

Although for almost twenty years I've worked as a lay leader of the New Israel Fund in the struggle to advance social justice, democratic values, and religious pluralism in Israel, I must confess that my first association to the question "What does Israel mean to me?" was not politics, not philanthropy, not the peace process, but poetry. I thought of a verse written by Elizabeth Barrett Browning: "How do I love thee? Let me count the ways."

Israel is not my home, but it is certainly a land that I love. Let me count its meanings—the land where so much of the ancient Jewish history I've studied actually unfolded and where a great many of the rabbinic texts I find so captivating were composed; a reborn sovereign Jewish state with which four generations of my family have been deeply involved; home to many good friends; a place I've visited more than forty times and where most people speak the new/old language I continue to study every week; a beautiful country brimming with its own enchantments and culture, special tastes and rhythms, and fascinating politics.

But there's something more. Israel means hope and responsibility. In one sense, that speaks to the promise of a secure and peaceful homeland for any Jew in search of one. Alas, the search for security and peace remains grueling. But the Jewish state means more than a port in a storm. Israel's rebirth means a chance to resume building a particular kind of society. When our ancestors left Egypt and received the Torah at Sinai, we headed for Israel; we accepted the obligation to create a society that for its time would stand as a proud model of social justice.

> And you shall not oppress a stranger for you know the feelings of the stranger, since you were strangers in the land of Egypt (Exodus 23:9). Justice, justice shall you pursue, that you may live and inherit the land (Deuteronomy 16:20). You shall not withhold the wages of a poor or destitute hired worker (Deuteronomy 24:14). When you reap your harvest in your field and forget a sheaf in the field, you shall not go back to take it; it shall be for the stranger, the orphan and the widow (Deuteronomy 24:19).

Several millennia later, the same obligation falls upon Israel and its supporters. Indeed, the existence of a modern Jewish state raises a number of profound questions. How will a people that for so long was a victimized minority and had so little control over its destiny wield power in its own state? What lessons will we draw from our long and painful history? And how seriously will we take the teachings of our ethical tradition on these matters? Israel is the central arena in which the Jewish people will forge answers to these questions.

One could explore these questions in terms of any number of issues: the peace process; the rapid growth of poverty in Israel, a nation once noted for its egalitarian economic policies; the complex relationship between religion and politics that has resulted in Israel's dubious distinction as the only democracy that does not permit Conservative, Reform, or Reconstructionist rabbis to officiate at conversions to Judaism, weddings, or funerals; the still lagging status of women in the first country to have elected a woman as prime minister; or even the quality of Israel's commitment to environmental issues.

Instead, let me focus on a particularly difficult issue, one that some may feel does not even belong in such a volume—relations between Israel's Jewish majority and its Arab minority, about 20 percent of the population. These are full citizens of the state who live inside the "green line," not in the West Bank. They are the descendants of the Arab community that lived in Israel before the 1948 War of Independence and who remained within the state during and after that war.

Before statehood, leaders of the Zionist movement affirmed their commitment to fair and equitable treatment of the Arab minority. In 1947, David Ben-Gurion, who would serve as Israel's first prime minister, delivered an address to the leaders of the Jewish National Fund on the responsibilities of the Jewish state to its non-Jewish citizens:

> In the Jewish State, Jews will not have any right that is denied to Arabs, Greeks, or Armenians, if they are residents and citizens of the State. Every citizen, Jewish, Arab or any other will be eligible to be elected to be president, prime minister, a justice of the high court or any other government office, important or minor. . . . We will need to concern ourselves with health and education, development and all the other services for Arab villages, no less than for those Jewish villages.

In his 1947 biography, Chaim Weizmann, soon to become the country's first president, offered a compelling explanation of *why* the Jewish state would not discriminate against its Arab minority:

> There must not be one law for the Jew and another for the Arabs. We must stand firm by the ancient principle enunciated in our Torah: "There shall be one law for the native and for the stranger who resides in your midst." . . . I am certain that the world will judge the Jewish State by what it will do with the Arabs, just as the Jewish people at large will be judged by what we do or fail to do in this State where we have been given such a wonderful opportunity after thousands of years of wandering and suffering. . . . Our security will to a great extent depend not only on the armies and navies which we can create, but on the internal moral stability of the country.

The confluence between the moral and pragmatic imperatives could not be more apparent—then and now.

Israel's Declaration of Independence duly promised political and social equality to all citizens. Needless to say, such promises are more easily made than kept. Although granted citizenship and the right to vote, the fact is that from the end of the War of Independence until

1966, Israel's Arab minority lived under sometimes harsh military administration. Traveling from one part of the country to another required a permit from the military authorities.

But despite much progress over the years, the gap between promise and practice remains large. A few examples paint the picture. Remember, the Arab minority represents nearly 20 percent of the population. A recent study by an Israeli nongovernmental organization—Sikkuy: The Association for the Advancement of Civic Equality in Israel—found that the Ministry of Construction and Housing and the Ministry of Science, Culture, and Sport both devote about 3 percent of their budgets to the Arab sector. According to the Statistical Abstract of Israel, the infant mortality rate among Arabs is twice as high as that among Jews. And Arabs represent only about 3 percent of those enrolled in graduate-level university programs.

The struggle for equality faces many obstacles. In 2001, Ariel Sharon appointed the first Arab, a Druze, ever to serve as a minister in the government. A survey conducted by the Israel Democracy Institute in 2004 found that 60 percent of Israeli Jews agreed that Arab citizens are discriminated against but that only 38 percent supported the right of an Arab to become a minister in the government. Among native-born Jewish youth, support for an Arab minister dropped to only 28 percent. A survey conducted by Haifa University in 2004 found that 64 percent of the Jewish public in Israel believes that the government should encourage Arab citizens to leave the country.

The enormous stresses of the bloody second intifada have rendered efforts to address the status of Israel's Arab minority paradoxically more difficult yet more critical. The Jewish majority questions the loyalty of the Arab community, and Arabs wonder how they can identify with a state that treats them as second-class citizens. But putting off efforts to address these problems will ensure that alienation and bitterness will continue to spiral, which in turn will only sow the seeds for greater conflict down the road.

There are, of course, voices in Israel and the American Jewish community deeply concerned with this issue, including a broad network of Israeli nonprofit organizations and the New Israel Fund, a partnership of Israelis and Diaspora Jews that helps fund many of them. And there are a handful of federations that have begun making grants to improve the circumstances of Arabs in Israel. As important as they are, these efforts are not enough to convince me that either American Jews or Israelis understand what's at stake here.

Now that we have a state with all the opportunities and risks associated with wielding power, what lessons will we take from our difficult history? The question of Jewish-Arab relations within the Jewish state confronts Israel and the Jewish people with a fateful choice. Will the scars of our suffering lead us to confirm the chilling observation of the Book of Proverbs (30:22): "The earth trembles when a slave becomes king"? Or will we use painful memories to strengthen our empathy in order to build a society that treats the "stranger" justly and fulfills our tradition's most noble aspirations? The injunction to treat the stranger fairly because we were strangers in Egypt occurs thirty-six times in the Bible. It's the most frequently repeated positive commandment—perhaps because it's so difficult to fulfill. Hillel doubtless had this in mind when he said, "What is hateful to you, do not do to your neighbor. That is the meaning of the whole Torah. All the rest is commentary. Now go and study!" (Babylonian Talmud, *Shabbat* 31a).

In college I was assigned a book written by the philosopher and cultural critic Stanley Cavell. I don't remember much about the book's content, but I've never forgotten its simple title: *Must We Mean What We Say?* As I consider what Israel means to me in light of the current state of Jewish-Arab relations in the country, Cavell's query haunts me. If we don't mean what we say, we make our tradition's central ethical teachings dead words in an old book instead of a living well of wisdom to guide us in the decisions we make in the real world. The depth of the Jewish people's commitment to those teachings will be reflected most clearly in the nature of society that Israel and those around the world who love it create in the Jewish state.

The struggle to build a just society is the life's work of all democracies. Has Israel made progress? Yes. Enough progress? No! Rabbi Tarfon, a Talmudic sage who lived in Israel almost two millennia ago, had it exactly right: "It's not for you to complete the task, but neither are you free to desist from it" (Mishnah, *Avot* 2:21).

The blessing of Israel's existence means that we who love it share the responsibility for building a just society in the Jewish state. We must approach this challenge with honesty and an unshakable hope in its favorable outcome. "*Od lo avdah tikvateinu*," proclaims Israel's anthem: "We have not yet lost our hope!"

William J. Bennett

William J. Bennett, a former secretary of education of the United States, is the host of the nationally syndicated radio show Bill Bennett's Morning in America *and the Washington Fellow of the Claremont Institute. He is also the chairman of Americans for Victory Over Terrorism.*

Why I Stand with Israel

The first piece I ever published in the popular press was a 1977 "My Turn" column in *Newsweek*. There, I lamented the fact that children were no longer identifying with heroes. I pointed out that to find a hero, to see heroism, one had to look no farther than Yonatan Netanyahu, who had died at Entebbe the previous year. Netanyahu was a hero, to be sure—but so, too, is the state of Israel a hero to many of us, even if so many others still think it appropriate to condemn and criticize it.

One of the premier political philosophers of our age said that Winston Churchill taught us to "see things as they are, and this means above all in seeing their greatness and their misery, their excellence and their vileness." When one looks at Israel and the Middle East, no task can be more important and, through the lens of moral clarity, no task can be more easily accomplished.

It did not take a great deal to see things as they really were on September 11, 2001—or on the days and weeks that followed. On

A version of this essay was published in the *Jerusalem Post*, May 7, 2002.

September 11, Israelis lowered their flags to half-staff in empathy with the United States. By contrast, Palestinians in the West Bank were cheering in the streets.

On September 11, we in the United States were forced to stare into the face, and feel the hand, of evil. Our very existence demanded that we fight back, not only to punish the wrong done to us, not only to protect our citizens and institutions, but to vindicate our democratic virtues.

Just after the slaughter that took place on September 11, many Israelis said, "We are all Americans now." The truth is, after September 11, we all became Israelis. Israel has been fighting a war against terrorism since the day it was founded, and this has been a war for the state's survival. It is not difficult to see that those who want to do Israel in—from Iran and Iraq to Hamas and the PLO—want to do the United States in as well. And, as is true in the case of Israel, our war on terrorism became, had to become, a war for our survival. Israel's war is our war, just as Israel's cause is our cause.

I am a Catholic, and many have speculated that Christian interpretations of the Torah are the reason many Christians support Israel. There may be something to that. But that is not my reason for standing with Israel, nor is it the reason the United States does and should stand with Israel.

We stand with Israel because Israel is a beacon of freedom and hope—to the world, generally, and in a more important sense, to the Middle East. In its very Declaration of Independence, Israel proclaimed that it would "ensure complete equality of social and political rights to all its inhabitants irrespective of religion, race, or sex; it will guarantee freedom of religion, conscience, language, education, and culture; it will safeguard the holy places of all religions." Israel has kept faith with the promise of its founding, a founding more similar to America's than perhaps any other nation's.

Israel is the only country in the region that permits citizens of all faiths to worship freely and openly. We need to remember that 20 percent of Israeli citizens are not Jewish. While Jews are not permitted to live in many Arab countries, Arabs are granted full citizenship and have the right to vote in Israel. (Arabs not only comprise a faction within the Knesset, but routinely side with Israel's enemies.) Arabs living in Israel have more rights and are freer than most Arabs living in Arab countries. Israel, in short, has shown the way in the Middle East; it has shown the way for freedom, for democracy, and for education.

And Israel has done all this while under continued pressure aimed at undermining and extinguishing its very existence. It was invaded by five armies upon its founding and has been threatened with annihilation ever since.

It should not have been surprising or worthy of condemnation that just after Yassir Arafat attempted to smuggle fifty tons of weapons into his Palestinian Authority in 2002, and just as his Fatah-affiliated al-Aksa Martyrs Brigades were perfecting their human-bomb-making capabilities, Israel finally said, "Enough!"

Israel then went into the territories to root out terrorists, to do what Arafat over the years had refused to do. That mission was of a piece with what the United States did in Afghanistan in rooting out the Taliban and al-Qaida. The pressure on Israel to cease that operation amounted to perhaps the greatest blurring of our moral clarity since September 11. That pressure was imposed on Israel in order to appease nations like Saudi Arabia, a repressive dictatorship that owes the United States a great many explanations, that deserves from the United States nothing.

Nor, by contrast, was it surprising that the first sentences uttered by Arafat upon release from his then confinement were libels against Israel as a "terrorist, Nazi, and racist" regime. This is what he always said, at least in Arabic. It was unfortunate he was given respectability in respectable redoubts; and his libels were similar to what other terrorists in our war have said about us. Lies pervaded Arafat's speeches, just as they have pervaded our direct enemies' speeches—and those lies have trickled down and out into the common criticisms of Israel heard elsewhere.

Just one of the lies that Arab terrorists have propagated about Israel, a lie that has taken on great currency throughout the world, and in too much common thinking, is that the Jewish settlements in the disputed territories are the greatest obstacle to peace in the Middle East. When I hear this, I am reminded of a lie from another context and another time: that blacks living as minorities in all-white neighborhoods in the American South were the cause of racial strife. They weren't—racists were the cause of racial strife.

There is no reason Jews should not be able to live in the West Bank unless there is a reason Arabs should not be able to live in Tel Aviv—which is to say, there is no reason at all. The freedoms to travel and live where one chooses are fundamental. To claim that certain lands should be free of Jews is to claim that the Third Reich had a moral point.

While many may prefer to forget their ugly history, I think it critical to remember it, for nowhere more than in the Middle East is history a prelude. Because of their animus against Jews, many leaders of the Palestinian cause have long supported our enemies. The grand mufti of Jerusalem allied himself with Adolf Hitler during World War II. Yassir Arafat repeatedly targeted and killed Americans.

Arafat was very closely aligned with the Soviet Union and other enemies of ours throughout the Cold War. In 1991, during the Gulf War, Arafat aligned himself with Saddam Hussein, whom he praised as "the defender of the Arab nation, of Muslims, and of free men everywhere." Israel, by contrast, has always been on the side of the United States, both as a strategic and as a moral ally. And the civilized world will never be able to pay its debt to Israel for bombing Iraq's nuclear reactor in 1981.

Today, more than ever, we cannot afford to criticize Israel for its war against terrorism, as we ignominiously did in that episode in 1981. Now, more than ever, we need to see things for their "excellence and for their vileness."

Those searching for heroes of democracy need look no farther than Israel, a country that has done more for more people, with fewer resources and under greater threat, than almost any other. We must never ignore the fact that if Israel loses its war against terrorism, it will lose its existence. To vindicate our own virtues and cherished beliefs, we should stand foursquare with Israel and apply pressure to the dictatorships in its neighborhood, not the other way around.

Moral clarity demands standing with Israel in its still unfinished war against terrorism, in its still unfinished work for survival. It is for these reasons and more, far more, that I count myself among the millions of Americans who see America's fate and Israel's fate as one.

Meron Benvenisti

Meron Benvenisti is a former deputy mayor of Jerusalem and the author of several books, including Conflicts and Contradictions: One of Israel's Leading Commentators Reflects on Israel, the Arabs and the West Bank; Intimate Enemies: Jews and Arabs in a Shared Land; and Sacred Landscape: The Buried History of the Holy Land Since 1948.

What Israel means to me is the most difficult question I can ask myself, precisely because it seems simple and obvious: it is the land in which I breathed my first and will breathe my last. One should not try to describe one's attachment to his or her mother; it is always greater than the sum of all its components.

In the early nineties I was asked to define my Israeli identity, and I answered, "I was born in the old Rothschild Hospital on Prophets Street, and my burial plot is ready beside my ancestors in the old Sephardic section of the cemetery on the Mount of Olives. The distance between these two sites is about a kilometer as the crow flies. In this space is my identity rooted; any attempt to depict it in complex—ideological, patriotic, or sophisticated—terms reflects, in my opinion, an immigrant's lack of connection. One doesn't demand from a native a declaration of attachment to his land."

My father succeeded in the principal mission that he took on: to make of me a "native" in my homeland. I have had no need for the ideological superstructure, the indoctrination, or the self-justifications. As I wrote, "For me the claim was a foregone conclusion. It depended only on my basic sense of belonging to the land. My starting point was 'native.'" I was not unique, and I do not give credit for this success to my father alone, but I can serve as a typical example of my generation—Jews born in Palestine in the 1930s. We and our older siblings are succumbing to natural attrition, and today no more than 1 percent of the Jewish population of Israel was born in the country and was kindergarten age or older at the founding of the state in 1948, and it turns out that our parents had no mean success: they did succeed in turning us into natives.

Our parents were busy with building a state and society from scratch. They trained us to follow in their footsteps, to implement the blueprints they had drawn up. They unapologetically groomed us to serve as an elite that would inherit the privileges they had amassed; they aspired that we, "the first generation for redemption," should be the very personification of "Israeliness," an object of emulation for the new-immigrant masses. The Hebrew we spoke—with its own peculiar slang—the community singing, the exceptionally informal style of dress, the sarcastic humor, the modern first names, the folk dances, the military and geographical knowledge, the rough exterior and sentimental interior of the sabra, the secularism—all were meant to aid in constructing a new image for the new immigrants, who would look upon us as role models, as products of the Israeli "melting pot," by whose example Israel's diverse ethnic communities would become truly one nation.

This synthetic Israeliness became, as well, a rallying point for world Jewry, a symbol of the new Israel that had risen from the ashes of the Diaspora communities destroyed in the Holocaust. Our parents could not have succeeded in creating the "new Israeli" had they not poured all their strength into our education. My father's devotion to this cause exemplified the energies invested by his generation and mine of educators—school and kindergarten teachers, as well as youth leaders—in this project. But their dedication and talent would not have sufficed were it not for the stirring message on their lips, a romantic tale of the rebirth of a nation, suffused with the loftiest social ideals. The real key to the success of this educational venture, however, lay in the amazing success of the whole Zionist enterprise. One found it easy to identify with the rousing saga of our struggle for national independence and to be full of pride in the part played by one's tribe—and oneself—in the marvelous success and in the knowledge that you had been here from the very beginning. And we, the young objects of this educational effort, took it all very seriously: we played at living the utopia, and we established a splendidly narcissistic society.

No wonder those who did not "belong" hated, envied—and emulated—us, and we had only ourselves to blame for their negative attitude. However, few of us felt that we were the beneficiaries of injustice or wrongful privilege. We hadn't stolen anything from anyone. On the contrary, we had given our all to "absorb" the others, those who had come because of persecution and because they had no choice, unlike our parents, who had immigrated of their own free will and out of a sense of ideological commitment to the realization of Zionism. Nonetheless, claims that we were arrogant, that we had an unjustifiable degree of control over the centers of political and economic power, and that we were contemptuous of the newcomers' culture grew in intensity as various groups of immigrants became more firmly established and began to demand their rightful place in the Israeli power structure.

Hatred for the elite made up of "native Israeli offspring of the founders" unites immigrants from the Arab world—who resent having been discriminated against and relegated to the margins of society and Israeli cultural life, their traditional family structure destroyed—and those from the former Soviet Union, who detest the socialist "left" and the remnants of the communist ethos.

There are, among my ilk, those who acknowledge the allegations of arrogance, feel guilty about our mistreatment of the "new immigrants," and make dramatic public apologies for our "terrible deeds" during the large-scale immigration of the 1950s. They are apologetic about their elitism and join ranks with their harshest critics, some even leading the chorus of recriminations—since they are such smooth talkers.

I, too, was once a part of this reproachful choir, but I have apparently mellowed with age; and now, as I enter the eighth decade of my life, my perspective has changed. I have been engulfed by a sweet nostalgia for my childhood and youth, and in addition to that, I am filled with pride and joy at belonging to the "tribe" of the founders' sons. What's more, I feel the need to defend myself against attack and even to launch a defiant counterattack of my own: "I am a proud

'Mayflower' descendant," "the salt of the earth." I feel no guilt or inferiority, nor do I regard myself as a robber. On the contrary, it is only thanks to us—the founders and their children—that our defamers and critics are here to complain. What would their fate have been had we not been here to welcome them?

The "nativeness" we had acquired was largely derivative, and thus is variously perceived as confused or as multidimensional, as suffering from vagueness and ambivalence or as actually being blessed with a wealth of nuance and the ability to accommodate a multiplicity of viewpoints. It is all in the eye of the beholder.

In the minds of some of us, "nativeness" finds its expression in the adoption of moderate political positions. In others, this "natural" connection to the homeland—free of ambivalence and requiring no self-justification—is actually liable to reinforce a tendency toward extremist attitudes, because of the deeply rooted perception that there can be but one "native" collectivity in the homeland and that the Palestinians, therefore, must be divested of their status as natives and must become mere resident aliens. For both Jewish "native groups," there is no longer any need to search out rights dating back to the biblical period or to postulate mythological roots in the homeland as a defense against attempts to portray the Zionist enterprise as a white settler society and therefore as being a form of illegitimate "colonialism." Today's thriving Israeli society—firmly planted in its homeland and having evolved a rich and varied culture in its own (Hebrew) language—requires no vindication, and anyone who dares to challenge its legitimacy risks being denounced as an anti-Semite.

When I was a youth, the Jewish community in Eretz Israel had to fight for its legitimacy, a minority compelled to defend itself against the claim that it was but a collection of immigrants scheming to take over a land that did not belong to them. Now, in my old age, the tables are turned, and the Palestinian people finds itself in the position of having to struggle for recognition that it, too, is a legitimate collectivity whose homeland this is, and not just a "gang of terrorists."

It is difficult to say which was the cause and which the effect: was my understanding of reality from a "native" point of view the outcome of the Zionist education I received, combined with the emotional affinity passed down to me; or had my disgust at witnessing the descent of both Israeli and Palestinian nationalism into the depths of extremism, xenophobia, violence, and killing awakened in me my "native" identity—one purporting to cast off nationalism and to pursue fellowship among Arab and Jewish "natives"; or was it all just a question of chicken and egg?

One way or another, I found myself inclined toward defining my worldview as "neo-Canaanite," whereas my political positions, as well as my attitudes toward other questions of identity, became increasingly esoteric, since public discourse was, and is, conducted within the "nationalist" model. Both Palestinians and Israelis emphasize and cultivate—and confront each other with—their respective national identities, and they affix this identity to the disputed territory. Both sides cling to aspirations of "self-determination" and to consequent claims of sovereignty over a defined piece of territory, and these aspirations also focus the debate on questions such as geographical partition and "unilateral separation."

The concept of a "native" or "neo-Canaanite" attachment to Eretz Israel/Palestine is not accepted in Israeli society for various and often contradictory reasons. It is regarded by the Zionist establishment and in right-wing circles as a betrayal of Zionist values and as undermining the privileged position granted by the Zionist establishment to those who act as if nothing has changed since the days of Theodore Herzl, Chaim Weizmann, and the pioneers of the second and third aliyot (waves of Jewish immigration to Palestine in the early twentieth century). This native, intimate connection to the land is perceived as negating one's connection to the Jewish people and, especially, to its sufferings—which have endowed this people with an absolute entitlement to a sense of self-righteousness as the "quintessential victim." Attachments suggestive of "post-Zionism" are perceived as anti-Zionist, which comes perilously close—in the view of the right—to anti-Semitism. Moreover, the Zionist left and Israeli post-Zionists are united in viewing those who identify themselves as neo-Canaanites with a degree of mistrust bordering on hostility. The Zionist faith continues to serve as a unifying myth within Israeli society, and the Zionist revolution is considered to be a "perennial revolution."

My "neo-Canaanite" position is summarized thus:

Objects created by human beings—by any human being—in this land combine to form a rich and glorious cultural heritage that influences the lives and experience of all who live there. No one has the right to rewrite or erase parts of it. The destruction of the cultural and human landscape, whether material or conceptual, would turn against the destroyer, leaving him impoverished and rootless.

"When all is said and done," as Mahmoud Darwish puts it, "the geography within history is stronger than the history within geography." And S. Yizhar's comment completes the thought: "The land, in its depths, does not forget. There, within it . . . suddenly, at different times, one can hear it growling an unforgetting silence; unable also to forget even when it has already been plowed and has already brought forth fair, new crops. Something within it knows and does not forget, cannot forget."

Only one who knows how to listen to the unforgetting silence of this agonized land, this land "from which we begin and to which we return"—Jews and Arabs alike—only that person is worthy of calling it "homeland."

So, what does Israel mean to me? As the celebrated poet Shaul Tchernichovsky wrote, "Man is but a small piece of land. Man is but an image of his homeland's landscape." I am a reflection of Israel's conflicts, antagonisms, and contradictions. I envy those who view the Jewish state as a glorious, unblemished symbol of their identity. I deplore their pathetic attempt to be more patriotic than I. I've earned my doubts, pain, and worries; I am as much a part of this land as its stones; it is only natural that I fear about the future of my grandchildren. What am I leaving them?

Theodore Bikel

Theodore Bikel has been a folk singer; a theater, film, and television actor; a radio host; the president of Actors' Equity Association; a political activist; a Jewish spokesman; and an author. He created the role of Baron von Trapp in the original Broadway production of The Sound of Music *and went on to play the role of Tevye in* Fiddler on the Roof *over two thousand times.*

A look at Israel today evokes thoughts about pride and passion, about peace and prejudice. There is much to be proud of when we look at the miracle that is Israel, 107 years after the first Zionist congress in Basel, 87 years after the Balfour Declaration, and 56 years after the establishment of the state. One could look at the achievements and at the very fact that Israel is alive and thriving and say, "*Dayenu*; is there a need to look much further?" But look we must, as Jews who have regard not only for our yesterdays but for our future and survival. Surely Israel is an essential element of our ethnic and cultural identity. The centrality of Israel to Jewish life in the Diaspora is quite properly paramount to the world Jewish community; yet there are moral and political pitfalls.

Jews outside of Israel have been reluctant to differ publicly—and even privately—with the policies of the government of Israel as they relate to questions impinging on physical security and military strategy. This reluctance was rightfully born of the feeling that the costs and consequences of any such policies would rest not on the shoulders of European, American, or Australian Jews, but on Israelis who have invested their lives in the creation and continuity of the state.

Yet it would be foolhardy to pretend that Jews the world over are not also profoundly affected by the choices any Israeli government makes. The meaning of our lives as Jews would surely be at risk, were

Israel's continuity endangered—not merely its physical continuity but its moral and ideological underpinnings as well. The course of the old Sharon government—before he had a change of heart and moved to a policy of a two-state solution—might well have endangered Israel's existence as a state that is Jewish, democratic, and independent. Not *either* Jewish *or* democratic, but both.

Equally endangered may be the world Jewish community because of perilous political attempts by the religious establishment within Israel—coalition partners of the government. These are attempts to delegitimize any but the most zealously Orthodox Jews by invalidating Conservative and Reform movements alike. We might be forgiven the note of fear that has crept into the discourse among ourselves and with our Israeli partners. True partners are able to disagree, argue, even raise voices—all in the interest of having the common enterprise flourish. What kind of partnership is it that accepts only yea-sayers and reacts with hostility in knee-jerk fashion to any signs of criticism or dissent? Either we are partners or we are not. If indeed we are, then it must be a partnership between fully recognized Jews in fact as well as in law. Let no religious divisions keep Jews apart. And who is to say that totally secular, nonreligious Jews have less of an attachment to their identity, less of a stake in Jewish survival, than those who only define themselves religiously? What of the legitimacy of culture and language, Hebrew, Yiddish, Ladino, or whatever other language in which Jewish creativity can be expressed?

Amid all these schisms there are frequent calls for unity. I firmly maintain that our strength lies not in unity but in diversity. In our past, there has always been disunity in one way or another, friction between scholars, strife between Pharisees and Sadducees, or between Hassidim and Misnagdim. What kept us alive was the sharp discussion, mind pitted against mind and man wrestling with God. Dialogue keeps one alive; acquiescence, on the other hand, leads to apathy, and apathy, to resignation.

The peace process is in deep trouble, partly due to certain elements that desire a radical shift from rational and democratic principles of governance to one that is shaped by messianism, extreme nationalism, and religious fundamentalism. Two sayings of the prophets come to mind: *Shalom, shalom ve'eyn shalom.* "Peace, peace, they mouth, yet there is no peace," and the other, an admonition not usually heeded by politicians in any country: *Tzedek tzedek tirdof.* "Justice, justice, shalt thou pursue."

The events that brought together Yassir Arafat and Yitzhak Rabin at the White House and gave rise to so much hope, expectation, and promise were also fraught with dangers and pitfalls we recognized even then. Alas, the world was not able to bask in the aura of this promise for very long. We have moved further and further away from the peace we all worked and prayed for and have become mired in a cycle of violence that has prompted even our most pacific instincts to be suppressed.

So much hope was placed in the Oslo Agreement and in the peace process that was to follow. The handshake on the South Lawn, a moving ceremony I attended as a guest, was a symbolic mutual affirmation of two peoples, bitter enemies in the past, of a firm intention to take the first steps on the road to peace. But in order to make this a reality, there had to be a genuine resolve on both sides, a promise to talk instead of shoot. No love fest was heralded, no suddenly discovered mutual affection; such naive notions cannot be in the vocabulary of pragmatic national leaders; leaders, moreover, who operate in the mercurial climate of the Middle East. There was a halfhearted smile that accompanied the handshake, a polite acknowledgment of solemn intentions; symbolism again. But symbolism can only go so far; reality must take over. As Amos Oz, the great Israeli writer and peace activist, wrote, "The moment of poetry is over and now it is time for the prose."

Yet the prose of politics in the Middle East is a bitter one. When Arafat was alive he was a leader of damaged reputation, a terrorist who failed to turn into a statesman. Arafat redux—neither peacemaker nor peacekeeper.

And Rabin is gone, too; his loss not Israel's alone. Murdered, and by whose hand? The myth that a Jew would not kill another Jew is no more than just that—a myth. Jews have killed Jews in the past. Within our own Zionist history, there have been such killings: the *Altalena* shot up by the Haganah in 1948, Chaim Arlosoroff murdered by right-wing opponents in 1933. And there is the ancient history of the Jewish kingdom before the Diaspora, when Jews were fighting and killing one another even while under siege from outside. We are not quite as noble as we like to believe. There is the constant contradiction in our claims of being *am s'gulah* (a people of distinction) on the one hand, and *goy k'chol hagoyim* (a people like all others) on the other; claims often made in the same breath. It is time to wake up to a stark truth: we Jews also sometimes thrive on intolerance one toward the other. Murder is only the starkest, the most obscene outcropping of the rhetoric of hatred. It does not just stop with the yelling.

I must confess that, as an American Jew, I strongly feel the burden of culpability that perforce rests on the shoulders of the American Jewish community. Baruch Goldstein, who massacred twenty-nine Arabs at prayer in a mosque in Hebron in 1994, was born and raised in the United States. His deed, a blot of shame on the pages of Jewish history, was perversely hailed by some in the United States and in Israel as the act of a redeemer. The extremist hawks among American Jews are guilty not only of exporting their rabid ideologies and nurturing them in their Israeli confederates, but of financing them heavily to boot. Far too many of the intransigent elements in Israel and in the territories who carried slogans of "Death to Rabin" were bred in the United States or else supported by big money raised in the United States. Everyone professed to be shocked by the murder of Yitzhak Rabin; but even before the end of shiva, voices were heard justifying the murder and a media appeal was created to raise money for the assassin.

After the assassination, the peace camp faced a heavy task. Predictions that the world and the Jewish community would be so shocked by the events as to be propelled to greater support for the peace process turned out to be wrong. Serious analysts warned then that one would have to continue not only to deal with former enemies but with new foes as well, foes of peace from within. That such foes could not all be contained—or detained—is obvious. One might try to draw them into the process, an uncertain task. The opponents of peace on the right, extremists claiming to be religious, would have to be reminded that long before you are permitted to reach for the voice of

God, you must heed the voices of man. An argument they would be unwilling to accept from learned rabbis, much less from Jews like us, secular leftist sinners.

For us, there was the shocking realization not only that Arafat turned out to be no partner for peace, but that he had never intended to be such a partner in the first place. Oslo and the handshake gave him the cachet of peacemaker; it also gave him half of a Nobel Peace Prize which, if he had had any sense of shame, he would have returned. In truth, for him Oslo was nothing more than an opportunity to obfuscate and spin wheels. In all the summit meetings, he appeared to be pacific, conciliatory, and seemingly accommodating, yet he withdrew as soon as real concessions were required. Because of his push-me-pull-you tactics, the pursuit of the peace process was fitful when it should have been steady, and stagnant where it should have been propulsive. He never meant for the Oslo Agreement to be implemented, and his intifada made certain that Israeli leaders were put in place who were as opposed to Oslo as he, leaders who helped move the process further and further away from a resolution.

Regrettably, Israel is making a colossal mistake by continuing to support the settlement enterprise. The settlements, perhaps the single most important obstacle to peace, undermine Israeli security and impede any progress toward peace. If there are ultimately to be two separate and sovereign states, then the settlements make all but impossible the completion of Israel's separation from the Palestinians, something that is critical for Israel's future as a Jewish democratic state.

The thought often occurs to me that far more dangerous than the conflict between Arabs and Jews is the conflict between Jews and Jews. The recent controversy about religious conversion is an ominous case in point. The halachic definition of "who is a Jew" is coming into conflict with demographic realities that cannot be swept under the rug. For example, of the 200,000 recent immigrants to Israel from the former Soviet Union, fully 50 percent are of dubious Jewish identity by halachic standards. They suffered as Jews, were jailed and escaped communist prisons as Jews, clamored for freedom as Jews, and finally found refuge in the Jewish homeland. Now, unless they can furnish proof of descent or "acceptable" conversion, they cannot even be married in Israel, because this modern democratic country has not understood the value of erecting a barrier between state and religion. The legitimacy of Conservative and Reform rabbis —some of unchallenged learning and scholarship—is called into question. Thus the issue has no longer become a question of "who is a Jew" but rather of "who is a rabbi."

This is wreaking havoc in Israel and especially in the American Jewish community, the strongest group of supporters and allies Israel has in the world. The only possible cure for this ailment is mutual respect for differing viewpoints, different modes of living, differing strains of thought. Unless there is a firm resolve to observe such respect, we shall be hopelessly torn asunder. And I do indeed mean mutual respect: secular and liberal Jews need to be mindful of the sensibilities of the Orthodox, just as the Orthodox need to refrain from imposing their lifestyle on all others. Respect is a two-way street, and when given, one returns respect for respect, tolerance for tolerance, and acceptance for acceptance.

I firmly believe that Jewish life, indeed any communal life, can be organized only according to democratic principles. The very antithesis to democracy is autocracy—or worse, theocracy. We are on dangerous ground here, with factions seeking to dictate to the rest of us and admitting of no definition but their own. It shames all those who have toiled in the service of the Jewish people and of the Zionist ideal, even laid down their lives for it, without the need for any declaration other than "I am a Jew—*hineni*."

Yitzhak Rabin had been a soldier and a man of war. Had he lived, he would have realized a vision of peace that is now in danger of being sacrificed on the altar of the idolatrous gods of expediency and intransigence. I honor his memory and grieve for our loss.

I trust that what you are hearing from me—even in my words of anguish—will be understood as coming from a man who is driven by a passion for Israel's survival. Not for mere physical survival, but for the continued existence of an Israel as a moral force rooted both in history and modernity. Those who maintain that there is a contradiction between the two are plainly wrong. The fusion of the two leads to the promise of a modern land, a twenty-first-century democracy:

modern—yet one that is founded upon the moral precepts of Jewish history and traditional wisdom.

My hope is for a return to a Zionism that is faithful to its founders, not one that is divisive and exclusionary, not one that labels all within or outside of Israel who do not share one single view as *posh'ey yisrael* or *soney yisrael* ("sinners" or "self-haters"). In this world of confusion, turmoil, and obfuscation, we above all must insist that our voice be the voice of sanity and deliberative reason.

Edwin Black

Edwin Black is an award-winning investigative author who has been nominated for the Pulitzer Prize eight times. His books include The Transfer Agreement: The Dramatic Story of the Pact between the Third Reich and Jewish Palestine, War against the Weak: Eugenics and America's Campaign to Create a Master Race, *and* IBM and the Holocaust: The Strategic Alliance between Nazi Germany and America's Most Powerful Corporation. *In 2004 he won the American Jewish Press Association Rockower Award for Investigative Journalism. His latest book is* Banking on Baghdad: Inside Iraq's 7,000-Year History of War, Profit, and Conflict.

My spiritual journey to Israel begins not at the foaming seashore of the Mediterranean where I played, or at the parched desert expanses of the Negev where I confronted the awe of nature, or at the lush Galilean kibbutzim where I once labored from sunrise to prove my worth and that of the nation.

For me, it all begins long ago in August 1943, in the terrifying darkness of a boxcar as a train swayed rhythmically, speeding toward Treblinka. Edjya, a thin, thirteen-year-old girl, sat on the boxcar floor, listening to the thudding rail ties, trying to understand the scream of terrible events befalling her family.

Her mother nudged her and whispered, "You're a skinny one, Edjya, always a skinny one," as she eyed the tiny vent at the top of the boxcar. "Quickly, up there," she said. "Edjya, go through." Her mother repeated. "Quickly, I said. We'll let you down slowly. Hold on to the towel."

Edjya inched out of the vent and down the horizontal wooden slats of the boxcar's exterior until her elbows and then finally her wrists cleared. With one foot resting on an exterior bolt, and hanging on to the towel against the wind, Edjya cried out, "Take me back up. I can't do it."

"Get ready," her mother instructed. "When you hit the ground, run, Edjya, run. And tell someone. Tell someone what is happening." Edjya jumped. On the ground, she was shot by militiamen and then buried in a snowy mass grave. But when Herschel, a teenage Polish forest fighter, came upon her leg protruding from the snow, he pulled her out to life and survival.

Edjya and Herschel are my parents. They did not end up entering Israel. As displaced persons, my parents made their way to the United States. I was born in Chicago and raised to understand that the Jewish people's post-Holocaust survival was embodied in the state of Israel. The walls in my childhood home were populated by green commemorative plates that framed portraits of Israel's founding fathers and mothers. Moshe Dayan's and Golda Meir's faces shone down on me as the heroes of the nation, and the nation always shone above as the hero of the Jewish people. Israel became my personal hero.

My first years in Israel were devotional. During my honeymoon, we labored at a kibbutz, hitchhiked through the country, slept in cheap youth hostels—anything to be in Israel and help build that country. When the disastrous Yom Kippur War drew to a close, I jumped on the first resuming flight from Chicago to do my bit, whether that meant washing floors or giving moral support.

In later years, as Israel's position became more secure, I struggled to understand her turbulent beginnings and the heartbreaking Holocaust-era decisions and selections that fired the bricks that built the state. I was a tormented fighter for truth in those days when in 1984 I revealed the Transfer Agreement. The best-selling book of the same title explained how the "deal with the devil," the pact between the Third Reich and the Zionist Organization, seeded the Jewish state by saving sixty thousand Jews and transferring some $200 million of their assets. I was so imbued with the strength of Israel that I embarked upon this sensitive issue even though it sparked tumult across the Jewish world. What is not known is that *The Transfer Agreement* was originally intended to be a trilogy; I refused to write the second and third volumes because the choices made during the later years of the twelve-year Holocaust were too painful even for me to chronicle.

But the book and the immense controversy propelled me into the forefront of the Jewish and Israeli media. I moved to Israel, where I fought the good fight any investigative journalist does with the powers that be. My weekly hard-hitting column, "The Cutting Edge," was syndicated in forty cities. Israel became an establishment to probe and expose even as I wrote articles exalting her strengths, and probed and exposed her enemies. Those were the best days of my life. I will never forget the air I was allowed to breathe on the *midrahov* in Jerusalem, the sand I was permitted to trickle through my fingers in the Negev, and the people I was permitted to know. No coffee will ever taste as bracing, no sunny day will ever shine as bright, no distant twinkle of village will ever sparkle as romantically as those seen and felt during my days and nights in Israel. Soul is Israel's most precious commodity. In 1986, when I left Israel to return to editorial duties in the United States, part of my soul remained in Israel. It remains there as deposit waiting to be reclaimed.

But in the nearly two decades since I returned, Israel's position has become increasingly more precarious. I discovered that attacks against Israel were too often just backdoor assaults against the Jewish people. Once Israel became the fortress of the Jewish people, she became the main target under siege. I found my energies and interests focused on the threats to her existence.

Today, Israel has emerged from its pioneering Zionist tradition, its romantic past when we sang "Hatikva" as El Al touched down at Ben-Gurion, and wept looking down when the plane dashed aloft for the return west. But to me, Israel still stands as the most important survivor of the Holocaust. With all its imperfections and magnificence, the nation itself is like a family—as long as it exists, the legacy continues. In Israel, mere existence is victory.

But that existence is ever more under attack, not only from those who wield bombs and missiles, but also from the subtlest movements in the international community seeking to isolate and batter the country. Here I have found my bond to Israel reinvigorated as I investigate the causes, underlying currents, and implications of the pernicious campaign to weaken and eradicate the Jewish state. If Israel cannot be driven into the sea, some would have the sea drive over Israel. I am among the multitude at the dike.

In 1943, my mother was hanging on to that speeding train by her fingernails, readying to drop to an uncertain fate. Israel is now hanging on even as the train accelerates, torn between the awful destination ahead and the uncertain fate below. Therefore, to love Israel, to know Israel, is simply to embrace the concept of Jewish survival, jumping from the train into the hostile woods.

Laura Blumenfeld

Laura Blumenfeld is a reporter for the Washington Post *and the author of the* New York Times *best seller* Revenge: A Story of Hope, *which explores her search for revenge on the man who tried to kill her father in Jerusalem in 1986.*

A Lesson in Vengeance

The pilot announced that we would be landing soon. I pressed my forehead against the oval window, craning for a glimpse of Israel. A strip of Mediterranean coastline unrolled below, then fogged over from my breath against the glass. Maybe the beach beneath the wing was Ashkelon, where Samson, the biblical avenger, killed thirty Philistines for cheating him in a riddle contest. He stripped their corpses, shaming them, to cover his own shame.

"As they did to me, so I did to them," Samson said.

Then he slaughtered a thousand more Philistines, swinging the fresh jawbone of an ass.

That was the thing about Israel—no pot of gold, no fountain of youth, but an episode of vengeance under every stone. Israel was a good country to enroll in for lessons in revenge. The archeology of revenge layered all the way back to the beginning of time. In Jerusalem lay the bones of Adam, the first man, and the world's first instrument of vengeance. Legend has it that Satan, tossed out of heaven, vowed to tempt Adam and his descendants to get even with God.

. . .

Condensed from *Revenge: A Story of Hope* (New York: Simon & Schuster, 2002).

My own revenge pledge was less grand, of course, though no less impracticable. My father had been shot in the head in 1986 while walking through Jerusalem's souvenir market toward his hotel. A death gang, members of a rebel faction of the Palestinian Liberation Organization, had targeted tourists—American, German, British—shooting them point-blank, a single bullet in the brain.

My father miraculously survived. To me, though, the gunman was more than just a man who wanted my father dead. He became a symbol of terror. Terrorism was not just about killing people, I thought, it was about dehumanizing them. How easily the gunman had stripped my father of his humanity. It angered me, and worse, it frightened me. In a world where people acted this way, no one was safe. I had to find a way to challenge the terrorist's way of thinking. Not with an act of violence. The revenge that I wanted was of a different kind, one that responded to the heart of the crime.

Six months after arriving in Israel, I found the gunman's home north of Jerusalem in Kalandia, on the edge of a barren gorge. I knocked on his front door.

"Come in," his mother said, smiling. "Would you like some orange soda?"

She drew me inside, into a dimly lit living room. Children were tucked into every shadow.

"That's him," she said, pointing. I followed her finger to the wall, to his photograph, saw his face for the first time and sank into the couch. "He tried to kill someone," she said in an easy voice.

"Who?" I asked.

"Some Jew," said the twelve-year-old on my right, shrugging.

He laughed and everyone laughed. I joined in too, as best as I could. Twelve years after the shooting, I had arrived unannounced on their doorstep one fiery July afternoon, a stranger with a notebook. I was a newspaper reporter from America, I said in Arabic, introducing myself simply as "Laura." Over cold soda and hot tea, I listened to their story.

"It happened inside the Old City, near the Western Wall," the gunman's brother said.

"He shot the man one time in the head."

"Why only once?" I asked.

"After the shooting, he threw the gun in the air," said his mother.

They started to chuckle at the comic scene: one bullet, a cowering Jew, the gun pinwheeling out of reach. The mother, laughing, smacked my thigh.

"After the incident, he came home and ate a big meal," said his sister-in-law. On the radio they heard a report of an American tourist who was shot in the head.

"He was proud, he was beaming," said a nephew.

"We were all with him politically," said his brother. "No justice comes from the Jews."

"And what about the man he tried to kill?" I said, blowing steam from my tea.

"It wasn't a personal vendetta," said the brother. "He didn't know the man. He did it so people would look at us. It was public relations."

"Won't someone from the victim's family kill one of your people?"

"No, there's no revenge. My brother never met the man personally. Nothing personal, so no revenge."

I drained my glass, burning my tongue. I had been sitting with them for over four hours. I couldn't sit anymore.

Come back, visit soon, they said as I left. They gathered on the front steps in the slanted pink light, arms and wrists and elbows all together, waving. My limbs moved stiffly, as if I had been holding them in an unnatural pose. I felt relief and then I felt something else. Inside a clamp came loose. All the swallowed heat rose from my stomach, stinging my chest and neck. "Nothing personal," the brother had said, "so no revenge." The heat was rising in my face, and prickled my scalp. It was personal. It was personal to me.

Could I make my father human in their eyes? Only if I hid my identity from them, I thought. They would come to know me—and through me, my father—as long as they didn't know who I really was.

What was the worst thing I could do to the gunman—the best

revenge? He was an ideologue, ready to kill. He had called my gentle, bookish father from suburban New York a "chosen military target." I set myself a goal that was outsized, naive, and most of all, elusive: I wanted him to realize he was wrong.

Over the next year, I got to know the gunman and his family. I visited their house every couple of weeks, spending hours in their living room, eating orange slices and drinking their dark, minty tea, admiring wedding photographs when a son got married, playing with the puppies when the German shepherd had a litter. I was so afraid they might uncover my identity, it took a bag of mental tricks even to smile. I joked with myself that I must never turn my head sideways, because if they saw my profile, they would realize that I was a Jew.

But they didn't. They wished me a Merry Christmas and the gunman himself described the shooting for me, justifying it by stating in his broken, angry English, "Our choice to the military struggle is a legitimate choice came on a historical basis that took into account the fact that the enemy we are facing is one who stands on a Zionist ideology which is racist in its basis and fascist in its aims."

Finally, after a year, I confronted him. The muscles in my back were clenched so tight, I stooped forward. For the first time, I spoke in Hebrew.

"I am his daughter," I said. "Laura Blumenfeld."

Omar Khatib, the gunman, looked flabbergasted. A little scared, shocked, and just as I had always hoped—shaken.

Thirteen years before, he had hid in an alley of the souvenir market, ambushing my father. Now I had ambushed him.

As the biblical Samson once said: "As they did to me, so I did to them."

A few weeks later, a letter arrived from Omar: "Dear Laura, You get me feel so stupid that once I was the cause of your and your kind mother's pain. Sorry and please understand. Of course I was shocked to know that you are David's daughter. I didn't sleep for almost two days."

My father, David Blumenfeld, also received a letter. "God is good to me that he gets me know your Laura," Omar wrote. "She was the mirror that made me see your face as a human person deserved to be admired and respected. I apologize for not understanding her message early from the beginning."

That was my revenge. Neither an eye for an eye, nor turn the other cheek. In a land of stark justice, I had found a third way: transformation. Getting even didn't have to be about destroying an enemy, it could mean transforming him, or yourself.

"It's good that Laura didn't say who she was the first time she came to us," said Omar's sister-in-law. "We would have closed the door to her, and closed our hearts."

But was it real? Could this tale be true, a bedtime story in a darkened world? Three years later I asked the question out loud, when I spoke to Omar by telephone. I had moved to Washington; he was at his home in Kalandia.

"It *is* a true story," he said, perplexed by my doubt. "A rare story like ours. In every public session I tell people about you. It brings hope to the heart of the people. I am preparing for a job that may suit my qualifications."

I tried to imagine what that might be.

"Diplomat," Omar said. "International relations. I will support the peace process and continue to move forward beyond the violence. Violence is not a way to gain our rights. I need to build my family. I need to build my home."

"Something constructive," I said.

"It is my promise—to you and to David," he said. "Say hello to your father."

I hung up the phone thinking back to the first time I saw Omar's house. His brother had dismissed my father's shooting as "nothing personal."

It was personal for me. Now it was personal for him.

It gave me a bit of hope.

Rabbi Shmuley Boteach

Rabbi Shmuley Boteach served for eleven years as the rabbi at Oxford University. He is a nationally syndicated radio host and a best-selling author of fourteen books, including Kosher Sex: A Recipe for Passion and Intimacy *and* Face Your Fear: Living with Courage in an Age of Caution.

That which I love I have always loved imperfectly. I am a religious man who loves God. But that has not stopped me from at times contravening His will. I am a family man who loves his wife and children. But that has not stopped me from at times acting with regard to my own selfish interests and not being as available to them as I otherwise might have been. And I am a Jew who loves Israel. But that has not impelled me to choose to live there, other than when I studied there as a student, or to serve in its army.

Yet, my love for Israel surrounds me constantly. It invades me. It never leaves me. I know it's real because I refuse to hear any criticism of Israel even though I am well aware of its flaws. Few things galvanize me more than rising to the defense of Israel, albeit in a safer arena than the battlefield, like my talk radio show or the op-ed pages of newspapers.

My love affair with Israel goes back to my childhood when my father used to hush us whenever Israel came up on the evening news broadcasts. He revered Israel and revered the courageous heroes who fought so that it might live. He taught me to love its soldiers and to admire those who sacrificed on its behalf.

I visited Israel several times as a child and remember the youthfulness of the country, the vibrancy of its citizens, the clean air of the Beer Sheva desert where my relatives resided, and the awe-inspiring holy sites at which I prayed. I especially remember a land of religious saturation, where Jews wore yarmulkes without any of the conflicts we American Jews experienced, and where Arabs proudly wore their traditional attire amid the burning desert heat (and Beer Sheva seemed to have as many Arabs as Jews).

My love for Israel increased alongside my commitment to Judaism through my teen years. By my fifteenth birthday I had decided to become a rabbi, and I chose to study in a yeshiva in Israel. Ostensibly, my decision had largely to do with my belief that the level of study there was far more advanced than in the United States. But just as important was my desire to breathe in the air of the Holy Land and experience the total immersion of a completely Jewish environment.

I impregnated every moment with activity. When we weren't studying, I was on the streets, talking to secular soldiers about religion, soaking up the incomparable atmosphere of Israel's outdoor markets, and surveying every inch of the country. My fixation with the land was less the fact that Abraham and Joshua had once trod on the same place and more the miraculous fact that the Jewish people, after two thousand years of exile, had reconstituted themselves as a living and breathing national organism in the ancient land promised to them by God. I looked upon the country as a never-ending miracle, and there wasn't a day that I took for granted.

It is now twenty years later, and Israel remains for me the embodiment and personification not just of Jewish, but of humanity's hopes. Israel is a symbol of how human potential, given enough willpower, can be translated into the actual, how millennia-old dreams can become reality. We humans are capable of making the desert bloom, of establishing a democracy in a region that has never known representative government. We are capable of practicing decency and repeatedly reaching out to our enemies, even as they vow to bury our children. We are capable of giving the vote not just to those who wish us well, but to those who wish us ill. We are capable of safeguarding human liberties, building courts and structures of justice, even as we face Herculean challenges related to security.

It might sound strange that a rabbi would view Israel as the apogee of human, rather than just Jewish, striving, but I have long believed in

Israel's universalism. For Israel has long illuminated for all the world how decent people wrestle with their conscience as they confront the highly imperfect world in which they are immersed. No country has ever behaved as Israel when faced with the seriousness of the threats that Israel confronts on a daily basis. The United States and Britain, two of the world's most respected democracies, responded to Hitlerism with the indiscriminate bombing of cities and civilian population centers. The United States later dropped atomic bombs on Japanese cities in order to spare the lives of its own soldiers in an invasion. The Arab countries that surround Israel—Jordan and Egypt in particular—that constantly accuse it of human rights violations had Palestinian intifadas of their own. But they dealt with them with gigantic massacres that included mowing down thousands of Palestinians with tanks and machine guns. Israel has instead focused on targeted elimination of terrorists and their leaders, and the building of walls to protect its civilian population centers from suicide bombers. Israel could have easily ended the threat against it by bombing hostile Palestinians to kingdom come. But that would have been unthinkable for a country that has placed decency ahead of its security.

That the founding of Israel was an inspiration to people the world over, and that its inspiration reached its apogee in the tiny country's gallant defense of itself by turning back numerous murderous armies in the victory of the Six-Day War, explains why the Arabs have been so dedicated to discrediting it. For the Arabs have launched a decades-old public-relations gambit—highly effective—to have Israel equated with the Third Reich. Destroying Israel's reputation was more important to the Arabs than even destroying the country. They wanted to darken Israel's light. For Israel represents to the entire world the triumph of democracy over tyranny and the victory of hope over fear, hardly a message that Gamal Abdel Nasser, Hafiz al Assad, Yassir Arafat, or Saddam Hussein wanted anyone to embrace.

Perhaps this was why my father always demanded such utter silence whenever reports on Israel aired. Israel's welfare was his welfare. His family had lived under Muslim rule in Iran. As a boy he faced constant beatings at school for being Jewish. His teachers never concealed the contempt they had for their Jewish pupils, who were always treated as second-class citizens. He and his twelve siblings lived in a giant tent in destitution and poverty. Through all this torment, what sustained them was the prayers they recited three times a day in which they verbalized the ancient Jewish dream of living freely as Jews in a land of their own. My father's grandfather had even undertaken the famous Persian-Jewish pilgrimage of walking to Israel, on foot, and returning to his family, an odyssey that took him three years to complete.

When my father's family heard that a Jewish army was fighting for its liberation against Arab assailants in 1948, they could hardly believe their ears. Could it be that Jews were standing up for themselves in the face of intractable odds? That people would fight for their rights in the Arab Middle East? Could it especially be that Jews, who had faced so many thousands of years of persecution and had just lost half their number in the Holocaust, would stand up proudly against their tormentors and carve a nation out of the desert sands? The spirit of Israel was infectious in my father's family, and just a few years after its founding they scraped together their pennies, boarded a plane for the first time in their lives, and flew to the ancient Holy Land.

After the horrors of September 11, I called the Reverend Al Sharpton, whom I had just debated on black-Jewish issues, and told him that he had an opportunity now to visit Israel and show compassion for the Israeli victims of Arab terror. Surely, such a visit would do much to foster much-needed goodwill between our respective communities. Sharpton agreed to travel with me to Israel. Nothing there made a bigger impact on him than when the Israeli foreign ministry took us to an absorption center for Ethiopian Jews. He sat with Africans who had been rescued from lives of oppression and tyranny. And I reminded Reverend Sharpton that in the history of the world, no nation had ever crossed the earth to bring Africans to a new country in order to liberate them. Previously, they had always been brought in chains into servitude.

I am amazed at how often non-Jews with whom I meet tell me that in their early twenties they traveled to Israel to work in a kibbutz. Invariably they will relate that it was the most memorable experience of their lives. When I ask them why, I usually hear something along the lines of, "It was like watching a dream. All these people, from so many corners of the globe, working to build a land they had never forgotten." They also mention to me how impressed they were that among the Israelis they lived with there was no hatred toward the Arabs.

Through the eleven years I served as rabbi at Oxford University in England, scores of German students who studied there would likewise recount to me their experiences in visiting Israel. They had gone to the Jewish state almost as a pilgrimage. Their consciences dragged them there in an effort to find cleansing. They would relate to me how, when asked where they were from, they were almost embarrassed to admit that they came from Germany. They expected to be cold-shouldered, and many of them would lie and say they were from a different European country—a futile effort, given the instant recognizability of the German accent. Yet, to a man and to a woman, they related to me that they were welcomed with effervescence and warmth. They too were treated as if they had come home, for Israel is a place where everyone who comes to find redemption can call home, a place where the sins of the past are enveloped by the promise of the future.

Paul Buhle

Paul Buhle is a senior lecturer at Brown University, a Yiddishist, and the editor of the multivolume Jews in American Popular Culture.

M y views on Israel have been shaped by an oral history engagement, as a non-Jew, with dozens of old-time Yiddish anar-
chists, socialists, ex-communists, and Labor Zionists, generations
whose expectations were very different from our current terrifying
reality. Even as I conducted fieldwork and the octogenarians pressed
upon me their Yiddishkeit and the need for me to make myself a
scholar of their traditions, the terror and tragedy of the 1982 invasion
of Lebanon unfolded, spurring the largest Jewish peace demonstration
in history. That I would join the circle of New Jewish Agenda was
inevitable. That I would make the continuity of a progressive, secular
Jewishness a large purpose in my future work was assured.

But the precise place of Israel in all this remains uncertain. My
special contribution seems to be exploring the central role of Jews in
American popular culture, the most influential culture of modern
times. Israelis are well known to be deeply affected by Hollywood, the
music industry, and even *Mad* magazine. But what does the consolida-
tion of a global culture in Israel, especially among the young, have to
do with its originating Jewish influences? If I am right, the experience
of the Diaspora produced in turn-of-the-twentieth-century Jewish
immigrants a unique ability to put themselves in the psychological
position of others, to "see" the music, theater, and movies—practically
everything but sports—that the non-Jewish masses would crave.

Yiddishkeit inspired a massive modern development that has now come nearly full circle in the nation whose founders decided against Yiddish, taken to be the linguistic symbol of defeat. No irony could be greater.

The existential circumstance of Israelis and Palestinians is shaped by these developments far more than reportage of competing nationalisms and mutually hostile religious-based impulses would suggest. My pessimistic (and widely shared) views are based on my observation of the need to conquer, so obvious in American leadership, so sharpened in the minds (and careers) of neoconservatives and their allies. Israel has been made, often against the will of Israelis, into something whose symbolic regional hegemony is ruled more important than the ability to live, work, and raise families in a land whose future is increasingly endangered by forces of mutual destruction.

My optimistic sense, an optimism of the will, is that Jewishness remains too strong to be overwhelmed by these developments, as proved by the strong sentiment against the current war and occupation, and against the Bush administration. This is a visceral American Jewish response to a society that seems to have relapsed, if only temporarily, to the 1920s, with Christian fundamentalism, rampant intolerance, and the latest version of red scares (minus the reds) on the march. It's a healthy response. It contains, in the younger generation, a wealth of idealism, precious little Zionism of the old kind, but a determination to see Jewishness survive and a spiritual belief that redemption is still possible. An Israel that is emphatically not the center of Jewish life, but nevertheless has an important role in Jewish life, must be part of that redemption from the old fears of war and destruction, and the new fears of wasteful resource-exhaustion, lunatic weapons-deployment, and ecological catastrophe.

Judy Feld Carr

Judy Feld Carr was awarded the Order of Canada for her work in clandestinely arranging for the rescue of the Jewish community of Syria over almost three decades. A former university lecturer in the subject of musicology, she has received many honors, including the Humanitarian Award of Merit from Haifa University. She is the subject of The Ransomed of God: The Secret Rescue of the Jews of Syria *by Harold Troper.*

I was not a child of the Holocaust.

My recollections of growing up in a very small Jewish community in northern Ontario include an early exposure to anti-Semitism.

As a six-year-old, before I knew who Jesus Christ was, my classmates in the Catholic school that I attended were accusing me of killing him.

I recall a Seder night when I had to drink my grandmother's delicious chicken soup through a straw, because of broken teeth and torn lips from a beating at the hands of students two or three years ahead of my class.

My grandmother—my Bubby—lived in Brooklyn, New York. Twice a year she made the trip to us, to the bleak, forbidding, and often frozen terrain that was the mining town of Sudbury. She spoke no English, but somehow the porters on the train understood her Yiddish-accompanied gestures, and she always endured the journey of two days and two nights in safety.

My Bubby paid me a quarter each week to learn Yiddish and to speak nothing else to her. We shared secrets known to nobody else in the family. I anxiously awaited her stays with us. Each visit brought something new, exciting, and joyful.

It was natural, therefore, that on one cold November day, I would, at age nine, obey her urging to sit with her in the bedroom that we shared, and listen to the radio. I did not understand why she gave me a pad of paper on which she had drawn two columns. The one on the right was headed "Ya," and the one on the left bore the word "Nein," both written in her cramped Yiddish hand.

She turned on my night table radio and told me to listen to a very important meeting, which she hoped would give the Jews a state.

This meant little to me, but it was exciting to be playing a game like tic-tac-toe. I, the scribe, was to make a mark with my pencil in one of the columns each time I heard the speaker name a country and follow it with the proclamation of a "yes" or "no."

For me, it was fun. For her, the anxiety showed on her face and by the way she gripped the sheets on the bed as the broadcast proceeded.

Dutifully, I made a mark in each column, depending on the speaker's "yes" or "no."

As the page filled, my Bubby became more and more agitated when she glanced at my pad and saw the growing marks on each side of the page. Her excitement became intense as those on the right side developed faster than those on the left.

Suddenly, after a certain "yes" had been announced, a roar of applause reverberated through the radio. My Bubby clapped her hands together and burst out crying. Her tears were tears of joy, as she exclaimed in Yiddish, "We have a Jewish state!"

She turned to me and told me that, although *she* would never see it, I must go to that Jewish state. Thus was my embarkation on a journey of Zionism.

I was still too young to grasp what a Jewish state meant. My father, who was a fur trader and hunter with the Indians in northern Canada, but a leader of the small Jewish community, explained that there was a country called Palestine where all the children in the schools would be Jewish—not just one lone pupil, as I was.

I did not even fully understand when my father rounded up a few Jewish children from other schools, but who went to the same "cheder" with me, to help in a secret project in the basement of our house. There, my family, aided by those children, laboriously hid hundreds of bullets of every shape and size among the fur pelts, packed and ready for shipment. As he was a hunter, my father had access to as much ammunition as he needed. It was only many years later, on my first visit to Israel, that I learned from one of the recipients of those shipments that the bullets—then more precious than the furs that surrounded them—helped the Haganah fend off the Arab attacks on the nascent Jewish state.

Those shipments from our basement destined ostensibly for world fur sales were sidetracked and delivered to skilled Jewish furriers who had survived the Holocaust and had set up business in Tel Aviv.

Over the decades, since Sudbury, my attachment to Israel has manifested itself in many and varied ways.

There have been extended visits, too numerous to count. I have taught at Hebrew University. I have frequently traveled the length and breadth of the country. My husband and I own an apartment in Jerusalem. We have walked home so many times after Kol Nidre to experience the silence and the sweet odor of the trees and blossoms that are that holy city.

We have a son, a daughter-in-law, and five grandchildren who live there who have been touched by the embrace of the land and its people. We have felt the fear for their safety and the joy of repeated reunion. All our other children have, at one time or another, been enveloped by the embrace of the land and its people.

I have had the honor of enabling hundreds of hapless Jewish refugees from Syria to find a new home among their own people, and give birth there to new generations.

Through all of this, I know deep within me that something surreal is afoot.

Among the horror of the barbaric attempts to kill as many Jews as possible, whether in the Holocaust or currently in their own land, I cannot help but realize that our survival as a people, as well as the survival of Israel as a state, has defied all reason and logic. The tribes, the civilizations, the myriad hordes of history, intent on our destruction, have all disappeared into the mists of time.

We, alone, remain, and we defy that reason and that logic.

Surrounded as it is, by millions who are still intent on that destruction, that land and those people continue to produce the unimaginable offshoots of a democracy and the inheritance from the Book—science, medicine, music, dance, and painting.

Above all, that land produces a people with a will to survive—again in defiance of that same reason and that same logic.

I, therefore, know, with a certainty born from the most unique history of any peoples that were ever on this planet, that my grandchildren and their children, and their children's children, will survive and flourish. And perhaps, one day they might just be recognized as that light among the nations, which so many of us believe to be our destiny.

Leon Charney

Leon Charney moderates The Leon Charney Report, *an award-winning nationally televised public affairs program. He worked with Israeli prime minister Golda Meir to help free a thousand Soviet Jewish dissidents who later immigrated to Israel, and he went on to serve as adviser to President Jimmy Carter on the Camp David Accords. He is the author of* The Charney Report: Confronting the Arab-Israeli Conflict.

Israel has a powerful meaning to me both intellectually and emotionally. It's the confluence of these two elements that makes Israel such a profound influence on the world as a whole and on Jews wherever they may be situated. It is nearly inexplicable, since it is the birthplace of the three great religions, and yet Israel is a Jewish state, and has created a base in the world for the Jewish Diaspora.

From a worldview in a civilized society, Israel is a beacon of democracy. In the area of the Middle East, which is fraught with totalitarianism, dictatorship, and religious fundamentalism, Israel remains a staunch and indomitable country encompassing basic freedoms for all of its citizens. Regardless of its internal machinations, which are many, Israel has not veered from its democratic principles and has chosen itself to be an outstanding democratic form of government. The country is a fusion of Western democracy and Jewish ideology. It is a proponent of civil rights to all of its citizens no matter what their religion or race. It flourishes with dissent and differences of opinion in both its government and its citizenship. At the end of the day, however, it never impinges the individual rights given to its citizens under their Declaration of Independence in 1948.

Israel per capita has more free world press and correspondence, and has greater access to its government than most countries in the world. It strives to be an example of moral authority in an immoral world. For religious and practicing Jews, it is a fulfillment of their biblical commandment to live a holy life in their ancestral holy land. The government is a phenomenal mixture of both religion and secularism. Many of its communal laws are based on Jewish tradition as interpreted by its chief rabbis; most of its other laws are based on British and Turkish law. Every citizen may experience either a secular or religious life or a combination of both. Many Jewish citizens of Israel have combined the biblical holidays into a form of secular holidays. These issues are ever changing and are being reinterpreted continually. This exercise affords a multitude of options for citizens and makes the place so energetic and full of vitality. Obviously, each adherent tries to influence the other. One might see this as a negative; I don't. I see it as a positive that allows the country and its citizens to voice their opinions in strong debate. Sometimes these arguments have been inflammatory, but at the end of the day the rule of law prevails. The result is a fascinating and interesting mosaic.

Perhaps more important than any of the above is that Israel means for all Jews a place of safety from worldwide anti-Semitism, which unfortunately has been part of world history for time immemorial. It is a citadel in the world for any Jew to find safe haven from persecution. It is the fulfillment of the promise of the modern Zionist dream to give a homeland to the Jewish people. It owes much of its birth to European anti-Semitism. The Jewish people for thousands of years wandered from place to place to seek a safe haven so that they could live a "normal life." History shows that this was an impossibility. The fact that Israel exists tells the world that past historical anti-Semitism can be resolved for any Jew by seeking refuge or citizenship in Israel. This was assured in its Declaration of Independence. Any and every Jew who seeks citizenship in Israel is granted the same by the fact that he or she is a Jew. How can one forget the Holocaust in which six million Jews perished? Had the country been in existence at that time, then the world would look totally different. Israel means a Jew will not have to suffer hatred, blood libel, and holocausts—the term "never again" exists because there is a Jewish state.

Israel, to me, means Jews worldwide no longer have to be ashamed of who they are. With the establishment of the state of Israel, Jews around the world can respond to any sort of anti-Semitism. Israel also makes the world accountable not only for its persecution of the Jewish people but also for the persecution of any people. By seeking to prevent another Holocaust, the Israelis also seek to stop the killing of other peoples. It is a shining example of basic human rights unseen in any other country in the region.

But above all, Israel means that after thousands of years of wandering, Jews have a home. It adds a dimension to the Jewish people that had not been available for thousands of years—pride and security. It is the unifier of a people who were once scattered worldwide.

This has given rise to a great intellectual, modern, technological state that has contributed great medical, scientific, and technological advances for the betterment of the world.

Israel means a successful integration of ancient traditions and history into a modern citizen democracy, a model for the Middle East that has struggled and is struggling with these issues.

It is an exemplar of hope in today's unsettled world.

Norm Coleman

Norm Coleman is a Republican senator from Minnesota and a member of the Senate Foreign Relations Committee.

I srael was a person, who became a nation, which became an ideal for me and the whole world. I understand that in Hebrew it means "striving with God and prevailing." To strive and prevail is the essence of being a Jew.

He began life as Jacob, a name that roughly means "wheeler-dealer," and it fit. He swindled his brother out of his birthright and won his wife Leah through clever negotiating tactics with her father. Years later, on his way to reconcile with his brother Esau, he encountered God in the form of an angel. He wrestled with him all night, not letting the angel go until he had blessed him. God gave him his new name, Israel. I sure love this athletic image of spiritual life—wrestling with issues and with God—more than a passive one. It was a different man who left the wrestling ring, no longer the guy who was "too clever by half." He was transformed to be the father of a nation.

The nation of Israel, I believe, was chosen by God to teach the world about Himself. Like a controlled experiment, God separated the Jewish people from the world so his truth could be clearly understood without intervening variables. Through the nation of Israel, the world came to understand law, family, the social contract, public health, caring for the poor, and so many other bedrock societal values.

President John F. Kennedy said famously that "life is unfair." The people of Israel have experienced that more than those of any nation.

They were enslaved by Egypt, conquered by Assyria, then Babylon, then Greece, and then Rome. The Romans eventually destroyed Israel's capital, Jerusalem, in A.D. 70. The nation in Diaspora suffered centuries of persecution throughout the world. The Nazi Holocaust ranks as the most unfair moment in human history. And consequently, the reformation of the Jewish state in 1948 ranks as one of the most just.

Israel, as our ally and a democracy in the Middle East, is a beacon of hope. If terrorism can be halted and peace between Israel and a Palestinian state takes root, the hope of democracy can spread throughout the region, and the world will be safer for all of us.

Israel survives after hundreds of other cultures have disappeared because God chose it, and it expresses a transcendent ideal. Life may be unfair, but as members of the family of Israel, we know that each human life has a dignity and potential because we are made in the image of God. This knowledge sets an incredibly high standard that we spend our whole lives reaching to attain.

That's why stuttering Moses became a great deliverer and leader. That's why a flawed man like David became a great king and "a man after God's own heart." That's why Esther could challenge a ruthless king and save her people from genocide, and why Joseph and Daniel could maintain their integrity in exile. Being part of Israel made them see themselves as part of something eternal and noble and ultimately true, and they lived accordingly.

And all the years of persecution and loss taught the Jews that the only real wealth is something they can't take away and that you can carry with you wherever you go. That is why family is so very important. That is why education is so very important. We carry around our true wealth in our hearts and minds, where it can't be confiscated, ruined, or smashed.

I often use the phrase that "a Jew is like any other person, only more so." I know I am part of a tradition and a culture that have made an incredible contribution to the life of this planet. I know that I am part of a nation that for some reason has always had a bull's-eye on it. But I know that right from the start, being a descendant of Israel means my life is all about "striving" and "prevailing," and I will do my utmost to fulfill that God-given destiny.

The Spanish rabbi Maimonides said, "We should all view ourselves as if the world were held in balance and any single act of goodness could tip the scales." That is the essence of Israel the person, the nation, and the ideal.

Richard Ben Cramer

Richard Ben Cramer is a journalist and author who was awarded the Pulitzer Prize for his coverage of the war in Lebanon. His books include How Israel Lost: The Four Questions.

Where I grew up, in a suburb of Rochester, New York, there was a temple called B'rith Kodesh—which (I now know) means Holy Covenant, though I never thought about it at the time. It was just B'rith Kodesh, as normal and established a landmark in my life as the public library, which was more or less across the street. The temple had a Sunday school to which I had to go. Why did I have to go? There wasn't any why about it. I had to go to Sunday school like I had to be bar mitzvahed, like I had to get through high school and go to college—those were my jobs. And I thought even less, at that time, about what they taught us in Sunday school. It was just Jewish stuff I had to learn, like my Catholic neighbors had to learn about saints, and Latin. At least we didn't have to go to confession.

It was Bible stories, mostly—Noah and the ark, Moses getting fished out of the Nile . . . that, and a lot of Jewish history, which mostly consisted of non-Jewish tyrants with lumpy names (like peanut brittle in your mouth)—Nebuchadnezzar, Ahashueras—who at different times in different places tried to do in the Jews. But then God showed up and smote them a Mighty Smite, and things were better till next

Excerpted from Richard Ben Cramer, *How Israel Lost: The Four Questions* (New York: Simon & Schuster, 2004).

Sunday, when the Jews were in trouble again. (It's like my friend Ilan Kutz says about Jewish holidays—they all pretty much add up to the same thing: "They tried to kill us. They didn't succeed. So, let's eat.") . . . All the stories were taught in a seamless succession, and no one made much fuss—certainly, I did not—about which ones came from the Bible, and which from later books, or from no books at all (like that impoverished little Hanukah story, which we all pretty much recognized as a plot to keep us from succumbing to Christmas).

And the last strand in this skein of woes was Hitler and the holocaust. Maybe this was taught with a little more heat because it had happened in the time of our teachers' lives. But there wasn't any more detail than we got about the Babylonians or Assyrians. Nevertheless, this Hitler business was my favorite Sunday school story. For one thing, I knew from independent sources (a series of wartime boys' books called *The Yankee Flier*—I'd inherited the set from my uncle, and read them all at least three times) that, in this case, God's Mighty Smite had arrived in the form of glorious U.S. Air Force squadrons, and George Patton's smashing Third Army—which, I felt, put *me* on the side of the angels. . . . And the other good thing was the end of this story—the creation of Israel—which I thought had potential to keep the Jews out of hot water for several Sundays in a row.

We didn't learn much about what Israel was. The teachers seemed to exult in it mostly because it was a place to speak Hebrew—which was another excuse for us to have to learn Hebrew. We did learn that Israel was a desert till the Jews showed up and made it bloom. We had to make it bloom, too, by slotting dimes into little cut-outs on a piece of cardboard with Hebrew writing on it—each dime would buy a pine tree to make Israel green. (It seemed to me, God ought to smite up some pine trees, while I used my dime for a big Three Musketeers bar.) . . . We were taught that the Arabs tried to kill off Israel at birth, by attacking all at once—which fact was presented as a modern confirmation of all the *other* stories. ("See? They're *still* trying to murder us.")...And we knew that Israel was definitely innocent and excellent: Ben-Gurion, Weizmann, Yigal Allon and Abba Eban were added to the roster of good-guys—on the same page, as it were, with Abraham, Isaac and Jacob, Moses and Aaron, Queen Esther, sage Solomon, King

David and a bunch of prophets. In fact, it was all one mud pie to us, straight from the Bible to Ben-Gurion—monotheism and zionism were both good isms the Jews thought up.

What I liked about Israel, apart from the fact that it was the end—last stop on the Sunday school train—was the slogan we heard every time the subject came up: *"Israel was a land without people for a people with no land."* . . . This was the tersest, most powerful storytelling—as good as all the other jingles that filled my head at the time: *See the U.S.A. in your Chevrolet . . . Winston tastes good, like a cigarette should.* (They were probably also the work of Jews.) But this was so neat a turn of phrase, and a turn of history, that it seemed to confirm for me the biggest of all Sunday school stories: the sense and economy, the goodness of God's creation. It all locked together in the end, neater than Legos—*a land without people for a people with no land.* That was what I knew.

It was a testament to my misspent school years that it was still just about all I knew fifteen years later. By that time, I was a reporter for *The Philadelphia Inquirer,* happily at work in that newspaper's New York Bureau. In fact, I was the New York Bureau, which was our only bureau—we weren't a rich paper at the time. My editor called me on the phone one day, in December 1977, and asked: "How fast can you be in Egypt?" I thought it was some stupid knock-knock joke. I said: "I give up. How fast can you be in Egypt?" But it turned out he was serious. The Egyptian president, Anwar Sadat, had just traveled to Jerusalem to propose peace—huge news. And now, it was announced, Menachem Begin, prime minister of Israel, would return the visit, at Ismailiya, Egypt, on Christmas Day. The paper had to do *something* to cover—but what could my bosses do? They couldn't uncover something *important,* like City Hall, or the Phillies! But the New York Bureau was already gravy—and in it was a Jew, who would work on Christmas. "I'll be there tomorrow," I said.

For the next seven years, I was a Middle East reporter, in and out of Israel a hundred times, and all over the Arab world. By the end, I thought I knew what I was doing. But what I had to learn first was the depth of my ignorance. On that first flight to Egypt, I could tot up my certainties on two fingers: The Jews were the good guys; the good guys always won. I never knew that much for sure again.

And when I got to Israel, a few weeks into my new career, my confusion was complete. Sure enough, there were the pine trees. (I was glad of that, and they'd done splendidly. Which ones were mine?) . . . For the rest, I was reminded of a line old Harry Truman spoke about his opponent: "It's not what he doesn't know that bothers me. It's what he knows for sure that's just plain wrong."

Those assholes honking at my rent-a-car, as I puzzled out some Hebrew road sign—were these the heroes of the Six Day War?

My first guide to Jerusalem, who cheated me out of a hundred bucks, and favored me with this axiom: "The good Arab it's the dead one."—was he the heritor of thirty centuries of humane Jewish wisdom?

And then I met the Arabs—live ones—and they were good: hospitable, dignified, rational, articulate and oppressed. But that wasn't the most surprising and disturbing fact that I had to work in. The true astonishment was, simply, *they were here*. They were here, their fathers were here, their grandfathers . . . for centuries!

What about the land with no people for the . . . well, you know the rest. In '48, the Jews, in fact, had no land. Okay. . . . But there was a people here!

I began to write their stories, too. Not the big picture—I didn't know the big picture. But I wrote what happened in front of my eyes, to people I had met and talked to. My newspaper was beset by protest—committees of Jews who came to complain, and try to lose me my job. "What kind of Arab apologist did you send there?" . . . "Is it really *Ibn Cramer*—is he an Arab?" . . . "Oh, we know his kind—the self-hating Jew!"

To their enduring credit, my bosses never told me about all the trouble—*for years*—which was a wonderful freedom . . . and a kindness to me, because I would have been hurt: by that time, I utterly loved the place.

Paul Eidelberg

> *Paul Eidelberg is an American immigrant to Israel and an internation-*
> *ally known political scientist, author, and lecturer, as well as the founder*
> *and president of the Foundation for Constitutional Democracy, with*
> *offices in Jerusalem.*

FROM ATHENS TO JERUSALEM: A SPIRITUAL JOURNEY

Israel is the culmination of a spiritual journey that began almost fifty years ago at the University of Chicago, where I was awed by the grandeur of classical Greek philosophy. In Israel, however, where I settled in 1976, the pinnacle Athens became the steppingstone to Jerusalem.

To encapsulate this journey, allow me to recall a dream I had before graduating the university. In that dream I found myself on a vast plain in which there appeared three tall pillars, one more distant than the others. On the first pillar was a bust of George Washington; on the second a bust of Plato; on the third a bust of Moses. The dream revealed the milestones of my spiritual odyssey.

While at Chicago, I studied under the greatest living political philosopher, Professor Leo Strauss, my first teacher. Anyone majoring *in* Strauss, as many did, was bound to have a more than casual interest in the idea of a philosophy of history. But whereas a teleology of history permeates the Bible of Israel, the idea appears foreign to classical Greek philosophy, in which Strauss gave many of his unique and deepest seminars. The Bible and philosophy, he emphasized, involve the most fundamental antithesis of Western civilization: revelation and reason—"Jerusalem and Athens: Some Introductory Reflections," the title of one of his most thought-provoking essays (*Commentary* 43 [1967]: 47–57).

For Strauss—who had also delved deeply in such Jewish philosophers as Maimonides and Judah Halevi—the progress of Western civilization depended on the continuing dialogue between revelation and
reason, a dialogue he regarded the most important in human life.
Although Jerusalem and Athens—the Torah and Greek philosophy—
were in substantial agreement regarding the moral virtues, they differed
as to the theoretical source and ultimate end served by those virtues.
The difference involves the very different ways of life of two cities,
Jerusalem and Athens, the archetypes symbolizing the antithesis of revelation and reason. While Strauss held that each archetype should be
open to the challenge of the other, he denied their final reconciliation.

After graduating from Chicago in 1966 with a degree in political
science, I wrote a trilogy on the statesmanship of America's founding
fathers. From their debates at the Constitutional Convention, the *Federalist Papers*, and their voluminous correspondence, I reconstructed
their mode of thought: their understanding of human nature and politics and their extraordinary knowledge of how to design the various
branches of government. Needless to say, my work was very much
influenced by Leo Strauss, by his profound seminars on classical and
modern political science, especially those on Plato and Aristotle,
whose greatness was only magnified by his seminars on Machiavelli
and Hobbes and Nietzsche, to mention only few of those who shaped
the mentality and behavior of modern man.

In 1971, a friend of mine, an orthodox Jew as well as a philosopher, introduced me to an extraordinary rabbi, Dr. Chaim Zimmerman, who was to become my second teacher. Rav Chaim was famous
for his prodigious memory. The Babylonian as well as the Jerusalem
Talmud and literally thousands of other Hebrew tomes were stored in
his memory as if his mind were a giant computer. But unlike a computer, his was a creative mind. He could interface Torah with science
and philosophy as well as with politics and thereby illuminate the
Torah as the paradigm of reason and of how man should live.

After a six-hour question-and-answer session with this genius, it
occurred to me that the 2,400-year Western antithesis of reason and
revelation may have been misconceived even by Strauss. In any event, I
came away from that 1971 mind-stretching session with a vague feeling

that such Western dichotomies as individual versus society, freedom versus authority, morality versus law, might be dissolved by a deeper understanding of the primary Jewish sources, of which I had only an "outsider's," not an "insider's," knowledge.

In 1972 I visited Israel for the first time, staying with the friend who had introduced me to Rav Chaim and who had made aliyah the previous year. I had just finished the first draft of *A Discourse on Statesmanship*, and we discussed its relevance to Israel. We concluded that what was lacking in Israel was *Jewish* statesmanship—meaning thoughtful application of a Torah-based philosophy to public policy. But to make a Jewish statesmanship credible in the predominantly secular state of Israel, it would be necessary to interface the Torah and modern science. How did I dare contemplate this formidable undertaking? It was not a subject of political science.

In 1973, Dr. Zimmerman made aliyah, as I did three years later. Strange: I was not a Zionist, and I had very little Jewish education in my youth. But if I was to come to grips with the antithesis of revelation and reason, it would have to be in Jerusalem.

And so, in 1976 I joined the faculty of Israel's Bar-Ilan University, a liberal as well as religious institution. It was not the university, however, but Dr. Zimmerman who prompted me to reexamine Plato and Aristotle from the advantage of deeper understanding of the Torah. Until his death in 1994, I visited Rav Chaim almost every week. During many of those weekly visits I heard him dictate two monumental works, *Torah and Reason* (1979) and *Torah and Existence* (1986). From him I learned that the Torah exemplifies not a religion so much as an all-comprehensive truth system, that Torah Judaism is based solidly on reason, that it illuminates the two domains of existence, history and nature. It was Rav Chaim who encouraged me to write *Jerusalem versus Athens* (1983). Note the difference between that title and Strauss's essay, "Jerusalem *and* Athens."

The thesis of my book, contrary to millennia of Western thought, is that philosophy originated in Jerusalem, not Athens. Placed in question was the revelation-reason dichotomy as well as the secularism that was undermining Jewish national pride and diminishing Israel among the nations. *Jerusalem versus Athens* was not merely an intellectual exercise. It was intended as a contribution to Jewish national redemption. I had come to a country lacking clarity and confidence in its purpose, but therefore unsure about its heritage. And I, too, had wondered whither are we going. In *Jerusalem versus Athens* I became dimly aware of a Jewish philosophy of history—a 2,500-year development in philosophy and science and world politics culminating in the re-establishment of the state of Israel. But how should one classify this state? It was reputed to be a democracy. It was also designated as a Jewish state—a controversial issue. Some preferred to call Israel the State of the Jews. But what was the mentality of the Jews who ran this state, and what if anything bonded them to the voters?

My first contact with an Israeli politician occurred in September 1976, the month after making aliyah, but prior to my beginning a twenty-year stint at Bar-Ilan University. My friend, General Haim Laskov, a former chief of staff, arranged a meeting between me and then Defense Minister Shimon Peres. Present at the meeting was Mr. Peres's mentor, Professor Yehoshafat Harkabi, head of Israel Military Intelligence, whose writings were then unknown to me. Mr. Peres queried me on U.S. foreign policy in the Middle East and how it might change if Jimmy Carter replaced Gerald Ford after the approaching November presidential election. Toward the end of the meeting, he asked what Israel's major problem would be after that election. I replied that regardless of its outcome, Israel would have to counter Arab propaganda about "self-determination of the Palestinian people." Professor Harkabi interjected, "That's irrelevant."

Harkabi's response indicated to me that something was dreadfully wrong with higher education in Israel, and therefore with Israel's policymakers. I soon found out: moral relativism. Harkabi was not only a self-professed relativist. He had dedicated his first book, *Arab Attitudes to Israel* (Jerusalem: Keter, 1972; see page 465), to Jews and Arabs alike, even though that book contains almost five hundred pages of unrelieved Arab vilification of Jews and Israel! (Harkabi's *Israel's Fateful Hour* [New York: Harper & Row, 1989], is also dedicated to Jews and Arabs.) Moral relativism, or its derivative, moral equivalence, placed the Jewish cause on the same level as the Arab cause. Since Jews were entitled to national self-determination, so were the Arab inhabitants of Judea and Samaria (the "West Bank") and Gaza. The abstraction—moral equivalence—trumped the antidemocratic mentality and genocidal intentions of the Arabs portrayed in Harkabi's book! It seemed to me that this moral equivalence was immoral.

In America, I had written extensively on the moral relativism permeating the social sciences, and I had warned that this doctrine was undermining the American tradition. And now, here I was in Israel, and the same doctrine was undermining the Jewish tradition. It was undermining the Jewish people's confidence in the justice of their cause. So pervasive and pernicious is this doctrine that, years later, I was prompted to write *Demophrenia: Israel and the Malaise of Democracy*. Politicians and academics afflicted by "demophrenia" (a neologism) dwell in a world of denial, incapable of facing the enormity of evil.

Since moral relativism denies the existence of universally valid or objective standards by which to determine what is good and bad, or whether the way of life of one individual, group, or nation is intrinsically superior to that of another, it rejects "Jerusalem" as well as "Athens," the archetypes of revelation and reason.

I had cast my lot with Israel, but Israel's government was dominated by Jews alienated from "Jerusalem" and indifferent to "Athens." No wonder the laws and policies of this government, generally speaking, are not quite Jewish and not quite wise. But then, neither is the structure of this government, whose institutions, I began to see, are not conducive to the survival of the Third Commonwealth. But if Israel is eternal, as the Torah affirms, must not the future harbor a Fourth Commonwealth? But I am getting ahead of my story.

With the establishment of the Third Commonwealth in 1948, Jews from a hundred nations returned to their ancient homeland as prophesied in the Torah. It was understood by the sages of the Talmud that these Jews would constitute a mixed multitude more or less influenced by gentile ways, that upon returning to Eretz Israel they were bound to establish a deeply flawed, indeed paltry, state. (See Babylonian Talmund, *Sanhedrin* 97a.). What else could one expect after nineteen hundred years of statelessness, of forced dispersion, persecution, and decimation? Religious as well as secular Jews were bound to return to their homeland with an enfeebled or *galut* mentality.

I came to know that most of the founders of the state of Israel were political or secular Zionists who had abandoned the Torah. Most were labor socialists. Most therefore harbored a split personality; for how can one be a solid Zionist or nationalist with Marxist and therefore internationalist leanings? I had no doubt which would prevail over the other, if only because of the profound influence of Marxism on the social sciences, in particular its atheism and historical relativism. Besides, the founders of the state brought to Israel a politics derived from Eastern Europe, with its emphasis on top-down party leadership. While they wanted to restore the dignity of the Jews, they envisioned a state in which Judaism, like Christianity, would be relegated to the home and the synagogue, would cease to modulate statecraft. However, because of Israel's crazy-quilt multiplicity of parties—a consequence of proportional representation—the political Zionists needed the cooperation of religious Zionists to form a government. The necessity of secular/religious coalition governments enabled religious parties to obtain public funds for Jewish education and preserve a modicum of Judaism in public life. It was a rather mixed marriage. Or as Rav Chaim put it, the religious politicians often used Torah for politics, rather than politics for Torah. This could not but engender cynicism among secularists and scorn among the ultra-Orthodox.

Not that the latter were beyond reproach. Still, it was the ultra-Orthodox who had preserved the Torah throughout the centuries of exile. They were skeptical about "modernity." Like "Straussians," they deplored the materialism and hedonism of the secular democratic state. Unlike the religious Zionists, they rejected the idea that the secular state of Israel could be an instrument of the redemption of the Jewish people. Such a state, they believed, was a continuation of the *galut* and would eventually disappear with the coming of the Moshiah. Although this position was argued by great Torah scholars, it was refuted in the first chapter of Dr. Zimmerman's *Torah and Existence* (which I had the honor of abbreviating for a popular audience).

However, it was the political Zionists who established the Third Commonwealth. It was they who facilitated the in-gathering of the Jews and developed the scientific-technological infrastructure that has thus far preserved this commonwealth against its enemies. These

Zionists had actually inaugurated the physical stage of Israel's restoration. This Israel, demonized by bigots, ignoramuses, and villains, is superior in various ways to gentile nations. Its generosity to countless immigrants, gentiles included, is unequaled. Its world leadership in medicine and biotechnology has relieved the suffering of countless people beyond its own borders, as have its charities to countries that have suffered various catastrophes. Its humane (but not always wise) conduct of war surpasses that of any other nation.

Nevertheless, it was becoming increasingly apparent to me that Israel exhibits all the shoddiness of politics. After examining its political system, I realized that it is this system that prevents the fulfillment of Zionism's goal: to restore Jewish honor in a secure Jewish state. Nothing of the sort can reasonably be expected of the state established in 1948 if only because of its inept and divisive system of governance. This state has the veneer of Western democracy—periodic, multiparty elections. But as David Ben-Gurion complained more than fifty years ago, the primary goal of the all-too-many parties that compete in these elections is "merely to divide up the positions of influence and the national budget." (See David Ben-Gurion, *Israel: A Personal History* [Tel Aviv: Sabra Books, 1972], 552.) Nothing has since changed.

To Israel's misfortune, the entire country constitutes a single parliamentary district. Citizens vote not for individual representatives but for a fixed, party-ranked list of candidates. Consequently, Knesset members (MKs) are not individually accountable to the voters—contrary to the practice of virtually all democracies (many of which are smaller than Israel in size and population). Moreover, since MKs owe their position and perks to their parties and not to the votes of constituents, they cannot function as judges of their government's policies as do legislators in virtually all democratic countries. Furthermore, since the cabinet consists of a coalition of party leaders in the Knesset, the absence of constituency elections enables the government to ignore public opinion with impunity.

These and other institutional flaws prompted me to write *Jewish Statesmanship: Lest Israel Fall.* There I showed, citing the *Federalist Papers*, that multiparty cabinet government is incapable of pursuing coherent and resolute national policies. Israel needed a presidential system of government with institutional checks and balances to ensure the rule of law. It needed a constitution designed to diminish secular-religious tensions. *Jewish Statesmanship* showed how to use democratic principles to make Israel more Jewish, and how to use Jewish principles to make Israel more democratic! Although the Torah is not a democratic charter, it insists on government *with* the consent of the governed.

The June 1992 Knesset elections provided proof that Israel cannot long endure under its existing system of government. That election produced a coup d'etat whose consequences threaten Israel's survival, a coup d'etat of which the vast majority of Israelis, including academics, were utterly oblivious! Here is what happened.

A potential coalition of Zionist and religious parties led by Likud chairman Yitzhak Shamir received 59 of the 120 seats in the Knesset. Opposing them was a Labor-Meretz coalition led by Labor chairman Yitzhak Rabin, which received 56 seats. By virtue of the remaining five seats won by two Arab parties, Labor-Meretz had a "blocking majority" that prompted President Ezer Weizman (recently a Labor cabinet minister) to ask Mr. Rabin to form the government. However, no previous Israeli government had ever depended on the participation of an Arab party. Conversely, no previous Israeli government had ever lacked the participation of a religious party! But such was the ultrasecular character of Meretz that all the religious parties had pledged they would not join a Labor-Meretz government!

No criminal investigation has been made of the matter, but the ultrareligious Shas Party betrayed its voters and made Mr. Rabin's left-wing government kosher. I was witnessing what any student of Aristotle would call a revolution, which apparently escaped the preoccupations of Israeli political scientists.

In any event, contrary to Labor's pledge to the nation, and in violation of the Prevention of Terrorism Act, but in dutiful recognition of its obligation to the Arab parties, Labor spokesmen engaged in clandestine negotiations with spokesmen of the PLO. These negotiations led to the September 13, 1993, Israel-PLO Agreement commonly known as the Oslo Accords. The principal architect of those accords, Foreign Minister Shimon Peres, had made it clear in previous years that he advocated Israel's withdrawal from Judea and Samaria (the "West Bank") and Gaza. This policy of "territory for peace" was utterly muted in the 1992 election campaign, since a substantial majority of the public was opposed to recognition of the PLO, which was listed as a criminal organization in Israel's penal code.

Oslo, I saw, was much more than a quest for peace. Oslo was part of a comprehensive plan to deconstruct, as it were, the historical memory of the Jewish people. Judea and Samaria constituted their historic heartland, the tangible link to the teachings of their prophets and sages. So long as Israel retained Judea and Samaria, most Jews in this country would remain bonded to those teachings. This bond had to be severed, hence Oslo. Consistent therewith, Labor–Meretz stripped the curriculums of the public schools of Jewish and Zionist content. If this were not enough to reveal the political revolution taking place in Israel, the words "Judaism," "Zionism," and "Eretz Israel" were expunged from the Soldiers Code of Ethics.

The revolution described above had been brewing in Israel's secular universities long before Oslo. These universities had imported from the West the doctrine of moral relativism, which leavened the mentality of Israel's ruling elite. As a consequence of this corrosive, subterranean doctrine, which thrives in democracies, Jews were embarrassed ruling Arabs whose spokesmen, in every Middle East tyranny, gulled the democratic world with the mantra of "self-determination for the Palestinian people." And so, what now endows Israel with legitimacy and its ruling elite with respectability is no longer Zionism but "democracy." The Zionism, or "particularism," of the founding has given way to "post-Zionism," to democratic universalism.

The Jewish state of Israel—the Third Commonwealth—was gradually being transformed into a "state of its citizens." Apart from amending the Law of Return to facilitate the influx of gentiles into Israel—presently more than 300,000 from Russia—how else could the ruling elite prevent the political ascendancy of Orthodox Jews, whose birthrate is twice that of secular Jews? Besides, hundreds of thousands of secular Jews had left Israel. The electoral base of the Labor Party was shrinking. The ruling elite became all the more dependent on the Arab vote. Oslo, or Labor's quest for peace—or was it for power?—required a shrinking of the Jewish soul or Jewish self-effacement. But this means that countless Jews who had come to live in Israel or who yearned to live in a Jewish state were being betrayed.

As I pondered the government's quest for peace in terms of Oslo, I began to feel I was living in an asylum. Oslo rescued from obscurity the godfather of international terrorism, Yassir Arafat. It allowed him to enter Israel, which he and his minions had pledged to destroy in stages. Moreover, Oslo required Israel to release and arm tens of thousands of Arab Jew-killers to prevent terrorist attacks against the Jewish state!

Summing up the character of the Third Commonwealth: it harbors basic intellectual and institutional flaws. Not only is its Jewish majority evaporating, but the policies of its government and the egalitarian agenda of its Supreme Court are transforming Israel into a state of its citizens, the penultimate stage of its demise. *Jewish Statesmanship* was intended to forestall this disintegration and facilitate the emergence of the Fourth Commonwealth, whose realization (God forbid) may require a future war. It would be tragic indeed and frightening had I not discerned the stirrings of this Fourth Commonwealth, for which I had been striving in the Third.

Whereas the Third Commonwealth was necessary for Israel's physical restoration, the Fourth is necessary for Israel's spiritual restoration. In *Beyond the Secular Mind* (1989), I show how Torah concepts can salvage the cardinal principles of democracy, freedom, and equality. Today these two principles lack ethical and rational constraints and thus prevent Israel from being a light unto the nations. In *Judaic Man* (1996) I refute modern psychology, which is based on the primacy of the emotions, and offer a conception of human nature based on the primacy of reason. But these books do not interface the Torah with the rigorous sciences, by which I mean, primarily, physics, cosmology, and microbiology.

Most inspiring in this regard is the work of the physicist Gerald L. Schroeder, whose *Science of God: The Convergence of Scientific and Biblical Wisdom* (New York: Broadway Books, 1997) provides the linchpin of my book *A Jewish Philosophy of History: Israel's Degradation and Redemption* (New York: iUniverse, 2004). (See also Gerald L. Schroeder, *The Hidden Face of God: Science Reveals the Ultimate Truth* [New York: Simon & Schuster, 2001].) This book, the culmination of my spiritual odyssey, envisions a restoration of Hebraic civilization, in which the antithesis of revelation and reason will cease to divide mankind. The overcoming of that antithesis may well be the purpose of Israel's rebirth, since that overcoming would sanctify the name of God and restore His presence among His people. *"This people have I created that they may relate My praise"* (Isaiah 43:21). To relate God's praise, the people of Israel would have to reveal, in finite ways, the infinite wisdom with which God created the universe. But if Israel is to enlighten mankind, it will have to become a nation in which freedom dwells with righteousness, equality with excellence, wealth with beauty, the here and now with love of the Eternal. This is what Israel means to me.

Stuart Eizenstat

Stuart E. Eizenstat is the former United States ambassador to the European Union and has held key government positions in several presidential administrations. He served as special representative of the president and secretary of state on Holocaust-era issues in the Clinton administration. Mr. Eizenstat is the recipient of the Courage and Conscience Award from the Israeli government.

I srael for me is more than another foreign country. Although I have worked with Israeli officials on a variety of political, economic, foreign assistance, and diplomatic issues over my government career, Israel is also a place where I have connections of family, of close friends, and of the heart. It is the fulfillment of a two-millennia-old dream of a homeland for the Jews, the Third Jewish Commonwealth in recorded history. It is a safe haven for Jews threatened around the world, one that, had it existed during World War II, would have saved millions from extinction. It is the repository of hopes for the future of the Jewish people.

When I was around twelve years old, following the death of my grandmother, my grandfather Esar Eizenstat, then well over eighty years old, decided to leave our home city of Atlanta, Georgia, and make aliyah in Israel. His children—my father Leo, my uncle Berry, and my aunt Ida—all tried in vain to change his mind, arguing that at his advanced age it was unwise to move thousands of miles away from the family. He was adamant. He wanted to die in the Holy Land, he said—nothing more, nothing less.

In the summer of 1965, after my first year at Harvard Law School (where Alan Dershowitz was my professor for criminal law), I had my first personal experience with Israel, through my grandfather. I made the first of what has become some thirty trips to Israel, both to see the country and to see my grandfather. I was taken by Israel from that visit, its mission to gather Jews dispersed around the world; providing a haven for distressed Jews from Arab nations to the Soviet Union; the physical beauty of the diverse landscape, from the Dead Sea to the Galilee, and the connection of the land to the history of the Jewish people I had learned during Hebrew school and Sunday school growing up in Atlanta.

While staying at the Hotel Monopol in Tel Aviv, I was shocked to see Jewish prostitutes, thinking that a Jewish state would be perfect, without the imperfections of other societies. Yet this taught me an important personal lesson. Israel was seeking to be a "light unto the nations," its biblical charge. But it was building a normal state. Normality is what the young Jewish state needed to have, not an unrealistically idealized state of dreams.

I visited my grandfather Esar, then well over ninety years old, in an old-age facility in Petach-Tikva, one of the oldest cities in modern Israel, and the location for the first great wave of aliyahs in the late nineteenth and early twentieth centuries. Remarkably, he had been self-sustaining for over a decade since his move from Atlanta. He was nearly blind, but he recognized me. We had an emotional reunion; I told him about his family in Atlanta, and he spoke to me in Yiddish. For me Israel was now not just a place, but a country with a blood tie, one that was even more strongly reinforced years later.

In 1980, following the conclusion of the Carter administration, my wife Fran and I were invited to Israel by Prime Minister Menachem Begin in recognition of my support for Israel-U.S. relations during 1977 to 1981. Here I again had an emotional family connection. Through some family research, I learned that there was a possibility that not only my grandfather Esar, who had died in late 1965, only months after my visit, but also my great-grandfather was buried in the main cemetery at Petach-Tikva. If this was true, it would be a startling finding, which would provide a connection not only to the modern state of Israel, but to pre-state Palestine as well. We were taken by an official from the cemetery to the gravesite of my grandfather, after I gave his date of death and full name. I then asked if he knew whether my grandfather's father might also be buried there, explaining I did not know his first name or even approximate date of death. Yet he immediately said he was buried here and that he could take me one row over to his gravesite. It was a powerful moment to see two generations of Eizenstats buried in the soil of Israel.

In subsequent trips over the decades, my wife and I learned of more and more live relatives on both my father and mother's side, from Haifa to Rishon L'Tzion, from Ramat Hasharon to Kibbutz Gan Shmuel and Jerusalem. This has been supplemented by scores of close friends in Israel we have developed, many of whom we have met during their diplomatic stays in Washington, including every Israeli ambassador to the United States, since we moved to Washington to work in the Carter White House. This web of family and friends has given Israel a very personal place in my heart.

Beyond family and friends, I have devoted a great deal of effort in my private life to another meaning Israel has for me: the place where the restoration of the Jewish homeland is being played out on a daily basis. It is remarkably fortunate for our generation that we are living at a time of the creation of the modern state of Israel, the Third Jewish Commonwealth, following two millennia of exile. The cataclysmic events of World War II, which loosened the chains of colonialism around the world, including Palestine, together with the Holocaust, which created a brief period of sympathy for the Jewish people, led the United Nations to create the state of Israel in 1947.

Israel is perhaps the only country created after the war that has not known one full day of complete peace with its neighbors ever since. I have engaged in a variety of activities to try to add what I could to help strengthen the Jewish state, still one of the world's newest nations. I have been the founding chairman of the American Jewish-Israel Institute of the American Jewish Committee, to build stronger ties between American Jews and Israel, and now serve as the chairman of the international board of governors of the Weizmann Institute of Science, one of Israel's crown jewels of scientific endeavor.

Israel will soon have the largest Jewish population of any country in the world, as its population continues to increase and that of the Diaspora tends to stay flat or even decline. We are the only major religious group whose numbers have actually declined worldwide. There were some 16 million Jews at the outset of World War II. Today there are around 13 million. Jewish continuity will increasingly be played out in Israel. Jewish art, culture, scholarship, and religion will increasingly be centered in Israel. That is why I have supported so many Jewish institutions in the United States that help Israel, such as the federation movement. It is why I marched in the streets in the 1980s with hundreds of thousands of others to demand that Jews in the then Soviet Union be permitted to emigrate to Israel and to the United States.

I have had many interactions with the Israeli government as a senior U.S. government official, from both the Carter administration and in my Holocaust restitution work in the Clinton administration. I did not check my religion or my feelings for Israel at the door when I entered government service. There was never an issue of dual loyalty. I was always cognizant that I was a U.S. government official who had to follow U.S. policy and act in the best interests of the United States. On the broadest level, our interests converge. But there are differences of policy from time to time. In the Carter administration it involved issues of U.S. sales of aircraft to Saudi Arabia and the expansion of settlements on the West Bank and Gaza.

During the Clinton administration, I helped negotiate a reduction in U.S. economic assistance to Israel that the government of Israel supported. I also was disappointed with the lack of support I received from the Israeli government when I was negotiating Holocaust restitution matters in Eastern Europe during the Clinton administration.

But overall, the interests of our two countries are so congruent, as two democracies with shared values, that there was never a sense that Israel's basic security interests would ever have to be compromised to accommodate U.S. policy.

In short, Israel has many meanings to me: a place where many of my relatives and closest friends live; a country where the Zionist dream is being played out on a daily basis; a country that holds the key to the future of the Jewish people worldwide; an ally of the United States; and an island of democracy, freedom, and stability in a sea of autocracy and often hostility in the Middle East.

Marc H. Ellis

Marc H. Ellis is University Professor of American and Jewish studies and director of the Center for Jewish Studies at Baylor University. Dr. Ellis specializes in modern Judaism and post-Holocaust thought and serves on the Council for Palestinian Restitution and Repatriation. His recent books are Israel and Palestine—Out of the Ashes: The Search for Jewish Identity in the Twenty-first Century *and* Toward a Jewish Theology of Liberation: The Challenge of the 21st Century.

What Israel Might Mean After

When I think of Israel, the first thing that comes to mind is its beauty—the landscape and its architecture, especially in Jerusalem. The shaping of Israel has transpired through time and memory; the struggles then and now to be just and free, the possibility of a covenanted people journeying through time with God. The Bible is the unfolding of Israel or, if you will, its blueprint. In Israel the Bible is past and present, as are the Jews, living in dual time, suspended between then and now, reaching toward a future.

When I think of Israel, I relive my first journey there in 1973, before and during the October war. The countryside was as beautiful and friendly as the war was ugly and frightening. I remember asking myself then if Isaiah's prophecy of peace would ever become reality.

When I think of Israel I imagine Palestine, the *before* of Israel, now the within of Israel, and how I became aware of both during my second visit in 1984. It was then that I met Palestinians who are Israelis and Palestinians who exist under occupation. I wondered then if these two peoples would ever come to agree that sharing the land was preferable to fighting over it.

When I think of Israel I remember Rabbi Judah Magnes, an American and a Zionist, who was the first president of Hebrew University. He argued for a Jewish homeland in Palestine alongside an

Arab homeland in a united Palestine. I think of Martin Buber, in exile from Nazi Germany and living in Jerusalem, working for the recognition of a binational sensibility so that Jews and Arabs could work together to achieve their separate but also connected destinies.

When I think of Israel I marvel in the expression of Jewish particularity, how it has survived through its provocative contributions to the world, especially the prophetic, and how Jews have survived catastrophe, the Holocaust being nearest yet by no means the first in Jewish history. I also marvel that Jewish particularity has continually opened itself to the universal, so that an embrace of Jewishness is an embrace of the world.

When I think of Israel my heart feels hope shadowed by despair. Could it be that after this long and incredible journey, we as Jews would settle for an expanded territory and a military prowess at the expense of ethical values lived in the world? That our independence would deny another people their independence?

When I think of Israel conflicting images come to mind. In Israel and the United States the Jewish community is divided; a civil war is being waged between the supporters of Israel who brook no dissent on its policies—I call them Constantinian Jews—and Jews of conscience, who say there is another way, a higher ground where Jews and Palestinians can live together in justice and peace. There are so many on each side, the known and unknown: the toupeed optometrist and failed mayoral candidate in a Southern town who use the synagogue as bully pulpit to beat down anyone who criticizes Israel; the children of Holocaust survivors who speak for Palestinians as a way of healing the wounds of their parents.

When I think of Israel I picture Ariel Sharon, a warrior prime minister. I also see Amira Hass, an Israeli reporter who lives in Ramallah. Both are Jews, both are Israelis, both are part of Jewish history. As a Jew I inherit and live with both; these two sides are the history we are creating and cannot escape. The struggle within the Jewish world will last my lifetime and beyond. Anyone who is serious about Jewish life cannot help but be affected, even scarred, by this civil war. It is our generation wrestling with what it means to be Jewish. Is it a wrestling unto death? Or will this wrestling bring life?

When I think of Israel I envision my children affirming their Jewishness as a path of justice and compassion, seeking a revolutionary forgiveness that has justice at its heart. For are not Jews *and* Palestinians both deserving a justice that looks toward a future worthy of our children?

Herein lies the meaning of Israel for my life: that when my children think of Israel, their images will be peaceful, affirming Jewish contributions to the world as their continuity rather than our suffering; and just, seeing that there is a place for Jews *and* Palestinians in this world and in this land that calls out to so many around the world as sacred and defining.

The alternative meaning is too horrible to contemplate: that when my children think of Israel they will ruminate on helicopter gunships and occupying soldiers as central to Jewish life. Then violence would be at the heart of the covenant and worse: we as Jews would become carriers of that violence as our witness to the world.

When I think of Israel the prophetic voice is near and alive. Jews of conscience carry this voice today as a sign of solidarity to our own heritage and as a witness for the future. One day Israel, the people, and Israel, the state, might embody this voice. But this can only come *after* a realization that dissent is a form of solidarity, a Jewishness in the world, that will outlast the anger and violence of this world that has invaded our own community.

Amitai Etzioni

*Amitai Etzioni, recognized as the founder of the communitarian phi-
losophy, is a professor at George Washington University, where he
directs the Institute for Communitarian Policy Studies. A former White
House adviser on domestic affairs, he is also the author of twenty-four
books, the most recent of which is* From Empire to Community:
A New Approach to International Relations.

Israel is for me, among many other things, a nation for whose existence I have risked my life several times (I served in the Palmach,
or the Israeli Commandos, both before and during the Israeli War of
Independence). It is a country that provides a home to my family,
who experienced the Nazis firsthand. It is a place in which my son,
daughter-in-law, four grandchildren, and quite a few other relatives
live. It is a nation that often makes me proud and whose government
policies sometimes trouble me, but a hell of a lot less than many other
governments, near and far, especially in the Middle East.

I pay special mind here about Israel as the only democracy in the
Middle East. Neocons often dream about turning the Middle East
(and the rest of the world) into "shining, prosperous democracies."
When this rarely works, they tend to define down what democracy
entails, referring to nations that hold elections but sharply limit the
freedom of the press, competition among political parties, and
the reign of the parliament as "democracy." The fact that the climate
in the Middle East is not too hot, the soil not alien, the people able to
form a true democracy, is highlighted only by one nation: Israel.

Critics are quick to point out that the Israeli democracy is not
without blemishes. And they find some real, and often imagined,
violations of human rights. In the process they measure Israel by some
ideal model that exists only in the back of their mind and disregard

that all democracies, especially those long besieged, have imperfections of their own. We would live in a much better and safer place if more nations of the world, and especially in the region, were half as democratic as Israel is, and half as attentive to human rights as it is. None of this should be read as condoning those violations of human rights that do occur, corruption, or any other defect. I merely suggest that fair-minded people best put these matters into a fair perspective.

I am stunned at the blind hatred Israel evokes, not only by the same dark forces that mean to do in all of Western civilization, the United States first, but by the numerous Europeans, and those on the American left, including some Jews who draw on their academic credentials (e.g., in linguistics) to write tirades about their own in such extreme terms it makes the paper blush and their ancestors turn in their graves like cement mixers. For them, Israel is often the disappointment that they previously found in the USSR, Yugoslavia, Sweden, and Cuba, all the nations that at one point or another were supposed to be their dream ticket, and then disappointed by being merely human.

I do not believe that criticizing the Sharon government's policies is anti-Semitic per se; if it is, most Israelis would have to be considered anti-Semites. I regret when Israel is treated as coequivalent with the policies of its current government (which, by the way, are by no means all off the mark). Nor can I ignore that *many* of those who are most vociferous in their denouncement of "Israel" are also anti-Semites, a despicable lot.

What is often lost sight of under the incessant anti-Israeli barrages is that most Israelis would give their right arm and then some to have a real peace with their neighboring countries, to play a key role in promoting mutually beneficial economic ties by sharing the technical knowledge and higher education that make for high-tech economics and expedited trade, and to work with progressive groups to advance democratic and human rights in the region and elsewhere. Sadly, these opportunities are missed, even by the nations that have a peace treaty with Israel.

Israel has sent literally hundreds of delegations of physicians, nurses, scientists, educators, agricultural experts, and members of many other professions and occupations to Egypt to try to build bridges and mutually beneficial arrangements. Practically all of these gestures of goodwill have been spurned by the Egyptians and they almost never reciprocate by sending their people to visit Israel. Similarly, tourism has been almost completely monodirectional, with Israelis streaming to Egypt and very few traveling the other way. This is a very cold and sad peace.

There are those who believe that if the United States would lean on Israel and resolve the conflict with the Palestinians, the enemies of the West would be appeased. Others, who favor "leaning" on Israel for their own reasons or political agendas, use this argument to demand that the United States force Israel to make concessions, even if those will endanger its survival and even if major Palestinian leaders openly state (to their credit) that they are happy to take half a loaf through negotiations—but then will go after the other half (whatever remains of Israel) with the same violent means as before.

I care a lot about resolving the Israeli-Palestinian conflict. I believe, in the Jewish tradition, that if one saves a single soul, it is as if he has saved a whole world. And I hate to see innocent people on both sides killed. Above all, I would give a great deal to see my children and grandchildren live in peace. However, it is a dangerous delusion to believe that the fundamentalist Muslims will cease to believe—correctly, by the way—that the West is undermining all that is dear to them: treating women as third-class citizens; severely punishing people for minor transgressions; dealing with all nonbelievers as if they were dog meat; putting their rigid interpretation of Islam above any decisions arrived by elected representatives; and using the sword to impose their worldview on others. Undermining Israel's existence—and all that it means to me and many millions of others—will not buy peace from the terrorists. All it will do is add untold anguish to people whose history of suffering is already quite overextended, and to my personal suffering.

Avner Even-Zohar

Avner Even-Zohar is the director of the Campus Division and Tzavta Program at the Israel Center of the San Francisco Jewish Community Federation. A native Israeli, he served in the Israeli army, including in the West Bank during the first Palestinian uprising (intifada) and in Lebanon.

FROM SAFED TO SAN FRANCISCO STATE

When I asked my grandmother why she has never left Israel, she answered, "Why? I have more than everything I need right here." Her brother once tried to create a family tree. He traced it back to the sixteenth century and said he thought our family has been living in the land of Israel continuously since the days of King David.

For generations, my family has lived in the upper Galilee, in the mystical town of Safed, Israel's highest mountain town. Known as the capital of Jewish mysticism, the kabbalah's most famous promoter, Rabbi Isaac Luria (and not Madonna, contrary to popular belief), lived and taught there. My great-grandfather's stone house is a short walk from Rabbi Luria's humble though magnificent synagogue.

Whenever my parents went on vacation, my grandmother schlepped me and my younger brother on three buses from Tel Aviv to Safed. We helped carry our bags along the narrow, shadowy alleys of the Old City to our great-grandfather's house. Safed is a city with more secrets than people, with a spirit of mystery in the air, like a riddle that has been waiting to be solved for three thousand years. But in Safed, I learned that time is not as important as spirituality.

My great-grandpa knew most of the people in his hometown. With his long white beard, and his beautiful eyes, this Torah scholar was a devout mystic. I'll never forget when he bought me a camera for my fifth birthday. I've long ago lost the photos I took, but memories of conversations with him and my grandmother are still vivid. At twilight on a beautiful summer day, as we were all sitting on the big balcony overlooking the pine trees and green mountains of Canaan, my grandma sat back, took a deep breath as if to fill herself with the splendor of it all, and told us a story that was anything but splendid.

"Of course I speak Arabic, how couldn't I? We had wonderful friendships with the local Arabs who lived among us, we knew them very well, they were our neighbors, and we did a lot of business with them. Muhammad made us shoes for the winter and sandals for the summer. For my five brothers and sisters and me, he was the best shoemaker. He often came to visit our house," recalled Grandma.

"But when I was nine years old it all changed. It was 1929 and Arab violence spread all over the country like a fire on a hot summer day. It could have been like Hebron," she said, describing how most of the ancient Hebron Jewish community was massacred by an Arab mob. "In Safed they were trying to do the same thing. An Arab mob flooded the streets, attacking any Jew in sight. We were hiding right here in the basement. All eight of us. I was only nine years old but remember it as if it was yesterday. And then as we heard the mob approaching our house, we suddenly recognized a familiar voice. Our friend Muhammad. He yelled out that the mob should put all the Jews in one house and kill them together. Not one by one. And I understand Arabic very well, but could not understand his hate. Frankly, I still don't to this very day. Muhammad, who often came to our house as like family suddenly wants to kill us all. And he was the one directing the mob to our house. Luckily, the British police arrived and escorted all the Jews to the local police station."

My great-grandpa was still angry about this irony. For four days, hundreds of frightened Jews were crowded into the police station. He described how the British police saved them but treated the Jews like prisoners while they let the Arab hooligans loot Jewish property for four days.

After the British let the Jews out, Grandma recalled how they found their house. In ruins. Their Arab neighbors had looted money, furniture, clothing. Whatever they didn't take, they burned.

And Muhammad? He continued living in Safed with his family; the British police did not arrest him.

"Believe me," said Grandpa. "Zionism won. Now we have our own state, our own army, and need no British mandate to protect us." Then he suddenly put his hand on my head and said, "Hopefully in a few years you will do your share."

I did. I served in the Israeli army for six years as an education officer and made it to captain. The Israeli army gives all its male and female recruits a medical profile ranging from 21 to 97. Why not 100? According to a military legend, only God is perfect, hence, we humans can only reach 97 percent of physical perfection. Others truly believe that the missing 3 percent is to be found in the incomplete male body—most male recruits are circumcised. I had asthma, so my medical profile was 45, but I still made it through the officers' course. As an education officer, I volunteered to serve in combat zones along the border with (and inside) Lebanon as well as the West Bank during the first wave of Palestine terrorism from 1987 to 1993. Currently I carry on the important job of education as director of the Campus Division for the Israel Center in San Francisco, which is part of the Jewish Community Federation. My job is to promote Israel education and balanced discussions on the campuses in the Bay Area. San Francisco is one of the most active epicenters of anti-Israel sentiment on U.S. campuses, so it is more than a full-time job.

I cherish the diversity and liberal thinking of the San Francisco Bay Area. However, I've discovered that many people here value open-mindedness and free speech, but not when it comes to the Jewish state.

I went to San Francisco State University on May 9, 2002, a few days after students and members of the anti-Israel faculty (there are quite a few) and staff had put on a hateful anti-Israel/anti-Zionist rally. Like most of their rallies, this one was blatantly anti-Semitic. It featured some of their all-time favorites: they would burn Israeli flags. The Israeli flags they wouldn't burn had swastikas instead of the Star of David. Some posters depicted a Star of David equaling the swastika. Others had grotesque cartoons of Jews with black coats and long noses. Others depicted Prime Minister Sharon as a dog. And a pig. They chanted slogans like "Two, four, six, eight, Israel is racist state," "Sharon is Hitler," and many more sickening ones.

I was there because in response, the pro-Israel, pro-peace students (and only a very few brave faculty) gathered for their own—much smaller—rally. Some of the outraged San Francisco Jewish community members showed up. There were about three hundred pro-Israel supporters and about eighty anti-Israel demonstrators. Although the university police built barricades between the camps, some people crossed them. I stood with a sign that said, "Would you like to be gay in Israel or in Saudi Arabia?" This was to illustrate the fact that Israel, the only democracy in the Middle East, is also the only gay mecca of the Middle East. While LGBT (lesbian, gay, bisexual, and transgender) people are being harassed, persecuted, arrested, and even executed all over the Arab world, Israel is home to a vibrant queer community with thousands of people taking part in annual pride parades in Tel Aviv, Jerusalem, and Eilat. Jerusalem will host the second ever world pride parade in summer 2006. In many areas, the legal status of queer people in Israel is more advanced than in the United States. For example, openly gay soldiers are in the highest ranks in the military. Israel has the world's strictest federal protection against workplace sexual discrimination.

But in the United States, the "open-minded" leftists and liberals show such blind hate toward Israel they are unwilling to see how Israel supports the same social causes they support in the United States and elsewhere. At that rally at San Francisco State, I saw a small group from the San Francisco queer community shouting, "Queers Against Israeli Terrorism." They ignored the fact that Israel is a safe haven for many gay Palestinians who under death threats from their families and government cross the border *into* Israel. Without Israeli protection, many of these Palestinians would be killed.

And then a young student introduced himself to me. Yousof was a graduate student from Saudi Arabia.

"Nice to meet you," I said. "Avner from Israel."

It was my first time meeting a Saudi Arabian. He ignored the gay issue and cut right to the point. "Were you born in Israel?" he asked.

"Yes," I replied.

"But your parents. Where did they come from?" he continued pressing.

"Both were born in Israel as well," I assured him.

"And your grandparents?" Since I knew where this stranger was going with this family tree inquiry, I did not mention my three Holocaust survivor grandparents and focused on the family of my maternal grandma. "They were all born in Israel and the family has been there since King David. We never left; do you know why?" Now it was my turn to ask.

"Why?" he said.

"Because it is our land; why would we leave it?" I told him about the continuous Jewish presence in the land of Israel, but he did not want to hear.

As the rally ended, dozens of anti-Israel students pushed the barricades toward the pro-Israel students and shoved them against the wall of the Student Center. The police intervened. The event was filmed and made the national news, a reason why the General Union of Palestinian Students Organization was expelled from campus for a year.

Many Jewish students are no longer shocked by the poisonous anti-Israel atmosphere on campuses. It is shockingly ugly. Sometimes when I am with Jewish students, I feel so proud to be an Israeli. I think of my great-grandpa in Safed. If he were alive today, he might say, "Zionism won; now we have our own state, our own army, and need no British mandate to protect us. But today you need to be an educator. In America. *You* must do your share."

Jane Falk

Jane Falk received her Ph.D. in linguistics from Princeton University and has drawn on those studies in her writing, teaching, and consulting. She lived and worked in Israel twice for several years and has lectured at universities both there and in the United States, including the Hebrew University, Bar-Ilan, University of California, Berkeley, and City University of New York. She is Modern Orthodox, now lives in Berkeley, California, and helps American and Israeli companies on how to bridge cultural divides.

TAKING LIBERTIES

The first time I visited Israel I was twenty-something—young, but hardly a child. Yet, a waiter at a Jerusalem restaurant exclaimed, "Good girl!" when he found no leftovers on my plate. In the San Francisco Bay Area, where I live now, the customer would withhold his tip for that remark.

I was further taken aback when I entered Binyanei HaUma, the main Jerusalem concert hall, to see the Israel Philharmonic. The ticket-taker glanced at my stub, rolled his eyes, shook his hand up and down, and mock-groaned, "Oooh, expensive!" What business was it of his?!

No less surprising was the passerby who stopped my friend in the middle of taking a photo of me and told him, "No, you're in the wrong place—the sun should be *behind* you." (Of course he was right.)

The longer I was there, the more I realized that such behavior was the rule rather than the exception. And while some might consider it intrusive, patronizing, or downright rude, the truth is, I was charmed from the outset. These Israeli strangers talked to me in exactly the way my family had during my upbringing in New York.

I was hooked on Israel from the beginning. A "disease," some call it, one that lasts a lifetime. It started with the visceral delight of walking the cobblestone streets of Jerusalem at the ebb of day when the stone buildings take on a pale sienna hue and the footsteps of our ancestors in Temple times are almost audible. Over time, a sense of home evolved, more so than it ever has in California and more deeply than in my native New York. But for me it was not so much because Israel is the Jewish homeland, or even because the majority of the population is Jewish, but mainly because the way the Israelis spoke to me made me feel surrounded by close relatives—that is, "at home."

In the waiter's remark I could almost hear my mother's triumphant voice as a clean spoon emerged in my high chair. When I grew up, she and the extended family, forever in and out of our Ocean Parkway duplex, expressed opinions about my every turn: "Cheap is not cheap," Papa proffered if I tried to impress him with my latest bargain. "Nice girls don't live on their own" was the mantra when I rented a tenement apartment in the Village. So even the Israeli saleswoman who persisted, ignoring my objections, "But the dress is perfect on you—how can you not buy it?" sparked nostalgia for long-ago shopping trips with my mother rather than annoyance. In Nordstrom's in San Francisco, if I solicit advice, the response is a sober "Do *you* like it?"

This feeling of home was strong enough to propel me to Israel when the Yom Kippur War broke out in 1973, though I was in the middle of graduate studies at Princeton at the time. My linguistics chairperson protested: "When a country is at war people usually leave, they don't *go* there." But he did grant me the leave, albeit reluctantly. So while my classmates remained safely squirreled in their carrels studying syntax, I spent three weeks picking oranges, replacing kibbutzniks who were on the front.

My enchantment with the way Israelis spoke bore out the assumption that had sent me to graduate school in the first place: that the key to relationships, the reason we "connect" to one person rather than another, lies in the communication. I came to discover that communication style can account for rapport with an entire culture as well.

For one thing, I love the Israelis' informality. It is refreshing to be able to call everyone by first name and to not be able to tell by the way someone is talking whether he is addressing the prime minister or a close friend. Israelis even use affectionate nicknames for their leaders—Ariel Sharon is commonly referred to as "Arik," for example. The casualness seeps into public discourse, too: the media reported the president as inviting Israel's first Olympic gold medal winner to his official residence—not to "congratulate" him, as every other president in the world would put it, but "to give him a hug!"

It's okay in Israel to pinch the cheek of a stranger's baby, or even to pat the belly of a pregnant woman you don't know. More than informal, behavior that elsewhere would be considered presumptuous is the norm. "Presumptuousness" is a culturally relative notion, I came to understand. For Israelis, the way you *embark* on a relationship is by being presumptuous. Taking liberties, verbally or nonverbally, that for others would only be appropriate in an *existing* close relationship—specifically, their sort of family one—is the way to bond. Indeed, it bonded me!

And Israelis like nothing better than to bond. So, in every setting, from a restaurant to a government office to the university, no matter their official role, personnel feel no compunction about offering you an opinion, a feeling, or a snappy retort. As a result, going about one's daily business, usually a humdrum affair, turns into a series of dramatic or fun interpersonal encounters. I heard a bus driver once, when asked by a passenger what his last stop was, quip, "Home, of course!" (Americans find it hard to believe that a sense of humor is a universal trait anywhere, but it is in Israel.)

Israeli parentalism can be moving. When my friend left her X-rays at the supermarket (in the Israeli health system, you are often the guardian of your records) and rushed back to retrieve them, the clerk who had held them for her moved close, touched her arm gently, and, brow furrowed with concern, whispered, "Are you all right, *momele?*"

I'm pushing sixty now, and still, on my most recent trip to Israel, the old Russian-born security guard at a small branch post office during a *chamsin* held out a cup of lemonade to me. "But it's your mug," I protested. "So what?" he insisted (and I actually took a sip, something I'd never do in San Francisco). After all, we were family.

Was the guard really worried that I, a complete stranger, was getting dehydrated? Did the supermarket clerk care what my friend's X-rays showed? Well, yes, to a greater degree than you'd find in most places, I'd say. Certainly, few Israelis would hesitate to help out if they see you are in trouble. And a sob story never fails to get you what you want from these softhearted sabras. "*Kol Yisroel chaverim*" ("All of Israel are friends") goes the national motto, and it seems to manifest at every moment.

There's another side of the coin, though. The sabra fruit, to which Israelis are likened, is prickly on the outside. Relatives can let you know what they think, and in no uncertain terms. My own are sometimes critical, sometimes brusque. They can give me an argument, don't worry about interrupting or inconveniencing me, and almost always think they know better than I do. So it is with Israelis. While this sort of treatment sometimes raised my hackles at home, from these strangers who had no real power over me, I was only charmed. During one of my sojourns (I travel back and forth often, and have twice lived in Israel for a few years at a time), when I asked a bank teller I'd never seen before in my life to put a rush on my new checks, she snapped, "Why didn't you order them sooner?" "Only in Israel do you have to explain yourself to the bank teller!" I laughed to myself, and mumbled, "I was out of the country" in my defense.

I stayed at a reasonably good hotel not so long ago and could not get the desk to comply with my wish that they hold my calls during certain hours. Finally, I took the receiver off the hook. In no time, a hotel employee was banging on my door, shouting, "Your phone is off the hook!" The hotel's obliviousness to my personal boundaries struck me as hilarious. But when my aunt refused to acknowledge the time difference between New York and California and would regularly call at 6:00 A.M. without apology, I was not amused.

And relatives feel no need to engage in social niceties. Government employees are especially notorious for their curtness. They think that "He's not here" is enough to say to a caller; that "I don't know" is a perfectly acceptable answer to an inquiry. By talking this way they are being direct, Israeli-style, not purposely rude (well, most of them, anyway). In their system, it's up to the caller to ask a follow-up question, such as, "Who *does* have the information?"

Even the student-teacher relationship is not sacrosanct, I discovered; when I was teaching cross-cultural communication at an Israeli university, one of my students yelled out, "That's wrong!" in the middle of a lecture. This forced me to interrupt the class, and provided a living example of cultural differences. He may have been stealing the spotlight, but he wasn't intending disrespect. On the contrary. For him, his interruption showed how involved he was, and challenging me was an invitation to argue, ergo bond. Argumentativeness, even when accompanied by raised voices, is a way of life for Israelis. It is a sociable enterprise, perpetuated perhaps by the culture of Talmudic study halls where students partner to argue the finest points of Jewish law. At the end of the semester I found a line outside my office of students waiting to argue for higher grades.

Laypeople attribute the Israelis' brusqueness to the inordinate degree of stress they are under. I'm sure that is a factor. But as a linguist, I don't think it's the main one. For one thing, biblical Hebrew has examples of sarcasm and complaining, even to God and His chosen leaders ("Were there not enough graves in Egypt that you brought us to die in the desert?" ask the Israelites of Moses). For another, like my grandparents, the founding settlers spoke the Yiddish of the small Eastern European shtetls, and that influenced their way of speaking Hebrew, just as it did my grandparents' English (hence the familiarity for me).

A language of intimacy could only take hold, however, because Israel is such a tiny country, no larger in area than the state of New Jersey, with a population under seven million. With its migrations from distant lands, speaking over a hundred different languages, there is probably no society in the world as diverse, yet 80 percent are Jews, People of the Book, with a shared history. On top of this, Israel has universal conscription—a people's army. The CEO of a company and its janitor could well have shared a foxhole. (No wonder they are on a first-name basis!) Also, Israel was set up quasi-socialist, less hierarchical from the start. And yes, the population has gone through a series of wars and gruesome terrorist attacks together. All these elements show up in the no-holds-barred way they talk.

Whether you are an immigrant or a tourist, whether you speak Hebrew or not, when you enter into Israeli society you are at the same time entering into a family—a particular sort of family—reflected in its apparently presumptuous familial communication patterns. If you have good associations with those patterns, as I do, or if you understand where the Israelis are "coming from," as I have tried to illuminate here, Israel easily becomes your home of the heart, as it has for me.

But change is afoot. In response to complaints, the Ministry of Interior has instituted a new "lexicon" for its clerks and secretaries, one that emphasizes "respect and dignity." Employees who answer the telephone are being trained to avoid saying, "I don't know" and rather to offer, "That's a good question, let me check." Instead of "Wait," they will say, "Could you wait? I have another call"; in the place of "You're lying" is "The information you gave me is incorrect."

My guess is that this generation of ministry clerks will have a hard time implementing the new protocol. It feels phony to them. Besides, they don't understand what all the hullabaloo is about. Their children, though, are another story.

Such "improvements" reflect the inevitable impact of globalization. Many younger Israelis, products of the Internet, American television, and foreign travel, react with the same distaste that outsiders do to the Israeli penchant for taking liberties, even of the parental type. When its own members start to find fault with their culture's characteristic behavior, it can mean the familial bonds are beginning to fray.

I lament this turn of events. I confess that at moments, Israelis can be hard to deal with, even for me—I don't always feel like an argument or an encounter. But the shift is worrisome. It may bring the Israelis more into line with the West, but will the demise of the stylistic glue contribute to lack of cohesiveness among them? And how will the young tourists like the one I once was feel they are among family if no waiter ever remarks, "Good girl!?"

Tovah Feldshuh

Tovah Feldshuh is an actress who has been nominated for three Tony Awards. She has appeared on the stage in Yentl *and* Lend Me a Tenor *and as Golda Meir in* Golda's Balcony, *on the television show* Law & Order, *and in the film* Kissing Jessica Stein.

What does Israel mean to me?

Courage. The Israelis have more courage in their pinky finger than I have in my whole life. Going to the supermarket in Eretz Yisroel is an act of courage. I love, admire, and will eternally raise money for Israel because I am well aware that she takes the bullets for me. She is my life insurance. My family has lived in America for more than a century. I never considered making aliyah to Israel because the U.S.A. has been so good to us and because I do not have the courage. I raise a glass to those who do.

Charles Fenyvesi

Charles Fenyvesi is a veteran reporter of the Israeli daily newspaper Ha'aretz, *the* Washington Post, *and* U.S. News and World Report. *He now edits the weekly electronic newsletter* Bigotry Monitor; *his books include* When Angels Fooled the World: Rescuers of Jews in Wartime Hungary, *an account of the rescue of thousands of Hungarian Jews—including the author and members of his family—by daring gentiles in Nazi-occupied Hungary.*

To me, Israel is family. Most of my relatives live in Israel, by now nearly all of them born and raised there. We greet one another with tight hugs that can go on for as long as a minute and with kisses on both cheeks. I am at home in their houses and apartments, and they feel the same way when they visit my nuclear family in the United States.

My Israeli cousins are descendants of two sets of two brothers born in a Hungarian village, first cousins who grew up in one household and thought of one another as brothers. Bedi, my mother's youngest brother, was a pioneer who left home at age sixteen and emigrated to the British Mandate of Palestine in 1929, Endre and Samuel arrived in 1949, and the fourth, my mother's favorite brother, Anti, in 1957. These founding fathers have passed on, but they are remembered fondly by the combined total of their eleven children whose children and grandchildren and great-grandchildren I can't keep tabs on. Aunt Kati, the wise but sadly childless family elder, estimates the current tally at well over sixty. I am in touch with all the adults, at least indirectly.

Of the four brothers, I was especially close to two: Anti, as good as the best home-baked bread, and Bedi, who could give you a lift like a slug of slivovitz at daybreak.

Toward the end of World War II, Anti fled across the Hungarian front line in the hope of joining the Russian army, only to be arrested and sent to a labor camp where he mined lead twelve hours a day for three years. When he was shipped back to Budapest at age thirty-five, he looked like a broken old man. He recovered, and ten years later he left for Israel, where he joined a moshav and raised cattle and chickens for more than two decades. Fair-minded and considerate, Anti was elected to the village council year after year despite his poor Hebrew, and he received kudos as a rare impartial referee at soccer games that sometimes stirred spectators to violence.

Across the road from Anti lived Bedi, who impetuously quit the kibbutz he had helped to found in the early 1930s. In the moshav, he switched crops every two or three years, gambling on new ventures that the Agriculture Department's extension agent suggested to him. Fellow villagers questioned his choices and then envied his success. When he was diagnosed with diabetes, he shrugged off the advice of doctors, who prescribed a strict diet. He loved cakes and would not stop eating them. "I want to live well," he said. "It doesn't matter how soon I die." His muscles declined so he could not stand up, and he lost his eyesight. Yet he remained a genial, ever-cheerful host. Surprising his doctors, he lived eighty-one years, and up to the end he could somehow identify each of his four children and sixteen grandchildren from a distance of six feet.

Bedi and Anti were the kind of people who made Israel grow. They both rejected notions such as that Jews should settle every piece of land occupied by Tsahal and that the state should entice settlers with economic benefits. After the 1967 war, they both argued for trading land for peace. They believed that power alone would never force Arabs to change their hatred of Jews.

The adult descendants of the four founders are mostly paired off, and the partners come from families that originated in Russia, Poland, Romania, Morocco, Iraq, and Yemen. Only two of my cousins married fellow Hungarians, one of them New York–born. Three children per nuclear family is the standard, but one cousin who married relatively late in life sired eight. Their worlds pivot around children, not careers or causes. None of them is rich, and none is on welfare. Farmers are the most numerous among them, closely followed by drivers of trucks and vans. Others earn their living in offices, schools, and hospitals, and doing social work. Their faces, their gestures, and sometimes their sense of humor remind me of relatives who perished in the Holocaust, as does their unconditional, reflexive love of our extended family. We agree wholeheartedly that *mishpachah* is the fixed point around which our lives turn.

Those I spend time with during visits or on the phone say that the present is the worst time of their lives, and it shows no sign of improving. They do not have ideas on how to end an era dominated by suicide bombers. They distrust their leaders whom they do not know personally; I distrust the politicians because I have met some of them. We agree that they are not up to the job that is admittedly impossible. Nevertheless, says Cousin David, we have to believe that there is a solution even if there isn't any in view; we have to keep hoping that a solution will be found. Somehow. Isn't life a search for solutions? There has got to be a way to peace. He questions the wisdom of occupation that he suspects has led to Arab despair, and he sighs and presses his lips together when referring to the extremism of the Jewish settlers west of the Jordan River. He grimaces when discussing Arik Sharon's wall that he fears will not stop attacks, and he frowns upon the humiliation of Arabs as an implicit state policy.

David's older brother Ilan, a truck driver now semiretired, supports a policy of "a strong hand," letting the Arabs know "who is the master." Yet he may be the only one in the family with several Arab friends whom he really, *really* likes, he says.

I love my Israeli cousins even when I disagree with their politics. I hold back no criticism and they don't either. But soon I realize that arguing with them is like arguing with myself.

Unlike most of their fellow Israelis, my cousins do not debate political issues at family events. They may express their dislike of a policy or a politician, and someone may offer a rebuttal. But they do not engage in the drawn-out shouting matches with escalating fury that characterize Israeli political debates. My cousins have other priorities. They have to get up in the morning, be at work or school on time, make a decent living, find spouses and friends, and raise children. They do not dwell on negatives. "We must go on living here," says Cousin Shosh, a practical idealist like her father Anti. "That's our politics." She calls for pursuing a full life, a good life. Indeed, the cousins eat more than they should, preferring spicy dishes whether inspired by Hungarian or Arab cuisine. They go on hikes inside Israel and travel abroad ("It's in our nomadic genes," they say) and visit one another ("It's a must"). They laugh a lot, and they get enthusiastic over a lovely female body or a boyfriend's wry sense of humor, the sharp early morning air of Jerusalem ("Maybe it will make us smarter"), and the scarlet sunset spilling over the Negev that has the color of an aged lion ("A hue that induces peace of mind"). They dance enthusiastically at weddings and outdo one another when giving eulogies at funerals. They love stories and argue passionately about their meanings.

The men have fought in some of Israel's many wars but it is hard to get them to talk about their time in the military. One day, Cousin Allon, burly and taciturn, was cornered into revealing how unbelievably heavy was his equipment that he had to carry on his back and how all his bones ached after each march "as if they were broken into small pieces." His refrain: "Tsahal is tough."

His uncle David was recently prodded to tell the story of how in the Yom Kippur War his unit took Mount Hermon from Syria on October 23, 1973, just as darkness fell. There was little shooting as the Syrians fled upon seeing the Israeli helicopters land and soldiers jump out of them. Night came quickly, and a system of watches was set up in case of a counterattack. David found a boulder that blocked the icy wind and went to sleep alongside it. When his turn to watch came at daybreak, he discovered that the boulder that protected him at night had a weather-beaten Hebrew inscription scrawled into it: "Kibbutz Maabaroth, 23.7.1942." He remembered his father Bedi telling him that he and fellow kibbutzniks once climbed the mountain, the highest peak in the area, and left behind a message.

Under cross-examination, David acknowledged that he had led his unit of a hundred men on what was initially considered a dangerous mission, and he was the first to jump out of the helicopter. No one under his command was killed, and he never had reason to fire his gun. "I am no war hero," he said. "I returned home from the war without firing a single bullet."

In the 1960s I substituted for Uncle Anti on guard duty one night. I walked around his village with a partner, a Moroccan Jew in his fifties who told me about how each town in his native land had a Jewish quarter and how relations were good except when Muslim extremists rose suddenly, as if out of the ground, and stabbed or shot every Jew they could find. But then they vanished as quickly as they came. Such is life, he concluded, and shrugged with an upward jerk of the shoulders and pursed lips, just like an East European Jew. But, he added, thank God, men and their moods do change, and a big change can come from one moment to the next.

I do not think that a foreigner would now be permitted to guard a village. Professionals do the job now, but even they cannot stop infiltrators from the West Bank entering on moonless nights, stealing cars or farm equipment and ruining what they cannot remove. My friend is no longer with us to tell me what he thinks. But I heard that his children endorse the idea of a high wall to keep out bad neighbors.

Brought up secular, my Israeli cousins speak of the Orthodox with contempt because "the black hats avoid hard work and military service." They are wide-eyed with wonder when I talk about our Hasidic ancestors who belonged to that small minority of Jews working on the land.

My uncles used to tell me that their sabra children had no interest in hearing about the *galut*, a term of contempt for the Diaspora. "This country is about the future," Uncle Bedi liked to say. "The past doesn't matter." His son David, a model farmer, is baffled when I mention the piles of compost and manure our great-grandfathers built and spread over their fields in the fall. David regrets his ignorance, as does his daughter Rinat, who finds that "the cut" with the past that her grandfather made "shut off" the next two generations from traditions such as practical Kabbalah, which she now knows that our ancestors applied on the land they first rented and eventually owned.

Yoav, Uncle Bedi's youngest son, is the most courteous driver of huge tractor-trailers. He is surprised when I tell him that our forefathers were proud owners of horse-drawn wagons as early as the eighteenth century. Each called himself a *balagola*, which in Hungarian Yiddish meant not just a coachman but suggested a Jew on his way up from poverty as he could carry his produce to the market and do commissions for others. With a wagon and just one horse, one could provide for his family. Recognizing the word *balagola* as borrowed from Hebrew, Yoav is tickled. As my first Hebrew teacher at age nine—I was twenty-two—he makes sure that I know that the word literally means "Master of the Wheel." It occurs to him that he earns a living the same way, though the tractor-trailer he drives is not his.

My Israeli cousins have an unstated, implicit belief in *tikun olam*—repairing the world—though few of them are aware that it is a Hasidic principle. They not only are hard workers but they keep trying new techniques—such as computer-controlled irrigation—and try to adopt and even invent new methods. They believe in updating and upgrading the equipment they work with, and they think that such an exploration is *derech eretz*—the right way, though they shy away from such Talmudic phrases and the solemnity they carry and the faith in divine direction they imply. Having been trained to respect made-in-America modernity and to disdain East European *galut*, my cousins find it hard to accept that despite oppression and anti-Semitism, viable Jewish worldviews existed before the birth of Israel, and that their dedication to hard work and their resilience in the face of adversity can be traced to *galut* villages they have never visited.

I thought of my family when filing from Washington breathless dispatches and ponderous commentaries for the U.S.-style *Jerusalem Post* and later for *Ha'aretz*, Tel Aviv's answer to *Die Zeit*. What would my cousins say, I often asked myself, for instance, when reporting an exclusive: the chilling analysis of a senior U.S. official after the first few days of the 1973 war. "Israel's survival hangs in the balance," he revealed, and "the odds right now are no better than fifty-fifty."

I did not question the senior official's sincerity, and I parsed his words with extra care. His face was chalk white; his stentorian voice at times trembled. I could surmise which side he was on in the policy debate of rushing arms to Israel—the question my cousins would surely ask but I would not. He knew how I felt when listening to the brutally candid U.S. assessment that turned out to be accurate even though Israel's government had held it back from the public. He was weighing the fate of my family.

I wish I could say that I was confident that Tsahal would eventually push the attacking armies back to the prewar ceasefire lines. I wasn't. Fortunately, my job did not call for boosting morale. I was a reporter assigned to convey the U.S. assessment the way I heard it, without a skew or a spin—a form of detachment not many Israelis appreciate. Nowadays when the war is fought inside the country and every passenger on a bus and each customer in a restaurant is a target for a suicide bomber, I tell myself that Israel will endure as it must and that it will return to the normalcy of a civil society one day. But I am not covering this war.

Israel will not be another failed dream of the century that is behind us, a black hole for ideologies. My sober uncle as well as his visionary brother would agree. Our lives need not unfold according to immutable ancient laws of hostility, and we need not rely on a divine promise as interpreted by self-appointed interpreters of His word. We can avert an evil decree, whether by a stern God who lost His temper or by frustrated politicians seething in hate.

I have faith in Israel's decent, hardworking, ordinary people, such as the members of my family. They may seem literal and pragmatic, at times too ready to fall back on the bottom line of military superiority and hesitant about devoting more energy to peacemaking and the many patient steps that must come before that. They are products of a system that won three wars and innumerable skirmishes. But at least some of them have an inkling that they must drastically revise their relations with the Palestinians, as one cannot live by gun alone.

It seemed a good sign when after a sixteen-year-old Palestinian suicide bomber killed three people in Tel Aviv in November 2004, his mother denounced the extremists who indoctrinated her son. But then Tsahal applied the routine punishment of demolishing her house, and the mother now praises the extremists. There must be ways to break out of the vicious circle of murderous attack and retaliation with punitive overkill and additional humiliation in bureaucratic contacts with the Palestinians. The sparks of ingenuity and flexibility inherited from *galut* ancestors should light up a path out of the current crisis that was created by an intifada unforeseen by the nation's smug politicians who thought they had a monopoly on initiatives and firepower.

Barney Frank

Barney Frank has represented Massachusetts in the U.S. House of Representatives since 1981. In 2002 he visited Israel and met with Israeli prime minister Ariel Sharon.

As a Jew, I have a strong emotional attachment to Israel. As a liberal committed to acting on the basis of universal norms, I have constantly on my mind the potential tension between the particularistic feelings that come from my own identity and those norms.

Fortunately, the case of Israel presents no dilemma in this regard. Wholly apart from my feelings as a Jew, strong support for Israel is the logical consequence of my political principles.

This does not mean that I have no disagreements with Israeli policies. Nations form a spectrum, with Norway and the Netherlands among the best, while North Korea, Burma, and Zimbabwe anchor the negative. By all of the values that motivate me, Israel is well on the positive side.

This is particularly impressive because Israel has maintained a vigorous, untrammeled, democratic politics from its very first day as a nation, despite facing constant, grave threats to its very existence.

The persistence of a vigorous democracy within Israel during this period of continuous national security threats of the highest order is an important refutation of the argument that democracy is a luxury to be enjoyed only by mature, wealthy societies that face no significant external threat.

. . .

It is true that the Israeli government has been guilty of violations of some rights of residents of the territories it administers in Gaza and the West Bank. Recognizing Israel's need for security, and accepting as I do the fact that it was forced in its own defense to take over those territories in the 1967 war, does not mean that every action of the Israeli government in Gaza and the West Bank is justifiable. But it is also the case that some of the most vigorous, informed, eloquent criticisms of the shortcomings of the Israeli government in this regard have consistently come from within Israeli society, and while those critics may not always have been popular, neither have they been suppressed.

The attachment of the people of Israel to democracy has most recently manifested itself in the painful decision to withdraw from Gaza, and the strong support that exists for withdrawal from at least some parts of the West Bank. The arguments against this have been trumped by the recognition that it is impossible for Israel to remain a Jewish, democratic state if it contains within its broadest borders millions of Palestinians hostile certainly to its Jewishness and in many cases to its democracy. It is still not clear how much of a withdrawal from the West Bank will occur. But the very fact that this debate is being carried on, given its painful nature for so many Israelis, underlines the centrality of Israel's commitment to the fundamental democratic principle.

The role of the official Jewishness of Israel is an issue for those attached to liberal norms. Objections to the status of Judaism, which come from those who have no trouble supporting the official Islamic nature of virtually all of Israel's neighbors, can of course be dismissed as pure hypocrisy.

But the fact that it is ludicrous for defenders of the existence of Saudi Arabia to object to the notion of a Jewish state does not entirely answer the argument. To me, the ideal state is neutral among religious and nonreligious people alike, while being firmly committed to protecting the rights of all to worship or not as they choose. But history does argue for occasional exceptions, and here the terrible fact of the

Holocaust and the failure of virtually all of the rest of the world not only justified but demanded the establishment of one country where Jews could always be sure of a haven. What realistic liberal principles call for in this case is a state that establishes Judaism as its religion, but extends to all others the basic freedoms that every human being ought to have.

Ethnic and religious minorities within Israel are treated far better than they are in any of Israel's neighboring countries, but still not as well as liberal principles require. As to the first point, if you are an Arab citizen of a Middle Eastern nation today, and you wish to denounce your government, publish newspapers critical of it, vote against its continuation in office, and in fact be represented in your country's parliament by officials who are free to speak their mind, you are better off living in Israel than in any other country in the area.

But the problem is that some of the most deeply religious people in Israel, as in our own country and elsewhere in the world, distressingly believe that it is not enough that they be free to worship as they choose, but that others be curtailed in their right to differ. One of the consequences of the centrality of the security issue in Israeli politics is that those whose primary goal is the establishment of a rigid religious regime exercise the balance of power, resulting in their having more influence over public policy than their numbers would justify.

On the question of Israel's compliance with liberal principles, one aspect of Israeli society gets far too little respect from those on the left who are harshly critical of Israel. That is the subject of the role in society of gay, lesbian, bisexual, and transgendered people.

For the past several years, gay male Palestinians have found refuge within Israel from homophobia in the Palestinian areas. The Israeli government has not loudly trumpeted this, but it has been one of the most humane aspects of Israeli policy and stands in very sharp contrast to the norm in its Arab neighbors. Nor is Israel's moral superiority here limited only to Arab refugees. Within Israel, gays and lesbians enjoy significantly greater rights than they do in most countries in the world. There have been several openly gay elected officials in Israel. Gay and lesbian organizations thrive, publishing newspapers, holding large parades—even in Jerusalem over the objection of some who would restrict the freedom of others in the name of religion.

In one gay-related public policy area in particular, I fervently wish Israel's example would be followed in the United States. The argument for banning gay and lesbian people from serving openly in the U.S. armed forces is that the presence of homosexuals in a military unit would cause such friction as to interfere with the unit's fighting capability. Those of us who have argued against this policy have consistently pointed to the other militaries in the world in which no such ban exists. The response we get is that the militaries to which we are alluding are not "real" armies. The rock on which this logic shatters is the experience of the Israel Defense Forces. Gay and lesbian Israelis serve openly and with distinction in the IDF, and I have yet to meet any American prepared to argue that the Israel Defense Forces have somehow been rendered ineffective in this regard.

No country in the history of the world has ever been able to govern a hostile population without some abuses. Young men and women forced to defend themselves and their country against hostility will on the whole behave decently, but will occasionally engage in cruelty; angry emotions will inevitably from time to time overrule judgment and principle. It is entirely legitimate for people to press the Israeli government to do more to minimize abuse. This is a reason to press for changes in Israeli policy, but not a reason to demonize the country. Israel is, by the standards of liberal principles, imperfect. It is also far less imperfect than any other nation in that part of the world, and most centrally considerably less imperfect than any other nation which has faced the constant security threats that have confronted Israel for its entire national life.

So in the end, my particularistic and universal impulses come together. As a Jew, I am very proud of the example Israel gives the rest of the world against the arguments of those who are constantly finding justifications for denying or deferring democracy.

Samuel Freedman

Samuel Freedman, a professor at Columbia University's Graduate School of Journalism, is a former staff reporter for the New York Times and currently writes the weekly column "On Education," as well as frequent articles on culture. He is a member of USA Today's board of contributors and has contributed to numerous other publications and Web sites, including New York magazine, Rolling Stone, Salon, and BeliefNet. He is the author of four acclaimed books, most recently Jew Versus Jew: The Struggle for the Soul of American Jewry, which won the National Jewish Book Award for Non-Fiction in 2001 and made the Publishers Weekly Religion Best-Sellers list.

LOVE DURING WARTIME

Around me in the departure lounge at Newark Airport, crowds formed beneath the monitors permanently tuned to CNN. The screen showed ambulances and blood and weeping, and the speaker broadcast a mixture of sirens and screams. I could hear the onlookers conversing feverishly in Hebrew, and without being able to interpret their words, I understood the essence. A few hours earlier, a suicide bomber had struck outside a disco on the Tel Aviv waterfront called the Dolphinarium, blasting apart twenty Israelis, most of them immigrant teenagers from Russia, so secular they were out clubbing on Shabbat.

All those Israelis there in the airport, so identifiable with their cell phones and wraparound sunglasses and Lycra tops, were taking the overnight flight to Ben-Gurion for the simple reason that they were going home. I was booked for pleasure—an invitation to participate in an academic conference at Tel Aviv University, as well as the chance to visit several friends. And I felt like I was the only American at the gate. Or, to put it more accurately, the only American Jew. There were a half-dozen American passengers wearing buttons with the slogan

"Hearts for Israel," all of them members of a solidarity mission of Christians.

Having learned of the Dolphinarium bombing from a news bulletin, my sister already had begged me to cancel my trip. I didn't dare call my wife and children from the airport, as I normally would, assuming they would know of the attack by now and make the same plea. I felt honor-bound to keep my commitment to the conference and too ashamed in the face of Israeli suffering to retreat to my Manhattan refuge.

In the years since that night in the airport in May 2001, though, I have come to date my special connection with Israel to that particular trip. Not because I felt braver or more virtuous or more Zionistic for having taken it, but because it began a process of discovering the Israeli soul, appreciating the resilience and spirit and gallows humor of a country under terrorist assault. As the novelist Nelson Algren famously said of Chicago, "Like loving a woman with a broken nose, you may well find lovelier lovelies. But never a lovely so real."

From childhood will into my adult years, I never made the typical trip to Israel for an American Jew of my generation. When my classmates and cousins were backpacking there or volunteering on kibbutzim in the late 1960s and early 1970s, I resisted doing what was expected. I heard all the usual stories of rude crowds at bus stops and macho paratroopers who picked up all the American girls. "Imagine a whole country of Puerto Ricans," said one of my high school friends after a summer trip to Israel. "Except they're all Jews."

As I grew into adulthood, I traveled to China, Japan, even Egypt, without giving much thought to seeing Israel. I made my way back into religious life after several decades of estrangement, yet I still bridled in the old, familiar way at the High Holy Days sales pitches for Israel bonds. Every time a theater-producer friend invited me along on the Israel tours he annually led, I prevaricated. I devoured news coverage of Israel, mind you, and read novels by Amos Oz and David Grossman. Something about actually going to Israel, though, just seemed so . . . so . . . predictable.

My work as an author finally provided a legitimate excuse. In reporting a book about the conflicts within American Jewry, I realized many of the tensions had roots or reflections in Israel, and I would need to conduct research there. So on a May afternoon in 1999, at the age of forty-three, I set foot on Israeli soil for the first time. And from the moment the taxicab climbed up the limestone slopes toward Jerusalem and I thought to myself, *So this is what they mean by the Judean Hills*, I recognized how perverse I had been in waiting so long. Those ten days were magical ones, magical both for the excitement of discovery and for the sense of illusion. I happened to be in Israel right as Ehud Barak was being elected prime minister, right when the Oslo optimism soared, right when Jews felt no hesitation buying bargain furniture in Palestinian villages on the West Bank or checking out the jazz clubs of Ramallah.

Within days of the outbreak of the al-Aqsa intifada in September 2000, that whole version of Israel vanished, vanished as instantly as if it never had existed. Initially, I clung to the memories of my first visit out of mere nostalgia. When I returned to Israel in the wake of the Dolphinarium attack for my second trip, though, those images served me well as counterpoint to the embattled nation I now saw. One morning during the academic conference, the whole room went quiet as several military jets could be seen through a picture window streaking up the coast toward Lebanon. Army radio played in every café. I stopped in to the gift shop at the hotel where I'd stayed on my first trip, only to discover the owner had gone broke and shut down. So barren of visitors was Jerusalem that when I hailed a cab to go from the Western Wall to the Mahane Yehuda market, the driver remarked sardonically, "I have the honor of driving the only tourist in all of Israel."

Yet those moments, the expected moments for an Israel at war, were not the ones that most affected me. What struck me far more deeply were the innumerable instances of normality, of daily life being lived as an act of defiance—browsing amid the throngs at an outdoor book fair beside Jerusalem's City Hall, sharing an Italian dinner at a shopping mall in Ra'anana. A high school classmate of mine, who had made aliyah twenty years earlier, lived in the Tel Aviv suburb and had a precocious young writer of a son named Tal. He was the one who kept cracking, as I shopped for sweatshirts in the university bookstore, "Don't you feel unsafe?"

I got a vital insight into the roots of that Israeli attitude on my final afternoon of the trip, when I had lunch with a diplomat from the Israeli Foreign Ministry. He showed me the hottest online joke of the moment. It was a graphic of a measuring stick labeled "ruler of attention and shock." On a numerical scale from 0 to 10, it rated the impact of various terrorist acts—2.5 for shooting at a settlement in the occupied territories, for instance, 7.4 for mortar fire on a development town. Even as Israelis cried and buried and mourned, and God knows there was plenty in the days after the Dolphinarium attack, they insisted on laughing in the face of existential threat.

One year later, I returned, this time to an even more beleaguered land. The son of a journalist friend of mine was becoming bar mitzvah, and as a friend I felt bound to take up the invitation. I figured I would try to defray the costs by working on a few freelance articles as well. Israel had just emerged from its bloodiest month of the intifada, March 2002, culminating in the suicide bombing of a Seder in Netanya. My hotel in Jerusalem was deserted, except for a touring dance troupe. My favorite neighborhood restaurants all had installed armed security guards, and even at that the tables were empty and only the take-out business was booming. The bar mitzvah reception for my friend's son was being held in the same Hyatt Hotel where a Cabinet minister had been assassinated in a Palestinian ambush several months earlier.

And yet again there was this principled refusal to buckle. I wound up writing an article about the nation's most popular television show, *Only in Israel*, which delighted in answering suicide bombing with satire. A typical skit had a romantic couple diving under their café table at every loud noise—a champagne bottle being uncorked, a balloon being pricked, a glass toppling and breaking. The daily newspaper *Ha'aretz* published a "People's Guide to Survival," which included such admonitions as "Don't wait for buses at a bus stop even if you are the only one there." The last in the guide's list of twenty-one rules was the only serious one: "Ignore all of the above and continue life as usual."

So did the Israelis I knew, and so, as a result, did I. I ate in an out-door café in the Shenkin district of Tel Aviv. I rode a public bus from Jerusalem to Kfar Saba. I went on morning runs from Liberty Bell Park onto Hebron Road and up to the army checkpoint near Har Homa. Maybe I was being stupid in my imitation of Israelis. Then again, as a New Yorker who had experienced September 11, 2001, I now had some domestic practice in staying strong.

By the time I made my most recent trip to Israel, in July 2004, the intifada essentially had been defeated, the separation wall was being constructed, and the American tourists were coming back. I grumbled at the fifteen-minute line in passport control at Ben-Gurion, at the wait for a table in the breakfast room of my hotel, at the insistent pitches of the Old City vendors.

I don't want to overstate the change; hundreds of lives had been lost and thousands ruined over the course of the terror campaign. I spent one day of my visit at Camp Koby, a program that combined recreation, camping, and therapy for children who had lost siblings or parents to Palestinian attacks. The camp had been founded by Seth and Sherri Mandell, two American immigrants, in honor of their son, who was bludgeoned to death in a cave on the West Bank several months into the intifada. As I sat with the Mandells at the side of the camp's swimming pool, watching the splashing and horseplay and listening to the yelps of joy, all of this pleasure coming from children who had grieved so much, I realized I was witnessing one more facet of Israel's unbroken spirit.

Since that trip to Israel, I have made one more, bringing my entire family during the summer of 2005. It was their first time, and I was pleased in a proprietary sort of way that they encountered Israel on the rebound, with lines at museums and restaurants, with the psychic wounds being dressed and healed. Grateful as I was to behold all the normality, deep inside I still cherished the country with the broken nose.

Leslie Gelb

Leslie Gelb is the president emeritus of the Council on Foreign Relations and cochairman of the International Crisis Group. A former correspondent for the New York Times, he was awarded a Pulitzer Prize in Explanatory Journalism and is an expert on U.S. foreign policy and national security.

M ine was the generation of American children who grew up selling paper bricks made in Sunday school to plant trees in Israel. It was the generation born just before the outbreak of World War II, and we began to grow up after the war. The bricks and the trees in Israel were mostly abstractions.

Being Jewish took on meaning far before we had any real sense of Israel. Many American Jews like myself knew what it was to be Jewish for the first time when we began to greet relatives who had survived the concentration camps. We went to the West Side of New York, to the docks, and brought home these strangers who were our relatives and who were Jews. They came here because most of their relatives were here. They did not go to Israel. Israel was still only a place we heard about in Sunday school or Hebrew school, a place far away like Kansas. We boys and girls who were born in the United States in the 1930s were Jewish boys and girls before we were Jews attached to Israel. Few of our friends went to Israel, and we knew few who lived there and visited here. Israel was Kansas City; Israel was Oz.

Though my career has been entirely about the world and about international affairs, and though I began to learn a great deal about Israel as I made my way through college and graduate school, a brief time as a professor, and a stint with U.S. senator Jacob Javits of New

York, and thence on to the Pentagon as director of Policy Planning, my first real sense of Israel, my emotional attachment to it, my passion for it, came from my parents.

In 1968 when I was working at the Pentagon, my mother and father retired from their life at a corner grocery store in New Rochelle, New York. They had come to the United States from Czechoslovakia in the 1920s and had never been abroad since their arrival in this country. My father talked often and passionately about Israel. Both parents were always worried about Israel, especially my father. He thought of himself both as an American and as an Israeli. Frankly, I could never tell which was the more dominant feeling. He would rise for both the American and Israeli national anthems. Some years after my wife Judy and I were married, she went with my father to see *Exodus*. At that moment in the film when Israel's independence was announced and when the dancing in the streets of Tel Aviv ceased and the crowd listened to Israel's new national anthem, my father came to his feet in the theater to join his voice with theirs— much to Judy's astonishment.

My father's most fervent dream was not to return to his home-land in Europe, but to visit his spiritual homeland in Israel. So in 1968, my parents embarked on their greatest travel adventure and flew to Israel.

When they returned, my father, Max, had been reborn, in a way possessed. He was so moved by what he saw there, so touched by the Jews having a homeland, so at home with this homeland. With tears filling his eyes, he told me over and over the story of his writing out prayers for the family on little white slips of paper and inserting them into the cracks of the Western Wall. His feelings, so strong and so uncomplicated, occupied my own soul.

Senator Javits, of course, spent a good deal of time on matters relating to Israel. He was a strong supporter of the Jewish state, and working with him on Israeli matters posed little tension. All that changed when I went to work in the Pentagon in 1967. I was there during the Six-Day War and during Israel's attack on the USS *Liberty*, an American eavesdropping ship in the eastern Mediterranean. The

Israelis said it was an accident, but the people in the Pentagon and particularly the military simply did not believe it and still do not believe it to this day. The moment was seminal. The U.S. military had up to this point very positive feelings for Israel. But in the flash of that attack on the *Liberty*, these feelings reversed. This reaction showed me how fragile Israel's standing really was among its American friends, how vulnerable. It convinced me that rational calculations of America's national interests, of who our friends were and were not, could fall easily to events. I saw very clearly then and thereafter that Israel's most enduring friends, particularly in the U.S. government, were those with an emotional tie to a country not because it was a Jewish state, but because it was a free and democratic state, like ours.

My own feelings, quite frankly, were tested some years later when I returned to government during the Carter administration. I served as assistant secretary of state for Politico-Military Affairs in the State Department and was responsible for worldwide arms sales, including sales to Israel. I recommended in favor of literally hundreds of arms and dual technology requests made by Israel. Specifically and most importantly, I recommended the sale of some of the most controversial weapons systems requested by Israel, including cluster bombs and night-fighting technology. Alfred "Roy" Atherton, then assistant secretary of state for Near Eastern Affairs, joined me in this recommendation, which we put in a memo and personally delivered to then secretary of state Cyrus Vance. Given Mr. Vance's and President Carter's opposition to the sales at that time, Roy and I didn't feel it was our place to let anyone know our views on this other than Mr. Vance.

Israeli diplomats in Washington gave us nothing but constant and terribly unpleasant grief. They thought that we, too, were opposed to the arms sales, and they simply unleashed a good deal of nasty talk in Washington. None of this upset me a great deal until they took the criticism up a notch. They leaked the story to the *Jerusalem Post* that accused me of being against the arms sales and referred to me as "a cold Jew." Now, I've been called worse, but my mother, Dorothy, never heard me called worse. She was in a nursing home at the time, quite alert and interested in world affairs, especially in

Israel. I'm sure it will surprise no one to hear that many of her friends telephoned her over the next days to read the good words of the *Jerusalem Post*.

None of this undermined my deep and abiding feelings toward Israel, but those feelings really were tested. I think many Israelis treat Jews who work in the U.S. government on Israel far harder than they treat others. And many of those Jews are tested by these Israeli attacks on them. Yes, I can understand the obsessiveness of Israelis about their security; I'd feel exactly that way in their place—and I feel that way in my place. It is important, however, for Israelis to learn that they should not try to destroy Jews or others in the U.S. government who don't see eye-to-eye with them. Yes, they should argue and be tough, but decency and restraint are called for. Not every bureaucrat or legislator will be a knight wielding a sword for Israel, but many of them can and want to be friends of Israel. Israelis need to be better aware of this.

Israel, of course, touched my life continuously in my years as a journalist for the *New York Times*. I wrote many stories about U.S. policy toward Israel and problems in the relationship. I came to see among many of my colleagues a certain duality of feeling about Israel. Journalists are largely sympathetic toward Israel as a Jewish state, but over the last thirty years or so they have become increasingly more sympathetic to the Palestinians. In the eyes of many of my journalistic colleagues, Israel's treatment of the Palestinians turned the Palestinians into the victims and the Israelis into the persecutors. I don't agree with that sentiment at all, but it is there in the media and it is growing. I hasten to add that I never felt any pressure whatsoever from my editors over the years to be anti-Israeli in my stories. I found the *Times*'s editors to be quite fair-minded and scrupulous when it came to reporting. But the sentiments are there and from time to time they reveal themselves. Israelis need to be more attentive in making sure that their story is told as often and as forthrightly as the Palestinian story. It will be a much harder job for them to do from now on.

I have no sense of conflicting loyalties between being Jewish and American, between being an American and a lover of Israel. I am an American. After that, I am Jewish and dedicated to ensuring that

American support is always there to help Israel to be strong and to work toward peace and security. These feelings grew inside me when Israel was only an abstraction, when I felt Jewish but with no particular feelings toward Israel, when I went through my career, which always involved me with Israel—and these feelings are now me.

Uri Geller

Uri Geller, a paranormalist and best-selling author, has performed for audiences around the world. He was born in Israel, where he spent his early years before moving to Cyprus at age eleven. He returned to Israel at age seventeen and served in the 1967 Six-Day War, in which he was wounded in action. Not long after, he began demonstrating his paranormal abilities in front of small audiences. By 1971 he had become so well known throughout Israel that when the prime minister, Golda Meir, was asked by a reporter to make a prediction about Israel's future, she replied, "Don't ask me—ask Uri Geller!"

The promenade from the port in north Tel Aviv is now complete, all the way to old Jaffa, and for the first time in my life I was able to walk its whole length without stepping onto the sand. It is an extraordinary path, with its vistas of brilliant blue Mediterranean and shimmering yellow beach.

I walked with my children and my wife; that is, they walked and I ran, leaped, and danced. My son kept urging me, "Calm down, Aba, cool it a couple of notches," but I could not. I was frantically invigorated by Israel, by the sunshine and the sounds, by the waves of nostalgia, by the architecture and the language, most of all by the sheer spiritual energy of the land.

We flew out on the day after New Year's Day, and it was as though I had connected my soul to a fuel pump as we touched down at Ben-Gurion Airport. We'd come to do a television show with the iconic Israeli singer Yoram Gaon, and the prospect certainly excited me, but it wasn't that which fired me up into the stratosphere. I was higher than a satellite the whole time, on nothing chemically stronger than honey and almonds.

Israel recharged me. Even now, back in England under January skies, I am abuzz with the brilliance of the coast and its culture. I cannot analyze the whole sensation, but I am certain that much of this must be rooted in the connections I make with my own past when I return to Tel Aviv. I scampered around the streets of Jaffa, pointing out the places where I had played, where my mother and I had lived, where I went to school, where we bought groceries, where my father found my first pet, a stray puppy.

I felt plugged in to the untrammeled energy that propelled me when I was a boy, before I learned to control the forces that made my career. It's great fun to be able to bend metal at will, but it's even more exciting to have that energy flowing wild and untamed through your body. I think every child feels this, in one way or another, but mostly we forget how to feel that life force as we grow up.

The buildings of Jaffa, many now refurbished, are a fascinating jumble of styles: Arabic, Bauhaus, Deco. And they are all low-rise, none of them more than four stories. Israelis love to talk of Tel Aviv as a rival to New York, but it is in Jaffa, where the spirit can soar unobstructed to the clear skies, that I feel real freedom.

Tel Aviv is named both for its newness and its deep history. The name was inspired by Theodor Herzl's Zionist novel, *Altneuland* (Old New Land). In Hebrew, Tel Aviv combines the concept of antiquity (*tel*, an ancient site) with joyous rebirth (*aviv*, springtime).

We roamed the waterside cafes and stared at the minarets, and I remembered how the streets were always jostling with soldiers when I was a young man here. Perhaps the military are warned to wear civilian clothes off duty out of fear of homicide bombers, but the sight of so many young people who were not in uniform gave hope to my heart.

On Yoram's show, I made a passionate plea for peace, urging Israelis to live side-by-side with Palestinians, pleading for an end to aggression on both sides. I have no patience with those militants, most of whom were not even born in my country, who demand blood sacrifices from my children's generation. The troubles have damaged tourism, of course, and it saddens me that so many Jews stay away from Israel now, when the country has most need of its friends overseas. There may be a greater risk to dining in Jaffa than in Milwaukee, in theory, but although you can get run over by a garbage truck in any city in the world, there is no place on earth that serves better food than Tel Aviv. The breakfasts were feasts from heaven. Succulent breads, sweet and savory; every kind of cheese, from the softest to the tangiest; all the fruits of Eden; strips of fish and scoops of spices; mouthwatering honey from the kibbutzim. I felt not only my body awake each morning, but my soul, as if I was realizing for the first time how God intended us to dine. We fill our faces with such junk most of the time, when there is a glorious storehouse of delicious and simple food ready to be spread before us in abundance.

Many Israeli families come to Tel Aviv for short breaks, taking advantage of the fact that foreign tourists are staying away. We chatted with a couple from the Sea of Galilee, who were clearly as happy as I felt myself, as we spread the thick honey in rolling coils across slices of dark rye bread.

One wonderful side effect of appearing on a show as popular as Yoram's was the rush of e-mails from old friends over the next few days—people whose faces I can still clearly recall, who sent notes such as this one: "You won't remember me, Uri, but we used to play basketball in the street where we lived."

Of course I remember! But there was one person I admit I could not recall at all, though my mother was delighted to see her old landlady again after so many decades. Her name is Lily, and we spoke on the phone shortly after I got back to England. "I held you in my arms," Lily told me, "and you couldn't have been more than one year old last time I saw you."

I shall have to return to Israel soon. I think Lily will be my excuse!

Judy Ginsburgh

Judy Ginsburgh is a multi-award-winning singer, songwriter, recording artist, cantorial soloist, and educator. Her most recent work, My Jewish World, *is a Jewish Early Childhood Curriculum for use in Jewish schools.*

ISRAEL: A JEWISH CONNECTION

Growing up in a small Southern community where Jews were very much in the minority, I primarily thought of Israel in a historical sense. Israel was the land of the Bible. It was the place where all the stories I was hearing in religious school took place. Israel was the land of Abraham, Sarah, Moses, and Miriam. To my childish imagination, it was a land of fairy tales somewhere far, far away.

My first real connection to Israel happened when I was about twelve years old. A member of my congregation had a relative in Israel—a young girl about my age—and we began corresponding as pen pals. She would write to me in Hebrew and I would write back to her in English. I would have her relative here translate her letters for me and eventually I learned enough Hebrew to be able to write to her in short sentences. We shared photos, souvenirs, and travel information. I learned about Israel through Adily, my pen pal. She made me want to visit Israel, not only to meet her, but to experience all that Israel had to offer.

When I was a senior in high school, my congregation planned a monthlong trip to Israel. I expressed to my grandmother how much I wanted to go. She offered to give me this as a graduation present. But I told her I would go only if she went along with me. I knew it would do my grandmother good to be able to take a trip like this, and she had never been to Israel, either. So, in March of my senior year, we flew to Israel.

It was definitely a life-changing experience. It was hard to believe that I was standing in this ancient land, this land that had become a homeland for Jews everywhere, this land that had blossomed into a paradise through the hard work of so many, this land that held so much of my heritage. I had so much to learn and it had so much to teach me.

I soaked in everything. I visited every historical site. I experienced the cultures of three religions living side by side after the Yom Kippur War. I saw the ravages of war, I sat with the soldiers on buses, I went to the discos and cafes, I spent time at an *ulpan* and a youth hostel. And, I met my Israeli pen pal. But the highlight of my trip was meeting Golda Meir and hearing her speak. An American-raised Jewish woman who was then the prime minister of Israel! What an impression that made on a seventeen-year-old girl!

When I returned to the States, suddenly everything I had learned in Sunday school made sense. My trip to Israel did not make me a Zionist and I never have had a desire to make aliyah, but the trip certainly strengthened my connection to being Jewish. It motivated me to learn more about my heritage as a Jew. It made me appreciate how hard my parents worked to keep a Jewish home and Jewish traditions in a place where there were very few Jews. I owe a lot to my family because there was never a time in my growing up when I felt ashamed to be Jewish. I was always very secure in the fact that I was Jewish and that I would raise my family to be Jewish.

I know that my trip to Israel had a huge impact on the choices I have made in my adult life. I never considered marrying anyone who was not Jewish. I met my husband Bob when I was a senior in college. We have been married for twenty-four years, and seventeen years ago, I brought him back to the small Southern town where I grew up to make our Jewish home. We are raising three children here and our youngest was bar mitzvahed in 2005. Our daughter is a counselor at our regional Jewish camp, and our son is president of our youth group and a counselor at a camp for handicapped youth sponsored by our Jewish camp program. All three of our children are proud to be Jewish and are giving of their time to Jewish causes.

When I lived in Washington, D.C., I developed and taught a hands-on, arts-infused Israel curriculum at a large religious school there. I know that my time spent in Israel helped me bring Israel to life in the classroom for these students. In 1986, I attended a Jewish educator's conference called CAJE (Conference on Alternatives in Jewish Education). I became a member of their board, and in 1998 I chaired their twenty-third annual conference.

For the past twenty-three years, I have made my living as a professional singer specializing in Jewish music. I sing throughout North America as a cantorial soloist, and I have released six award-winning recordings for Jewish families. In my concerts, my goal is to help children and their families feel proud to be Jewish, to make them curious to learn more, and to pass down my passion for all things Jewish to another generation.

In 1994, I began Jewish Entertainment Resources as a hobby. Jewish Entertainment Resources is a database of Jewish performers from all over the world. We now host a Web site that features information on a variety of Jewish performers, an international Jewish concert calendar of Jewish cultural events throughout the world, and educational resource information for Jewish performers and presenting organizations.

I look at what I have accomplished so far in my life and almost 99 percent has to do with something Jewish. My grandmother gave me a wonderful gift. She gave me much more than *just* a trip to Israel. She helped a small-town girl with very few Jewish role models to be able to make a lifelong connection with a land that holds so much promise for Jews everywhere. That trip to Israel allowed me to grow as a Jew and to bring what I have learned back to my roots and beyond.

One of my favorite anonymous sayings is, "I've learned that you shouldn't go through life with a catcher's mitt on both hands. You need to be able to throw something back." This has become my motto and I try to live by it each day. I hope that I can give something back to another young Jewish girl growing up in the South and, through my example, inspire her to be proud of her Jewish heritage and give back to future generations.

Nathan Glazer

Nathan Glazer is a contributing editor of the New Republic, professor emeritus at Harvard University's Graduate School of Education, and coeditor of the Public Interest. He is the author of several books, including We Are All Multiculturalists Now and Beyond the Melting Pot.

I t is perhaps an indication of my unsuitability to participate in this joint enterprise that I almost immediately edited the title in my mind to "what Israel meant to me." That would be an easier question to which to respond. Israel, of course, has undergone many changes in its half-century of independent life, and what Israel (or Palestine, as we called it when I was a student socialist Zionist—the name then did not belong to its Arab residents alone), meant to me in the early 1940s could not be unaffected by the great changes that have transformed the Yishuv of those days into the ten times larger and more complex Jewish nation of today. But it is not Israel's drift away from a youthful and naive dream of socialism that has affected my relation to Israel. Yes, the first article I wrote on Palestine, when I was a freshman at City College, for the socialist New Leader, edited by Daniel Bell at the time, was a paean to the labor federation the Histadrut, describing its reach and power in the Yishuv of the 1940s. One of the first book reviews I published was of a sympathetic study of the kibbutz. These little communal settlements played a much greater role in the Yishuv of those days than they do in the Israel of today. These features of the prestate Yishuv contributed to my enthusiasm for the Zionist project,

---

Written in April 2004.

but it is not their decline that has reduced me in recent years to silence on the issue of Israel.

I was recently reminded of what Israel meant to me up until the mid-1970s, a better time all in all than today, by some lines of Christopher Hitchens, writing of his first meeting with Edward Said in 1976:

> Palestinian resistance to Israeli occupation was in its infancy. . . . Egypt was still the Egypt of Anwar Sadat . . . who was only two years away from the Camp David Accords. . . . It was becoming dimly apprehended in the West that the old narrative of "Israel" versus "the Arabs" was much too crude. The image of a frugal kibbutz state surrounded by a heaving ocean of raving mullahs and demagogues was slowly yielding to a story of two peoples contesting a right to the same twice-promised land.

About that time or somewhat earlier, in the wake of the 1973 war, I was connected briefly with a group that took the name "Breira," in opposition to the common slogan of the time, "Ein Breira." That slogan asserted there was no alternative to continuing the occupation of the territories until the Arab nations were willing to deal with Israel. The Arab states had refused in any way to recognize the existence of Israel, except to occasionally try, unsuccessfully, to destroy it. For them, there could be no discussion, no compromise, with the "Zionist entity."

Breira's position was that there was an alternative, one in which the occupied territories would be given up for peace, and the sooner the better. We thought that was also the position of the Labor government, which then ruled Israel, but it was dawning on us that this was not the case. A decisive rejoinder to the notion that Israel should try to negotiate a deal was, "How could one make a deal when the other side refuses to enter into negotiation?" I am not an expert in the arcana of Arab-Israeli history, but there is apparently some evidence now that, despite the public position of the Arab states, even in those days there were some contacts, some possibilities for discussion and negotiation. Perhaps there was no possibility of an exchange of the occupied territories for peace (we all know how many complexities are evaded in that apparently simple formula). But some arrangement along those

lines seems never to have been seriously contemplated, by the Labor
government or the Likud government that shortly succeeded it. It is
understandable that a threatened and encircled people enjoying the
additional modicum of security given by a few more miles between
them and the Arab armies were loath to give them up. But what was
the alternative?

The settlement policy, whatever its justifications—and I found
them from the beginning weak or outlandish and the policy itself
clearly potentially disastrous—has been maintained both by Labor
and Likud governments, and has been sustained and intensified since
the Oslo Agreement of 1993, in which both sides seemed to accept
two separate states. But the settlement policy makes the possibility of
a two-state solution—the only possible solution, if there is ever to be
one—ever more remote. So many of us look aside and refuse to contemplate the reality: the checkpoints to defend the settlements, the
engrossing of water supply and land for them (the few thousand settlers of the Gaza Strip held a grossly disproportionate share of the
land and water of that overcrowded patch), the special roads built to
connect the settlements, the permanent intrusive military presence in
Arab areas to man checkpoints and defend roads, the division of the
potential Arab homeland into fragments that cannot connect with
each other, the frustration and anger of the people subjected to such
policies.

How do we respond, when the Israeli novelist David Grossman
writes that "the Israeli eye is already trained to skip over the small
items in the newspaper: the Palestinian babies dying at roadblocks, the
children fainting from thirst in the refugee camps because Israeli
officials control the water supply, thousands of families whose homes
are being bulldozed on the ground of being 'illegal construction'"?
And this was written in 1998, before the recent intifada, which made
matters much, much worse. Yes, we know the routine responses to
such reports; we have used them ourselves—after all, the Israeli newspapers do publish these items, Israeli human rights and civil rights
organizations attack such policies in the courts, the courts are independent, there is nothing like this self-criticism and correction in the
Arab world, and so on. And then we add that the Arabs brought it on

themselves through refusing to accept a reasonable (to us) deal and responding with terrorism.

But after all this, there still remains the reality of a heavily armed encirclement and occupation of Palestinian areas that has destroyed Palestinian institutions and made life for the population unbearable. We cannot forever pride ourselves on the fact that Israel after all is (as yet) far from pursuing a policy of transfer or expulsion of the Arab population.

Yes, we know Israel is a democracy, with (almost) equal rights for all, and its Arab population, even when deprived of some rights, is still better off economically and politically than the people of almost any Arab country. We know that these measures are required by security against terror. All true enough. But these measures certainly affect "what Israel means to me," and must affect what Israel means to anyone who accepts the primacy of equal rights and lawful procedures, and the protection of the life and liberty and property of citizens and residents by the state.

This passage from David Grossman, and similar ones I could have given, are from a recent article by Jacqueline Rose in the *London Review of Books*, a journal fiercely hostile to Israel, and which regularly publishes Edward Said and even more severe opponents of Israel and Zionism. But there are many other sources in the Israeli press for similar items. How can such accounts not affect "what Israel means to me?"

Perhaps there were no practical alternatives to the policies Israel has pursued for the last thirty years or so. Yet when blowing up the family homes of terrorists and killing their leaders has had no apparent effect in reducing the violence, one would think such tactics would have been reviewed. Perhaps had Israel been more forthcoming, as the people of Breira and the many peace-oriented groups that have succeeded it proposed, the result would have been only the strengthening of an inveterately hostile Arab population and Arab world, continuously aiming at the destruction of Israel and its people. Perhaps there was no way in which Israel could have reduced Arab hostility. But the way it did act certainly ensured and deepened the hostility.

So whatever Israel meant to me, what does it mean to me now? How does one respond to a country of fellow Jews that is permanently endangered, even if one thinks this situation has been exacerbated by Israeli leaders (supported indeed by the Israeli electorate)?

It is hard to see any alternative now to the situation of permanent war and preparation for war in which Israel now lives. If Oslo didn't work, there is no reason to believe the "road map to peace" can work. If the major settlement groups of the West Bank remain and are defended, any possible Arab Palestine becomes a group of barely connected fragments, and no Palestinian government will accept that as a permanent solution. But then how does a democratic polity uproot 250,000 settlers, 5 percent of the Jewish population—and voters—for a possible peace, one that in any case must remain uncertain?

So one defends Israel, certainly one does not join its enemies, one understands how things have come to this pass, but one must be bitter at some of the leaders who made a difficult situation worse. We in the Diaspora had no right to intervene in the decision-making that has resulted in the present situation (though all of us involved in the fate of Israel do intervene, on one side or the other). It is the Israelis who are endangered and who bear the consequences of their policies. Our task then is reduced to using the power of the American Jewish community to keep American influence and strength in the balance on Israel's side, to the degree that that is possible. One cannot contemplate the alternative.

J. J. Goldberg

J. J. Goldberg is editor in chief of the Forward, the English-language newsweekly published in association with the Jewish Daily Forward.

It was during the summer of my tenth year, in 1960, that I had my defining Israel experience. I was attending a Zionist summer camp in upstate New York, the same camp my father had attended during the Depression, sponsored by the same Labor Zionist movement my grandfather had helped to found before World War I. In a way, I had been preparing for this all my life.

The camp was modeled on the Israeli kibbutz. Each day we studied Hebrew, learned the songs of the Israeli pioneers, raised our own vegetables, scrubbed our pots, and washed the toilets. We were taught that by doing these things, we were taking our place in the ranks of the movement that had built the Jewish state. Our comrades, David Ben-Gurion, Moshe Dayan, Golda Meir—a graduate of our own Milwaukee chapter—were shaping a new future of independence and pride for Jews everywhere. Our camp was our training ground, preparing us to take our place in Jewish history.

On the last morning of camp, we lined up to salute the counselors who were departing the next week for the movement's yearlong kibbutz training program. I saw my destiny: to be a kibbutznik, to join, as the Hebrew song said, in building and being rebuilt in Labor Israel.

My life followed that path, more or less, for the next twenty years, through youth movement activism, college organizing, Zionist education work in Jerusalem, and finally membership on a kibbutz, until a time came when I left. It was years before I found a new life's mission, and that new mission, journalism, remained tentative, a work in progress, for a long time. It still has the quality, a quarter-century later, of a second love, satisfying in an adult way but never with the passion of a first love. It suffers, too, from the continuing presence of that first love. For while I no longer live in Israel or work on a kibbutz, the animating vision of Labor Zionism continues to define my relationship to Israel—and beyond that, to Judaism, to the United States, and to the world.

In 1963, when I was thirteen, I went with my kid brother to spend the summer with cousins in Israel. We traveled the Jewish state from top to bottom, climbing up wadis and poking through archaeological digs. In between, we hung out at home in suburban Haifa. Looking back years later, I remain surprised by how familiar Israel felt that first time, as though I were settling comfortably into a world I had constructed in my mind so precisely that everything fit.

I went home in late August 1963 to start high school. My after-school hours were divided between school clubs, where we debated civil rights and the escalating Vietnam War, and the youth movement, where we studied Zionist philosophers, taught pioneer songs to the smaller children—and debated civil rights and Vietnam.

After high school, I packed off to Israel for the movement's year course. It was September 1967. The Six-Day War had ended weeks earlier. Israel was on a high. American teenagers were coming in droves as volunteers, students, and tourists. The country was thrilled to have us, but a trifle wary. We were a distinctly foreign body, with our long hair and beads, our portable stereos blasting rock 'n' roll—and worst of all, our drugs.

Those of us who had come as committed Zionists, perhaps one-tenth of the ten thousand–odd volunteers, were in a bind. We wanted to be taken more seriously than the day-trippers. We knew about Ben-Gurion and the pioneers. We meant to settle here. Yet, we shared the long hair, rock 'n' roll, and weed. We wanted to be part of Israel, but on our own terms.

I must have been shaken more than most of my friends by the gap in perceptions. Come spring, when we met to discuss our roles in the movement back home, I announced that I was through with Zionism. If our task was to lead the Jewish people, the work was in the United States, where most Jews lived. Telling Jews to settle in Israel seemed pointless. Ironically, I actually liked Israel. I felt at home. But my mission, in my teenage mind, was with the Jews, not Israel.

I enrolled at McGill University in Montreal, naively planning to study Yiddish, the language of the Diaspora. My plan collapsed in the first week. My Yiddish skills were hopeless. My Hebrew studies, meanwhile, advanced to medieval poetry and classic prose style. My Zionism seemed incurable. Sealing my fate, I was recruited to the campus arm of the World Zionist Organization and spent my free hours writing pro-Israel polemics and planning curricula. Soon I was flying around North America to attend conferences and debate anti-Zionists.

Zionism became my career. After college I went to work in Jerusalem as a conference planner for the World Zionist Organization. Over the next two years, I walked every inch of Israel, sat in seminars with some of Israel's most promising young academics and army officers, and spent endless hours in late-night conversations with Palestinian intellectuals and West Bank settler pioneers.

After a few years I left Jerusalem and joined with a group of movement friends to start our own kibbutz. I spent the next three years as the kibbutz business agent and secretary, roaming from the warehouses of South Tel Aviv to my familiar political haunts in Jerusalem. Three years later, I left Israel, for a combination of minor reasons that I still do not understand after thirty years. But only half of me returned to the United States. Half stayed there.

Following interludes as a New York cabdriver and a California surfer, I settled into a career as a journalist. Mostly I have been reporting for Israeli journals on Jewish life in the United States and for American Jewish journals on Israel and the politics of the Jewish community. I have spent the years traveling back and forth, maintaining close friendships on both sides of the ocean, deeply involved in the politics and culture of both societies, watching the two communities up close, from inside.

What I've learned over the years is that American Jews and Israel are best described—with apologies to George Bernard Shaw—as two communities separated by a common faith-heritage. The bonds that unite us are strong and many-faceted, but the chasm dividing us is deep and wide, and it is growing wider by the year.

For now, the bonds between us are greater than the divisions. Above all, we are the two main centers of Judaism in the modern world. That one fact defines us more than any other in the minds of most Jews and in the eyes of much of the world. We share dreams of the same past glories and tragedies. We construct our communal lives around the same calendar and the same symbols. We are the two great communities that emerged intact from the ashes of European Jewry to carry on the three-thousand-year tradition of Judaism.

What has emerged in these two young communities, however, has turned out to be very different—from what came before and from each other. Each of our communities, Israeli and American, has come to reflect one half—different halves—of the European Jewish civilization that spawned us. Each of us, thinking we are natural heirs, assumes that the other understands the Jewish tradition the way that we do. But we do not. And so, all too frequently, we bewilder each other.

European Jewry was an organic civilization, rooted in a conscious, voluntary faith system but encompassing every aspect of daily life from language to garb. American Judaism inherited the voluntary faith part. It became a culture consisting of daily choices by which Jewish Americans affirm their heritage and separate themselves from their neighbors. Israel, by contrast, inherited the daily ordinariness of life in an all-encompassing Jewish society, the Jewishness of language and neighborhood.

This quotidian normality is Zionism's success and its weakness. Zionism set out to normalize the Jewish condition, to remove from Jews the abnormality of living what the founding fathers saw as the stunted life of an oppressed nation cowering in the shadows of history. They intended to remake Judaism as the daily culture of a reclaimed Jewish nation. They expected that once Jewish sovereignty was reborn, the Diaspora would disappear as Jews returned en masse to their homeland, "as naturally," one early Zionist wrote, "as a hat settling on a head."

They were half right. A sovereign Jewish homeland arose in which Judaism once again consists of the daily routines of normal life in a normal country: speaking a Jewish language, serving in a Jewish army, shopping in a Jewish supermarket. The rebirth of the Jewish nation has become the greatest guarantor that Judaism will continue into the future, dependent not on the whims of individuals but on the collective might and will of a sovereign state.

But they were wrong about the Diaspora. It did not disappear; on the contrary, it was strengthened. The image of reborn Jewish nationhood gave new heart to Jews around the world.

It's important to note that it was the image of Israel, not its reality, that gave American Jews strength. They had little connection to the Israel of soil and concrete. Like Jews for centuries before, they looked to a spiritual vision of a heavenly Jerusalem that hovered in their mind's eye just above the earthly Jerusalem. Yet the strength it gave them was real. In the devastating wake of the Holocaust, the spiritual sustenance flowing from Israel to the struggling communities of the Diaspora was the very stuff of life.

To Israelis, by contrast, it was merely ironic. Israel—the real, earthly one—was intended to replace the Diaspora, not revive it. Jews were supposed to relocate en masse to the land of Israel, not return to their old Jewish ways—reinvigorated, of all things.

Over time, Diaspora Jewish life has become more and more of a conundrum to Israelis. Most of Israel's Jewish population now consists of people who were reared in the Jewish culture of daily Israeli life. For those Jews, to whom being Jewish consists of speaking a Jewish language and riding a Jewish bus, what can it possibly mean to live as a Jew in Cleveland?

The incomprehension, it must be said, is mutual.

One evening in 1987, early in my reporting career, I was working late in the newsroom of a local Jewish weekly when the phone rang. A deeply agitated woman with a Yiddish accent wanted to alert us that the Jewish community center had just hosted a speech by a Palestinian terrorist. The speaker urged Israel to "give in to the PLO. He said

Israel should be talking to Arafat, that murderer." I expressed concern and asked for details. Did she know the speaker's name? Yes, she said, she had written it down: Yehoshafat Harkabi.

I didn't have the heart to tell her who Harkabi was: a former chief of Israel's military intelligence, a onetime senior adviser to Golda Meir, the first authoritative Israeli to warn of the Arafat threat. Of late he had written a series of books arguing that Arafat and the Palestine Liberation Organization had changed direction, that it was time for Israel to sit down with them. No Israeli security expert knew the Palestinians better than he did.

But there are some things about Israel that you just can't say to American Jews. It is not the real Israel to which they turn their eyes, but the Jewish homeland of their dreams and nightmares.

The best description I have ever heard of our gap of mutual Jewish incomprehension was offered to me several decades ago by a young Israeli professor of Holocaust studies, Arye Carmon, who has gone on to head a Jerusalem think tank, the Israel Democracy Institute. American Jewry and Israel, Carmon said, are like two siblings, offspring of the same mother, who were orphaned as young children and raised in different households.

If fate had permitted the two infant cultures to grow for another century in organic relationship to the mother culture, they might have evolved into adult cultures that had more in common with each other. But the mother was cut down when the two offspring were still in their infancy. American and Israeli Judaism were forced to become the central streams of the Jewish cultural tradition before either one was remotely ready.

Each retains characteristics of the mother, but they grew up to become very different adults, barely recognizable to one another. How they might look today if they had been raised together under their mother's nurturing tutelage, we can never know.

We have no choice but to go forward, trying our best to understand what we were and must be to one another. For each of us is part of the other—in many ways, the best part.

Ari L. Goldman

Ari L. Goldman, the author of The Search for God at Harvard, *is a professor and the dean of students at Columbia University's Graduate School of Journalism.*

One of my most favorite people in the world was my cello teacher, Heinrich Joachim. He had a wonderful career as a cellist, playing with the New York Philharmonic and other world-class orchestras. He was known for the rich sound he was able to draw from his instrument. When I would go to Mr. Joachim's home for lessons, he would sometimes bring out another instrument that he loved, the viola da gamba. The gamba is a Baroque predecessor of the cello that has five strings and a lighter, tinnier sound.

As everyone knows, cellos are hugged as much as they are played. And the physical sensation of the instrument is a powerful one. One day Mr. Joachim stopped playing, embraced his cello, and nodded to the viola de gamba that stood off in the distance.

"This is my wife," he said of the cello. "But the gamba is my mistress!"

That is how I often feel about Israel. The United States is my wife. This is where I make my home. This is where I do my work and raise my family. But Israel, there in the distance, is my mistress.

Our romance goes way back. The first time I stepped onto an airplane, it was to go to Israel. It was 1963, and my father sent me on a summer Israel program as a bar mitzvah present. The program was sponsored by the Rabbinical Council of America, an Orthodox group. I was the first one in my family to make the journey.

Israel was a hardscrabble land back then, technologically backward and poor. There was no Old City of Jerusalem to visit and no occupied territories to worry about. There was a tangible sense of idealism, with dreams of "making the deserts bloom," along with a constant fear of doom.

This was well before Israel proved itself as a military power. Arab neighbors constantly flexed their muscles and Israel's existence was seen as tenuous, at best.

Nothing was ever the same for me after that summer in Israel. When I said the Grace after Meals, the prayer for Jerusalem took on new meaning. When I studied the Torah, Jewish history, and later the Talmud, the names and places were tangible. Yavneh, Safed, Tiberias, the Negev, Mount Zion, Masada, the Dead Sea.

Since I was thirteen, I have returned to Israel more times than I can count. Over the years, I have forged connections with new places and new people. I watched my grandparents go on aliyah in the 1970s and my father follow suit in 1993. Numerous cousins and friends also made the move.

Shira and I went for our honeymoon in 1983 and we returned to Israel with our three children twelve years later, when I was a visiting professor at Hebrew University. We lived in Jerusalem for one glorious year, but left, always knowing we would return. I came back with groups of students from Columbia University in 2000 and 2001. And our family continues to go for holidays and family life cycle events.

Sometimes I feel like the Alan Alda character in *Same Time Next Year*, the 1978 movie about a chance meeting between a man (Alda) and a woman (Ellen Burstyn) at a romantic country inn. The two, married to others, resolve to meet each year on this, their secret anniversary, for an annual tryst. Over the years, of course, they change. Family and personal troubles are raised and sorted out. They ultimately find much more in each other than the sex that first drew them together. They help each other through.

I feel that way about Israel. I am not ready to make a commitment to the land; perhaps I never will. But I feel tied to her in a way that I know helps me and I hope helps her, too.

Monty Hall

Monty Hall is the cocreator and longtime emcee of the television game show Let's Make a Deal.

I was born and raised in Winnipeg, Canada. We had a large Jewish population and they were all passionate Zionists. All the women belonged to Hadassah and the men belonged to a Zionist organization, and everyone planned and hoped and dreamed of a homeland for the Jewish people. My mother, the late Rose Halparin, became the national vice president for Hadassah and eventually the national chairman of Youth Aliyah in Canada. She spent years traveling from coast to coast speaking on behalf of Youth Aliyah, the organization that rescued the surviving children of the Holocaust in Europe and brought them to what was then Palestine and later, of course, Israel.

It was only natural when growing up that I would become an ardent Zionist myself, watching my mother's work and identifying with her dreams. In later years I started raising money for Israel by speaking throughout Canada and, after moving to the United States, I have continued to speak to the present day.

Any person who makes a trip to Israel will be overwhelmed with so many different emotions, ranging from historical and biblical references to the struggle of the Israelis to exist. By their accomplishments in medicine and science, the museums, the universities, the hospitals, and miraculously the ingathering of Jews from around the world. My first trip and subsequent trips produced the same emotions. However, there is one story that can sum up my history and my connection with the state of Israel.

Although I have been involved in every aspect of Israel, raising money and serving on the boards of several universities and hospitals, and so on, I was fascinated by the organization of the Israel Tennis Centers. This group was dedicated to giving the children of Israel a sense of normalcy. When most Israeli children were growing up defensively, there was not much opportunity for them to have what children in the United States have—the freedom to participate in sports in an organized manner. The Tennis Centers provided them with such an outlet. I have traveled around the United States and Canada with children from Israel, staging exhibitions and raising funds for this organization, which has established tennis centers throughout Israel.

When a new stadium was built in Ramat Hasharon, many of us from the United States attended the opening. On that day the Canadian Davis Cup team was to play the Israeli Davis Cup team in an exhibition. The defining moment came when the Israeli team was introduced in the following manner: "This player is Shlomo, whose mother came from Russia and whose father came from Libya. This is Yitzhak, whose mother came from Poland and his father came from Yemen." And another player whose father came from Morocco and his mother came from France, and so on. As the team was introduced and all these countries were named as the birthplace of their families, I realized that these were the children *of* the children whom my mother spent her whole life saving and bringing to a new life in Israel.

My emotions were overflowing. I wept. This was what my mother had been working for—what I had been working for—what we had all dreamed of. Not only saving the children, but giving them a land in which they could grow and enjoy freedom. These were not just tennis players. This was the building of a new nation—how important Israel was to these children, how important Israel is to me.

Joshua Hammer

Joshua Hammer, a former Jerusalem bureau chief for Newsweek, *is the author of* A Season in Bethlehem: Unholy War in a Sacred Place. *He is currently a Nieman Fellow at Harvard University.*

I grew up in a secular Jewish family in Westchester County and New York City—the kind of clan that acknowledged its cultural-religious roots with annual Passover Seders, sporadic trips to shul for Rosh Hashanah, bar mitzvahs in Reform temples, and not much else. All of my great-grandparents had escaped Russia and the Ukraine for the United States in the late nineteenth century, and no close relatives had perished in the Holocaust. Yet there was no doubt about my family's Jewish identity or of our profound belief in the state of Israel. One of my most vivid memories from childhood was hearing the news that the Israeli army had defeated the Arabs in the Six-Day War and captured the Old City of Jerusalem. Unleashing a banshee yell, I leapt in ecstasy through the hallways of Public School 6 on the Upper East Side of Manhattan, drawing the curious stares of both students and teachers. The one-eyed hero of the 1967 war, Moshe Dayan, was as much an idol to me as the faded stars of the New York Yankees—Mickey Mantle, Whitey Ford, Mel Stottlemyre—then sinking fast into the American League basement.

Israel maintained its hold on me through my teenage years, even as my connection to my Jewish roots became ever more tenuous. Perhaps it was my growing interest in international politics, or my nascent career as a journalist, or some vestige of tribal pride, but I still followed the Israeli story—the Munich Olympics massacre, the Yom Kippur

War, the election of Menachem Begin, the Camp David Accord of 1978—as if it were an intimate drama involving members of my own family. Then, in the spring of 1981, at the tail end of a yearlong backpacking trip through Asia, I made an impulsive decision to visit the country whose travails and triumphs I had followed so closely. My younger brother had taken a leave from college to live in Jerusalem, and one balmy night in May, I landed at Ben-Gurion Airport and then caught a bus to his tiny apartment on a back alley in the Nachla'ot neighborhood, a ten-minute walk from Jaffa Gate.

It might well have had something to do with that sibling reunion, after a lonely odyssey through fleabag hotels in third-world hellholes, but my arrival in Israel felt like a homecoming. Seeing Israel in the flesh—young soldiers with knit *kipas* on their heads and Galil rifles slung over their shoulders; Orthodox Jews at the Western Wall, davening before the heavy tan blocks of Jerusalem stone—moved me beyond all expectation. A visit to Yad Vashem, the Holocaust memorial in West Jerusalem, filled me with a sense of guilt over my stunted Jewish faith. How could I deny my origins, I asked myself, when so many had died solely because they were Jews? Over the next weeks in Israel I wrestled with fundamental questions—whether to make aliyah, whether to incorporate Jewish ritual and faith into my totally secular life in the United States. I spent Shabbat with a Hasidic family in Mea She'arim, made a pilgrimage to Masada, even enrolled in a yeshiva in Jerusalem where many lapsed American Jews like me immersed themselves in Torah and Talmudic scholarship. When I returned to the United States my spiritual awakening faded fast, but my pride in Israel had solidified.

The following two decades evoked a more complicated response. Israel's invasion of Lebanon in 1982 and the clashes I observed in Hebron and Ramallah as a freelancer during the first intifada of the late 1980s suggested trouble in the Israeli national psyche, internal divisions, a loss of the moral clarity that had defined the state in its first decades of existence. The Israel Defense Forces metamorphosed from defenders of a fragile nation to an occupying force, and though Israel's leaders defended this new role as a temporary condition, justified by the nation's security needs, as time passed the occupation was becoming a permanent state.

In January 2001, when I returned to live in Jerusalem as *Newsweek's* Middle East bureau chief, the familiar sense of homecoming was tempered with more ambivalent emotions. Nothing seemed clear-cut anymore. True, the breakdown of the Camp David talks of July 2000 and the orchestrated campaign of violence that followed could be blamed to a great degree on the failings of Yassir Arafat. True, the suicide bombings carried out by Palestinian militants were atrocities that nothing could justify. But what about the relentless expansion of Jewish settlements across the West Bank, or the killings of thousands of ordinary Palestinians in the name of suppressing terror?

The past four years have been terrible years, a time when dialogue seemed drowned out by the roar of F-16s and the boom of suicide bombs. Each side clings passionately to the righteousness of his cause and his version of history; each accuses the other of heinous crimes and admits no wrong. Israel has retreated behind an ugly concrete barrier—the security fence—resting more or less secure against the threat of terrorist attack. But it often appears as though Israel's leaders want it both ways: to isolate their Palestinian neighbors behind a separation fence, then continue to dominate them, carve up their land, regulate their movements, all to fulfill the territorial imperatives of their most irredentist citizens. The Israel I once knew and loved has moved close to becoming an apartheid state, enforcing its will through the barrel of a gun. I still admire its cacophonous democracy, its vibrantly heterogeneous society. But more and more I've come to feel like an estranged relative at the family dinner table, searching in vain to recapture a lost bond.

David Harris

David Harris is the executive director of the American Jewish Committee, an organization founded in 1906 out of concern for the welfare and security of Jews living in Russia but whose mission today is described as dedicated to safeguarding "the welfare and security of Jews in the United States, in Israel, and throughout the world."

L et me put my cards on the table right up front—I'm not dispassionate when it comes to Israel.

The establishment of the state in 1948; the fulfillment of its envisioned role as home and haven for Jews from around the world; its wholehearted embrace of democracy and the rule of law; and its impressive scientific, cultural, and economic achievements are accomplishments beyond my wildest imagination.

For centuries, Jews around the world prayed for a return to Zion. We are the lucky ones who have seen those prayers answered. I am ever so grateful to witness this most extraordinary period in Jewish history and Jewish sovereignty.

And when one adds the key element, namely, that all this took place not in the Middle West but in the Middle East, where Israel's neighbors determined from day one to destroy it through any means available to them—from full-scale wars to wars of attrition; from diplomatic isolation to international delegitimation; from primary to secondary to even tertiary economic boycotts; from terrorism to the spread of anti-Semitism, often thinly veiled as anti-Zionism—the story of Israel's first fifty-six years becomes all the more remarkable. It is a tale of nation-building entirely without precedent.

Here was a people brought to the brink of utter destruction by the genocidal policies of Nazi Germany and its allies. Here was a people shown to be utterly powerless to influence a largely indifferent world to stop, or even slow down, the Final Solution. And here was a people, numbering but 600,000, living cheek by jowl with often hostile Arab neighbors, under unsympathetic British occupation, on a harsh soil with no significant natural resources other than human resources in then Mandatory Palestine.

That the blue-and-white flag of an independent Israel could be planted on this land, to which the Jewish people had been intimately linked since the time of Abraham, just three years after the end of World War II—and with the support of a decisive majority of UN members at the time—truly boggles the mind.

And what's more, that this tiny community of Jews, including survivors of the Holocaust who had somehow made their way to Palestine despite the British blockade, could successfully defend themselves against the onslaught of five Arab standing armies that launched their attack on Israel's very first day of existence, is almost beyond imagination.

To understand the essence of Israel's meaning, it is enough to ask how the history of the Jewish people might have been different had there been a Jewish state in 1933, in 1938, or even in 1941. If Israel had controlled its borders and the right of entry instead of Britain, if Israel had had embassies and consulates throughout Europe, how many more Jews might have escaped and found sanctuary?

I witnessed firsthand what Israeli embassies and consulates meant to Jews drawn by the pull of Zion or the push of hatred. I stood in the courtyard of the Israeli embassy in Moscow and saw thousands of Jews seeking a quick exit from a Soviet Union in the throes of cataclysmic change, fearful that the change might be in the direction of renewed chauvinism and anti-Semitism.

Awestruck, I watched firsthand as Israel never faltered, not even for a moment, in transporting Soviet Jews to the Jewish homeland, even as Scud missiles launched from Iraq traumatized the nation in 1991. It says a lot about the conditions they were leaving behind that these Jews continued to board planes for Tel Aviv while missiles were exploding in Israeli population centers. In fact, on two occasions I sat in sealed rooms with Soviet Jewish families who had just arrived in

Israel during these missile attacks. Not once did any of them question their decision to establish new lives in the Jewish state. And equally, it says a lot about Israel that, amid all the pressing security concerns, it managed, without missing a beat, to continue to welcome these new immigrants.

In the mid-1980s, I saw firsthand Israel do what no Western, much less Arab, country had ever done before—bring out black Africans, in this case Ethiopian Jews, not in chains for exploitation, but in dignity for freedom. These Ethiopian Jews, numbering tens of thousands, had lived as Jews since the time of Solomon and Sheba and had yearned for a return to Zion ever since. In our lifetimes, their dreams came true, though the perilous journey out of Ethiopia cost the lives of thousands who fell victim to bandits, unforgiving terrain, and hunger.

And how can I ever forget the surge of pride, Jewish pride, that completely enveloped me in July 1976 on hearing the astonishing news of Israel's daring rescue of the 106 Jewish hostages held by Arab and German terrorists in Entebbe, Uganda, over two thousand miles from Israel's border? The unmistakable message: Jews in danger will never again be alone, without hope, and totally dependent on others for their safety.

Not least, I can still remember as if it were yesterday my very first visit to Israel. It was in 1970, and I was not quite twenty-one years old.

I didn't know what to expect, but I recall being quite emotional from the moment I boarded the El Al plane to the very first glimpse of the Israeli coastline from the plane's window. As I disembarked, I surprised myself by wanting to kiss the ground. In the ensuing weeks, I marveled at everything I saw. To me it was as if every apartment building, factory, school, orange grove, and Egged bus was nothing less than a miracle. A Jewish state was unfolding before my very eyes.

After centuries of persecutions, pogroms, exiles, ghettos, pales of settlement, inquisitions, blood libels, forced conversions, discriminatory legislation, and immigration restrictions—and, no less, centuries of prayers, dreams, and yearning—the Jews had come back home and would be masters of their own fate.

I was overwhelmed by the mix of people, backgrounds, languages, and lifestyles, and by the intensity of life itself. Everyone, it seemed, had a compelling story to tell. There were Holocaust survivors with harrowing tales of their years in the camps. There were Jews from Arab countries, whose stories of persecution in such countries as Iraq, Libya, and Syria were little known at the time. There were the first Jews arriving from the USSR seeking repatriation in the Jewish homeland. There were the sabras, the native-born Israelis, many of whose families had lived in Palestine for generations. There were local Arabs, both Christian and Muslim. There were Druze, whose religious practices are kept secret from the outside world. And on and on.

I was moved beyond words by the sight of Jerusalem and the fervor with which observant and even not-so-observant Jews prayed at the Western Wall. And I was particularly struck by the youth and their dedication to the state. Coming from a nation that was at the time deeply divided and demoralized, I found my Israeli peers to be unabashedly proud of their country, eager to serve in the military, and in many cases, determined to volunteer for the most elite combat units. They felt personally involved in the enterprise of building a Jewish state.

To be sure, nation-building is an infinitely complex process. In Israel's case, that nation-building began against a backdrop of tensions with a local Arab population that laid claim to the very same land, and tragically refused a United Nations proposal to divide the land into Arab and Jewish states; as the Arab world sought to isolate, demoralize, and ultimately destroy the state; as Israel's population doubled in the first three years of the country's existence, putting an unimaginable strain on severely limited resources; as the nation was forced to devote a vast portion of its limited national budget to defense expenditures; and as the country coped with forging a national identity and social consensus among a population that could not have been more geographically, linguistically, socially, and culturally heterogeneous.

Moreover, there is the tricky and underappreciated issue of the potential clash between the messy realities of statehood and, in this case, the ideals and faith of a people. It is one thing for a people to live their religion as a minority; it is quite another to exercise sovereignty as the majority population while remaining true to one's ethical standards. Inevitably, tension will arise between a people's spiritual or moral self-definition and the exigencies of statecraft, between our highest concepts of human nature and the daily realities of individuals in decision-making positions wielding power and balancing a variety of competing interests.

Even so, shall we raise the bar so high as to practically ensure that Israel—forced to function in the often gritty, morally ambiguous world of international relations and politics, especially as a small, endangered state—will always fall short?

On the other hand, the notion that Israel would ever become ethically indistinguishable from any other country, reflexively seeking cover behind the convenient justification of realpolitik to explain its behavior, must be equally unacceptable.

Loving Israel certainly doesn't mean overlooking its shortcomings, including, in my judgment, the excessive and unholy intrusion of religion into politics, the marginalization of non-Orthodox Jewish religious streams, the dangers posed by political and religious zealots, and the unfinished, if undeniably complex, task of integrating Israeli Arabs into the mainstream.

But it also doesn't mean allowing such issues to overshadow Israel's remarkable achievements, accomplished, as I've said, under the most difficult of circumstances.

In just fifty-six years, Israel has built a thriving democracy, unique in the region, including a Supreme Court prepared, when it deems appropriate, to overrule the prime minister or the military establishment, a feisty parliament that includes every imaginable viewpoint along the political spectrum, a robust civil society, and a vigorous press.

It has built an economy whose per capita gross natural product exceeds the combined total of its four contiguous sovereign neighbors—Egypt, Jordan, Lebanon, and Syria.

It has built universities and research centers that have contributed to advancing the world's frontiers of knowledge in countless ways. Two of its scientists recently shared the Nobel Prize in chemistry.

It has built one of the world's most powerful militaries—always under civilian control—to ensure its survival in a rough-and-tumble neighborhood. It has shown the world how a tiny nation, no larger than New Jersey or Wales, can, by sheer ingenuity, will, courage, and commitment, defend itself against those who would destroy it through conventional armies or armies of suicide bombers. And it has done all this while striving to adhere to a strict code of military conduct that has few rivals in the democratic world, much less elsewhere—in the face of an enemy prepared to send children to the front lines and seek cover in mosques, schools, and hospitals.

It has built a thriving culture whose musicians, writers, and artists are admired far beyond Israel's borders. In doing so, it has lovingly taken an ancient language, Hebrew, the language of the prophets, and rendered it modern to accommodate the vocabulary of the contemporary world.

It has built a climate of respect for other faith groups, including Baha'i, Christianity, and Islam, and their places of worship.

Step back from the twists and turns of the daily information overload coming from the Middle East and consider the sweep of the last fifty-six years. Look at the light-years traveled since the darkness of the Holocaust and marvel at the miracle of a decimated people returning to a tiny sliver of land—the land of our ancestors, the land of Zion and Jerusalem—and successfully building a modern, vibrant state against all the odds, on that ancient foundation.

In the final analysis, then, the story of Israel is the wondrous realization of a 3,500-year link among a land, a faith, a language, a people, and a vision. It is an unparalleled story of tenacity and determination, of courage and renewal. And it is ultimately a metaphor for the triumph of enduring hope over the temptation of despair.

Mark Helprin

*Mark Helprin is a novelist and political commentator. He served in the
Israel Defense Forces in 1972 and 1973.*

TURBULENCE

Long after I first came to Israel as a volunteer in June of 1967, when I
was 20, I learned (I observed day by day) what it is in particular that
allows Israel to be more than just a Jewish Singapore. That June was
the most buoyant month of my life, and when victory was unques-
tioned, Jerusalem was of gold, Israel had no gravity, and neither did I.
In the back of an air force truck that had stopped at Sdeh Boker, I
took a bag of peaches from an aged Ben-Gurion, who, tzaddik-like,
without a word, blessed the boys who were taking care of the planes.
The dominant form of transport seemed to be the motorcycle with
sidecar. There was no Coca-Cola, no Black September, no Intifada.
The selfless concentration of the founders existed simultaneously with
the relief and relaxation of victory. For one giddy moment, the effects
of achievement did not undermine the benefits of aspiration. And
then, inevitably, they did.

But even as history reasserted itself and times grew, if not more
difficult, then less heroic, the passion that seems to flow up from the
Land of Israel in great and invisible waves did not subside. Of course
it never does, no matter what the difficulties. Some claim to see in

Previously published in the *Jerusalem Report* in May 1998.

the quality of the light, or feel in the quality of the air, or sense in the quality of silence, of Jerusalem and elsewhere—at the tops of mountains, in the Makhtesh Ramon, on the beaches of the Mediterranean—an indication of this passion, a special and, at times, even an unnerving intensity. This is quite so, and it is not merely a geological effect, or the remnant spell of history. It is the turbulence of earthly things in the presence of God. Embrace this turbulence, for it is the wellspring of action and the heart of the nation. All else, every secular dream, image, and effort, every religious practice and definition, every monumental thing like war or nation-building, is merely its faint echo.

Susannah Heschel

Susannah Heschel is the Eli Black Associate Professor of Jewish Stud-
ies and the chair of the Jewish Studies Program at Dartmouth College.
She is the author of numerous studies on modern Jewish thought,
including Abraham Geiger and the Jewish Jesus and Insider/
Outsider: Jews and Multiculturalism, coedited with David Biale and
Michael Galchinsky.

MY ISRAEL

Israel occupies both imaginary and physical space in my landscape. In
my childhood, Israel took shape through the Hebrew songs we sang
in school, pioneer songs about working the soil. In my mind, I was
one of those pioneers, and milk and honey would gush forth from
the dark earth as I imagined myself shoveling and planting and har-
vesting. Yet it was not so much the content of those songs as their
spirit, the warm melodies, the brisk beat, and the circle dances that
left us all breathless. That spirit was in marked contrast to the more
somber, plaintive melodies of prayer, usually in a minor key, that
spoke of longing for redemption and sadness over exile. Israel seemed
fresh, energetic, and young.

As a small child, I was taken by my parents to Israel on two occasions. These were the early years, when the country was still very poor
and struggling, and beggars were everywhere. Still, I found it extraordinary, as a five-year-old, to be walking on the same land as King
David and the prophets. During those visits, we spent most of our time
in Jerusalem, which was still a village, and the rhythms of that city have
stayed with me forever. The glow of the stones in the late afternoon

This article originally appeared in German translation in Mein Israel, ed. Micha
Brumlik (Frankfurt: S. Fischer Verlag, 1998).

sunset gives the whole city its golden, magical hue, but Friday afternoons were the most moving. The intensity of the morning grocery shopping, the crowded stores, the nervous rush of early afternoon slowly dissipated and the streets gradually emptied. Everywhere one could smell delicious dinners cooking. In the evening, walking from the synagogue, sounds of Friday night melodies being sung upstairs in dining rooms filled the streets, and it seemed that everyone was part of one large family, distributed at many tables. I could knock on any door and feel welcomed and at home. On those occasions I felt a sense of wholeness as a Jew that I have never experienced anywhere else.

With each visit, even as an adult, came a feeling of resentment that I had been raised in the United States rather than in Israel. I resented the gulf that separated me from Israelis, the gulf of language and mentality. I felt guilty that these Jews were placing their lives at risk for the sake of all Jews, while I sat comfortably in the United States. When the terrorist attacks began, I wanted more than anything to be there. What right do I have to escape the danger, I thought; isn't it shameful enough that by being born after the war, I escaped the last generation's murders? During my student years of travel to Israel, friends and family warned me of the bombings that continued, but I couldn't justify staying home. How could I claim that my blood was redder than theirs, my Israeli brothers' and sisters'?

To this day, there is nothing comparable to Shabbat in Jerusalem. It is not an idolatry of the land, or any sense that Israel as a physical space is holy. Rather, because Jerusalem is filled with memories, which form the core of religious experience, it becomes the occasion for moments in which God's presence is palpable. Throughout the centuries, Jews longed for Jerusalem, a longing inscribed in our prayers, yet most of us could only dream about Jerusalem, not actually enter it. When I am in Jerusalem today, I feel accompanied by streams of Jewish longing. It is as if the metaphors of the psalms suddenly become reified, as if the hills are truly singing and dancing, and I want to shout hallelujah.

Yet there is also Israel the physical land, the political reality that so often stands in sharp, ugly discordant clang with my religious experience. Zionism promised refuge and security, escape from anti-Semitism, violence, and the Western tropes of Christian disparagement of Jews. Not theological constructs, Jewish–Christian friendships, political guarantees from various governments, but a state of and for the Jews would be the first and only place of safety. Even more was promised: not only was the Zionist state for the Jews, but it was also to be a new kind of state, promising a political system of justice that had never before existed in history, under any rubrics.

The Zionist vision drew heavily on religious impulses embedded in traditional Jewish liturgy, and so the experience of Israel that I had as a child was of a dream come true, an otherworldly situation that seemed to have a divine power behind it. Just a few years earlier, European Jewry had been murdered, and now the governments of the world declared the establishment of a Jewish state. With the quality of the miraculous that was attached to Israel, it seemed inconceivable that the State could ever do wrong and commit evil.

Such feelings remained strong during the Six-Day War. Few periods of my childhood remain as vivid as those tense weeks during the spring of 1967. The increasingly hostile tone of political rhetoric in the Middle East was combined with threatening troop movements, which reached an emotional peak with the withdrawal of UN peacekeeping troops stationed in Egypt. It was the sort of emotional atmosphere of a waiting room at a hospital's intensive care unit, a sense that Israel's life and death were hanging in the balance, and with it, the life or death of all Jews. My friends and I left school early every day and volunteered to raise money for Israel. At the New York headquarters of the United Jewish Appeal, I heard about donations to Israel from American Jews of their entire life savings, of their homes, and of their businesses. The end of the war, in June 1967, brought an emotional release that was extraordinary. Sheer joy was mixed with tears over the disaster that might have occurred, and the celebrations were tinged with expressions of the profound vulnerability we had all felt. My father was a refugee from Europe, as were most of my parents' friends, and the 1967 war was an especially terrifying reminder of the Nazi years. The years of PLO terrorism that followed, especially the Munich massacre, the Ma'alot school invasion, the hijacking at Entebbe, the murder of Leon Klinghoffer, the UN declaration equating Zionism with racism, among other horrors, reinforced the feeling that all Jews were vulnerable, and that the security promised by the State could be destroyed at any moment.

The dramatic change for me came during my student years in Israel, in the late 1970s. Suddenly, for the first time, I began to observe something new: I saw Israel not only as a vulnerable target of hatred, but as an occupying force denying democracy to the occupied territories, degrading Palestinians, and serving as an obstacle or even opponent of peace. I was in Israel when Prime Minister Yitzhak Rabin approved the Camp Kaddum settlement, the first Jewish settlement in the West Bank territories. I noticed the roadblocks at which police stopped Arab cars, marked by a blue license plate, and detained them in long lines for hours, while permitting the yellow-plated Jewish cars to drive on. I heard new kinds of voices, voices of racism, in which Jews said, "The only good Arab is a dead Arab." I saw Orthodox Jews, most of them American émigrés, swaggering around their encampments on the West Bank with guns in holsters, like cowboys in the movies. The machismo that prevailed had no use for female students and scholars; I was told that just as every man goes to the army, every woman must donate her womb to the State, producing as many babies as possible to surpass the demographic threat posed by the high Arab birth rate.

My depression and alienation from Israel were profound, and I kept away from the country for ten years. Zionism seemed lost, and I was pessimistic about ever recovering a relationship to the state. Gradually, though, I came into contact with like-minded Israelis and American Jews, people who, like me, were critical of Israeli government policies in light of the Zionist promise. As I began to return to Israel on a regular basis, conducting research and lecturing, I found a new kind of community and a much deeper engagement in the state. I now go to Israel not simply to receive religious nourishment, but as a participant in the effort to shape the country, to fight for its proper direction and for the fulfillment of the promises of classical Zionism.

In truth, it is only in Israel that I find a certain kind of religious inspiration. Yet today I have also found an intellectual and political stimulation in Israel that is similarly extraordinary, not to be found elsewhere. The problems of the nineteenth- and twentieth-century political heritage, of nationalism and democracy, religion and state, ethnicity and multiculturalism, patriarchy and feminism, theological truth versus tolerance, face most countries in the world, yet they seem to receive their sharpest focus in the intellectual circles of Israeli society. Israel may not be what the Zionist dream envisioned, a political light to the nations, but it may offer the best chance for confronting and resolving the conflicts that all countries are facing in this century.

In recent years some Jewish theologians have insisted that a central role be given within Judaism to the religious significance of land, arguing that Judaism should not be defined as a religion of time, because that would be un-Zionist. Yet the land cannot be holy in itself, as land; Jews do not worship soil. Rather, the land can be the site for holiness to be created. Jewish tradition, it seems clear to me, teaches that God is not dwelling any more in Israel than anywhere else, because God is not reached through the physicality of space, but rather is met in moments of faith, in holy time. Instead, Israel is so deeply entwined with Jewish history and faith that it possesses the ability to inspire a revivification of religious spirit. The task of the Jew, my father wrote, "is to humanize the sacred and to sanctify the secular." That duty is most important in the political realm, because power, he wrote, can become "demonic when detached from moral meaning, from moral commitment."

My commitment to Israel is a transcendent one, a hope that through resolution of its problems, other countries will be able to benefit from its insights. The vision of Zionism is not diminished, but is transformed into a challenge. The state of Israel is not a panacea, but a measure of moral fiber, a demand that justice prevails over power. The state of Israel is not a gift to the Jews, or an achievement on their part, but a test of the integrity of the Jewish people and the competence of Judaism.

Jews today are challenged with the question, How does one live in the city of God, in the land of the Bible? We ask about life in the realm of the sacred, while Germans ask about life in the face of the demonic. Our tasks are diametrically opposed, but perhaps just as complex as those facing Germans, who wonder how they should live in the land of Auschwitz. For both of us, the political never stands alone, but is intimately tied to the moral and theological realms of our existence. How we assume our responsibilities and the obligations they entail is the ultimate test of our worth as human beings.

Rabbi Marvin Hier

Rabbi Marvin Hier is the dean and founder of the Simon Wiesenthal Center, a Jewish human rights agency, and its Museum of Tolerance. He is the founder of Moriah, the center's film division, and he has received two Academy Awards—one for coproducing The Long Way Home, *which followed the lives of Holocaust survivors, and the other for coproducing and cowriting* Genocide, *a documentary on the Holocaust.*

Whenever I cross the Atlantic, I take comfort in tracking the plane's route on the navigation map, and watching it hug the coast of Greenland. I guess it's comforting to know that there is an airport out there, just in case of an unforeseen emergency.

There are many who view Israel that way, as every Jew's emergency-landing spot. Truth be told, some may prefer Regent's Park, Beverly Hills, or the Hamptons, but as the recent planeload of French Jews arriving in Israel can testify, it's great to know that there is a land out there where they are always welcome. Indeed, in 1938 at the Evian Conference, the whole world was trying to find such a spot that would welcome Europe's Jews. But not a single country, including the United States, would grant them even emergency residency rights. As the Australian delegate told the conference, "Australia doesn't have a racial problem and is not interested in importing one."

But I think this notion of Israel as every Jew's second home overlooks Israel's true meaning to Jews.

In a penetrating comment on Jewish destiny, the great biblical commentator, Rashi, cites the following midrashic parable to explain why so soon after the miraculous Exodus from Egypt, the Amalekites attacked Israel: "It is a parable of a father who carried his son on his shoulder and then went on his journey. Soon the son noticed an article he wanted and asked his father to retrieve it for him. This occurred once, a second time, and finally a third time, until suddenly they passed another man walking toward them. The son called out to him (to the stranger), 'Have you by any chance seen my father?' At that moment the astonished father rebuked his son, 'You don't know where I am?' (after he had carried him all this way). So in anger, he threw his son to the ground and a snake came and bit him."

For me, this parable sums up best what Israel means.

When World War II ended, Jewish civilization was threatened with extinction. We had lost one-third of our people, the best and the brightest in the death camps that became Hitler's inferno. Only a bleak future awaited us. What contribution could such a morally wounded people make to mankind? Many predicted mass assimilation. Indeed, many did just that. After all, how many young people in 1945 were talking about Jewish continuity? To the world at large, the Jews had lost their compass. They appeared helpless, a community of perennial victims with whom no one wanted to associate.

Then came the notion of the Jewish state. A larger than life "father" image, forged out of the furnace by a band of Zionists swimming against the tide. This "father" image reached out and picked up his forsaken children and carried them proudly on his shoulder, restoring meaning and pride to the name "Jew."

As the years passed, and Israel took its place among the community of nations, a great renaissance occurred. Our self-confidence was restored and a rejuvenation of Jewish life began. No more the victims, Jewish schools and synagogues sprang up everywhere, on campuses and in suburban communities. Jews were bold enough to wear their yarmulkes again and take pride in their ancient heritage. There was a proliferation of books and films.

Even the anti-Semites changed their slogans. They no longer depicted Jews as emaciated, skeleton-type figures from Auschwitz. Instead, they were now depicted as aggressive soldiers wearing the Star of David.

Sadly, many have forgotten the contributions of this new "father" who picked up his children and carried them on his shoulder.

Unfortunately today, Jews invited to the White House, or to 10 Downing Street, or to the Elysée Palace think they got there all on their own. They have forgotten how lonely it was after World War II, how unwanted Jews were in the bastions of power, how difficult it was to get a meeting with President Roosevelt even to discuss the fate of Europe's Jews during World War II.

We have had a partner in all of our great accomplishments since the end of the war, and that partner has been the state of Israel.

Yes, it is true that if a grave crisis struck and Jews were in danger again, Israel would be there for us. But it is equally true and must never be forgotten that there would never have been such a rebirth of Jewish life were it not for the fact that among the flags flying outside the United Nations, there now flies a blue and white flag, a flag that has restored our hope and our pride in the prophetic promise that the destiny of the Jewish people will never be forsaken.

Arthur Hiller

Arthur Hiller is the former president of the Academy of Motion Picture Arts and Sciences and the director of several movies, including The Out-of-Towners, Love Story, *and* Man of La Mancha. *He was awarded the 2004 Israel Film Festival Humanitarian Award in recognition of his leadership in the motion picture industry and his support of humanitarian causes in the state of Israel.*

I feel an emotional tug thinking about how to express "what Israel means to me." There are so many things it means.

I was attending university in Canada when Israel became an "official" country for the first time since the Romans expelled them from their Judean state over two thousand years ago. The UN resolution took effect in May 1948, and Israel was immediately attacked by five different Arab armies. It became a major act of defense, and Israel was asking many countries for volunteers for their defense forces. I volunteered but they turned me down because I was married. I drove down to Seattle to try to volunteer from the United States but again was turned down because I was married. My wife agreed to volunteer, too, but again, "No."

Why did I volunteer? Because I wanted to stand up for the only place of refuge for the Holocaust survivors of Hitler's extermination program. They had been turned down by *every* country. I had flown with the Royal Canadian Air Force on bombing raids when the Allies were trying to stop Hitler's attempt to take over all of Europe—and to wipe out every Jew. He failed the takeover but he did massacre six million Jews in the Holocaust. I feel if there had been a Jewish homeland, an Israel, there is a good chance there wouldn't have been such a Holocaust. I did it for the survivors of that horrible period.

Now Israel has become an inspiration for me. When I think of the dozens and dozens of times in history that the Jewish people have been killed or driven from their homeland countries or from this land that is now Israel, Jordan, and Palestine—and some of it Egypt, Syria, and Lebanon—and that they have survived and worked their way back without ever starting a war, it just amazes me. Not only to return but to form the *only democracy* in the Middle East. One that has the moral values of the Judeo-Christian ethic that we in the United States and Canada, and so few other countries around the world, cherish and live by. It's such a symbol to all of us in our own small way. You can't give up. You have to hang in there and work and work to achieve your dreams no matter how impossible the situation seems.

Israel hangs in not only as the one democracy in the Middle East, but with the highest standards of living and care for its people whether they are Jewish or not. It's the only Middle East country with uncensored press or television. It's the only Middle East country where you're free to have differences of opinion and free to have artistic expression.

Only in Israel can women travel without having to have the permission of a male relative—and women are almost half the work force. Israel is the only country in the Middle East that has freedom of religion and the only one that has free and fair elections and laws against discrimination and hate crimes.

In Israel, Arabs have 12 of 120 seats in the Knesset (the Israeli parliament), and they are professors at the universities. Arabic as well as Hebrew is an official language. All the Arab municipalities receive government funding—and all this while Israel stands alone in the Middle East as a democratic country. It's a whole different attitude of treating people fairly and equally.

I don't think you'll find Jewish people in these positions and situations, or with this freedom in Syria, Iran, Libya, Saudi Arabia, and so on.

I remember my wife and me on our first visit to Israel in the late 1950s and as we taxied from the airport toward Jerusalem, we were astounded to see, on one side of the dividing fence separating Israel and its Arab neighbors, miles and miles of flat sand and dirt, and on the other side, miles and miles of greenery and development. Then it hit me again that this people who had survived so many massacres, wars, and being pushed out of its land, had determinedly returned; and now with this small area of mostly barren land it had been given as a state, had turned it into a thriving country of industry and work opportunities and care for the settlers and for the thousands of refugees and immigrants. The Palestinians got almost ten times as much land, but despite the wealth of some of their leaders and of their wealthy Arab neighbors, this land remains sand and desert and has not nurtured work and development and business growth but instead nurtured poverty and hate and now suicide bombers who have been taught hatred for Jews in their classrooms and in their mosques. The latter has resulted in death to thousands of innocent Israeli civilians, young and old.

Again it hit me that this is a problem created by the Arabs themselves who would not let their refugees become citizens (except Jordan) but instead kept them in refugee camps. All this despite the millions of Arab oil dollars. Once again it struck me how determined and caring and doing the Israelis were—and all this while in a struggle for survival, a struggle that we learn daily is far from over.

It makes me see again and again how fortunate we are to live in the United States. We had our struggles to achieve our wonderful democratic country and I'm proud that we, and sometimes Great Britain, stand up for Israel in the UN and provide so much humanitarian help for Israel.

For Israel, the current situation and conflicts are life-and-death struggles. I admire their determination and dignity of purpose with high ethical standards as they try to make their country safe *for* democracy, while the countries around them try to make the Arab world safe *from* democracy.

Judd Hirsch

Judd Hirsch is an Emmy and Tony award–winning actor who has appeared on television and stage and in film. He starred as Alex Rieger in the television series Taxi *and went on to star in the Broadway plays* I'm Not Rappaport *and* Conversations with My Father.

I am an American. I was born to a country that had already attained its freedoms. But I am a member of a very young country with a very young history based on escape from the tyrannies of regal power and religion.

What can I know of the yearnings of a people whose history is steeped in loss—of identity, of homeland, and of respect for the only thing that has bound them as a people, their beliefs?

It's not easy to understand how a nation can reclaim itself after five thousand years of banishment, occupation, and inhumane treatment by so many peoples of the world. Perhaps it only desires the same freedoms we exacted out of a bloody revolution. Or perhaps it yearns for freedoms of a different nature: the freedom to exist and be acknowledged by others in their existence; the freedom to defend itself from once again losing everything; freedom from bigoted hate by other peoples and religions.

But somehow I have faith that this nation, this people, this idea called Israel will give back in kind to a world that grants these freedoms.

David Horovitz

David Horovitz *is the editor of the Israeli news magazine the* Jerusalem Report *and the author of two books,* Still Life with Bombers: Israel in the Age of Terrorism *and* A Little Too Close to God.

It was a Russian immigrant who asked me, after I had been living here for about eleven years, "Why?" He was a thin, high-cheek-boned young soldier named Alexander who had the misfortune to be serving with the Israel Defense Forces in Khan Younis, an over-crowded, impoverished refugee camp town in the Gaza Strip. As part of my army reservist's service, I had given a lecture at his base—this was a few years before the army's 1994 pullback from most of Gaza—and he approached me at the end. Why? he wondered, gen-uinely puzzled. Why was I living in Israel?

"Because I'm Jewish," I said, "and because Israel is the home of the Jews."

Was it difficult being Jewish in England (where I spent the first twenty years of my life), Alexander wondered, like in the old Soviet Union? Was I denied a place at university, as he had been? Kept out of certain jobs? Forbidden to travel overseas?

No, none of that, I had to admit. There was an undercurrent of anti-Semitism, the odd snide remark in the streets, a fight here and there. But no, there was nothing life-threatening.

Parts of this essay were amended by the author from his two recent books about life in Israel, *A Little Too Close to God* (New York: Knopf, 2000) and *Still Life with Bombers: Israel in the Age of Terrorism* (New York: Knopf, 2004).

"So," he persisted, "why uproot yourself from such a haven of Western culture and civilization for a conflict-bedeviled strip of desert in the Middle East?"

I talked about the rare opportunity to live in a Jewish state, about building a liberal, democratic society, and about spreading the notion of equality through the benighted dictatorships and theocracies of the Middle East.

Alexander had no reaction.

I started speaking faster, about how the Holocaust could never have happened if we'd had a land to call our own. I said that only an independent, strong Israel could guarantee Jewish safety, and that I wanted to help build that Israel.

Alexander stared back blankly.

Desperate by now, I talked about my children growing up as native-born sabras, suntanned, healthy, speaking Hebrew with a proper, rolling *r-r-r-r-resh*. They were certain, unlike in the Diaspora, to marry into the faith, to keep their Judaism alive.

Nothing. Alexander clearly thought I was insane.

Okay, then. Last chance. "The weather," I blurted out. "The weather. I really came because of the weather."

For the first time, he looked interested.

"Ten, eleven months of the year, in England," I told him, "it rains. Not let's-get-this-downpour-over-with-and-then-the-sun-can-come-back-out rain, but wheezy, whiny, apologetic rain, struggling to reach the ground, leaking in rivulets down the back of your neck and into the tops of your Wellington boots. The day starts off sunny. But you shouldn't be fooled. In ten minutes, it can cloud over and start spitting on you. And it will do that every day except the one when you remember your extra sweater, your boots, your raincoat, and your umbrella. That day, it will stay sunny right through. The next day, you'll forget your umbrella, and it will piddle on you again."

"Ahh," said Alexander, fully comprehending now. "The weather, sure. Makes sense." And off he went, a pale Russian kid in his oversized green Israeli uniform—whistling, puzzle solved—to peel his potatoes, patrol the jails, or do whatever it was he spent his miserable new-immigrant army days doing.

Such improvised explanation notwithstanding, the truth is that I can't drag myself away from this country—and it's more than sunshine that keeps me here. A few years back, we spent a summer vacation with my wife Lisa's parents, played racquetball with her old school friends, sweated in the health-club sauna, kept the gray cells mildly active with chess matches contested on an inflatable board in the pool of a friend's back garden. It was divine; sheer untroubled bliss. We did not watch the news or read the papers and did not miss them—for about five days. Then I started feeling an indefinable kind of itch. Life was just too serene, too easy. What was the point of it? Was this what I had been put on the planet for? I started reading the papers again, watching CNN International. Absurdly, I even began feeling guilty about being away from Israel, not only missing what was happening, but somehow letting the country down. It was only when the plane touched the tarmac at Ben-Gurion Airport, and I knew I was back amid the strain and tension of the Middle East, that I could relax.

Most journalists would identify with some of that—with the helpless frustration of being away when news is breaking. But with me and Israel, it runs much deeper. Whatever my misgivings over this or that government policy, this is the only country to which I feel an emotional connection, a personal stake. This is the only country where I feel personally affected by national events—by election results, by Supreme Court decisions on the status of non-Orthodox Judaism, by a rise in the murder rate, by a spate of horrific cases of family violence, by the turnout at demonstrations. I would never have engaged in sweating, terse conversations with relatives and friends over British politics in the way that I do over our political differences here. In no other country would I have felt personal pride in the way we have absorbed a million ex-Soviet immigrants, or in the smooth functioning of the field hospital our army erected in a day to save refugee lives and help birth refugee babies on the Kosovo-Macedonia border. In no other country would I feel bereaved and obsessed by the relentless toll of terrorism, and furiously frustrated by international misperception of its causes. Nowhere else would I feel affronted by the weekly death toll on the roads, elated at a local scientific breakthrough, delirious that "my" beauty queen had won the passé Miss World pageant (Liora

Avergil, 1999), and that "my" transsexual pop singer had triumphed in the supremely irrelevant Eurovision Song Contest (Dana International, 1999). This is the only country I could ever love like that.

Life in Israel has been anything but easy these past few years. We have been battered by a strategic terrorist onslaught, whose perpetrators aimed not merely to "liberate" the disputed territory of the West Bank, Gaza, and East Jerusalem, but also to terrorize the rest of purportedly undisputed sovereign Israel. They told us in bloody capital letters, by targeting us in West Jerusalem, Tel Aviv, Haifa, Netanya, and pretty much every other population center in the country, that their struggle is not confined to the land beyond Israel's pre-1967 borders, which they are assuring the international community is all they seek for their state. Rather, the battle extends across our entire country. As Hamas openly confirms, it is a battle for control of all the territory between the Jordan River and the Mediterranean Sea.

Nowhere, absolutely nowhere, has been off-limits to terrorism—not even predominantly Arab areas, not even the Hebrew University campus, which, because of the large number of Arab students, we had assumed would be left unscathed; the main cafeteria was blown up in July 2002. We have been denied the assumption that governs normal life in the free world—the assumption that the people with whom you come into unremarkable contact in the course of your daily routine value the divine gift of life. In fact, in the Israel of the age of terrorism, we make the opposite working assumption: that wherever we go, in any relatively large grouping—whether it's to shop, eat out, or cross at a traffic light—somebody may be lurking who seeks nothing more fervently than to kill himself—or even herself—and as many of us as possible. To shut the front door in the morning has been to enter a kind of grisly lottery, with no guarantee that we and our loved ones will make it home safely at the end of the day. There's not an Israeli who hasn't felt the chill wind of terrorism in the bitter years since fall 2000.

We have proved incredibly resilient as bombers target our civilian population and as we suffer an additional onslaught from an intellectually dishonest international community. A large body of world opinion misrepresents what has happened here to falsely condemn us as the architects of our own misfortune, arguing that the Palestinians had no alternative but to resort to terrorism because we did not offer them viable terms for coexistence and because of their daily suffering amid the closures and curfews and the "apartheid wall" in the West Bank. In fact, of course, the government of Ehud Barak accepted President Clinton's thoroughly viable blueprint for peace while Yassir Arafat did not, and the restrictions on Palestinian movement, rather than the cause of the terrorism, are defensive measures that were introduced to curb the waves of terrorists crossing our open borders.

Why have I been prepared to stick all this out, and subject my children to it? Because just two generations ago, Lisa's father, who grew up in Lodz, lost almost his entire family—his parents, and all but one of his seven siblings—murdered in Nazi concentration camps, and he survived the camps himself only through a combination of astonishing resilience and good fortune. Because my father, together with his siblings, had to be dragged out of Germany by his parents in the nick of time, severed from the place they had never conceived could be anything other than home to them. Because the Jews have been refugees for centuries, the appreciated, tolerated, despised, or loathed minority, but always the minority, dependent for survival on the good graces of others. And now our nation of refugees has restored its ancient refuge. And if that refuge, this homeland, falls again, I see no reason to expect a flowering of Jewish culture, a stabilizing of Jewish demography, a sensitive integration of Jews around the world. Anything but. So I'd like to think I've been putting my family through this for our own sakes, a shortish-term risk for a hoped-for long-term benefit, for my children and for their children and for their children's children.

Our lives are coinciding with a rare moment in human history when the Jews are sovereign in their own country, making our own choices about our own destiny. I relish the opportunity to help shape that future. And along with the rest of my astonishingly resolute countrymen and women, I don't want to be terrorized into giving it up.

Erica Jong

Erica Jong is the author of the best-selling novel Fear of Flying. *She has written seven other novels, nonfiction, including* Fear of Fifty: A Midlife Memoir, *and six volumes of poetry.*

FALLING IN LOVE WITH ISRAEL

I never wanted to go to Israel when I was young. Growing up in a sophisticated, assimilated New York Jewish family, I had a horror of kibbutzim and the kind of American Jewish kids who summered at them. Let them dance the hora in Negev, I thought, I'm going to be dirty dancing in a Paris boîte on the night of Quatorze Juillet. I thought of Israel as the opposite of all the elegance and grace I craved in life. Big-breasted girls wearing khaki and rifles and picking dates! Goody-two-shoes Zionists making the desert bloom with berries, barbed wire, and babies. Spare me. Cole Porter and Noel Coward were my idea of cool, not Ben-Gurion.

What an ignorant little twit I was! I went to Israel for the first time after I was fifty (the occasion was a poetry festival in Jerusalem) and I fell so in love with the country that since then I have looked for every excuse to go back. The Mediterranean landscape, the exuberance of the Israelis, the way politics is a matter of life and death there—all these things beguiled me. Not to mention the archeological sites, the immersion in ancient history, and the sheer passion of the people for

This is a revised version of the essay "Out of Time: Israel's Negev Desert," which appeared in *Travel & Leisure* in January 2000.

politics, music, and literature. Of course, it didn't hurt that most of my books are translated into Hebrew and are popular in Israel. But it wasn't merely ego. It was a genuine appreciation of the earthiness of a country I had been too uptight to visit when I was in my teens.

Many writerly trips had been proposed through the years, but none came off. (On one occasion twenty years before, I was offered a grant to live and write in Jerusalem for several months at Mishkenot Shananim, but I was breast-feeding my daughter in Connecticut.) Fate conspired to make me wait to discover Israel in 1997, when I finally went to read poetry in Jerusalem and was utterly smitten. So smitten that I found a way to go back to Israel two years later—this time to the Negev desert, where I gave lectures and seminars on American Jewish writing and writers at Ben-Gurion University in Beersheva.

I arrived just after Passover in April, when the desert is blooming, and I left before the hot weather arrived—a perfect time to see the Negev. Again I was struck by the richness and variety of this tiny country, and I wondered why I had been so resistant to Israel in the past.

Perhaps it's because Israel represents a threat to certain American Jews. We're afraid we'll lose our souls to the Jewish homeland and never be able to return to the United States. Our very concept of home may change.

The more you travel in the Middle East, the more you realize that Jews and Arabs share as many qualities as they do divisions. The abundant, almost rambunctious hospitality, the appetite for ancient history, the olive-oil based cuisine, the relentless quest for water extend across national boundaries. In many ways, the most exciting thing about the Middle East is its people and their irrepressible ardor. No wonder they fight so bitterly. They are so alike. Should they ever become friends, they may be as passionate friends as they once were enemies.

Optimistic? Very. But ancient history shows us the consistency of peoples' needs through the ages: a caravan route, water, a place to bury the dead. Gods come and go but peoples' needs remain constant. Ben-Gurion was right. If the desert can flower, anything can happen.

Israel is such a small country (the geographical size of New Jersey, with a spirit as big as the United States and Russia and China combined) that it is possible to see Jerusalem, Tel Aviv, the Sea of Galilee, and the spice routes of the Negev all on the same trip. Jordan's Petra is easily accessible, too, and forms the logical end point of a trip that follows the spice traders' trail from the Dead Sea. If the peace process really succeeds this time, travelers and archeology buffs will be the real winners, since the abundant ancient remains in the Middle East are only isolated from each other—and us—by political barriers.

My travels in the Negev took off from Beersheva, where I was based at the university. There's no denying that Beersheva is an ugly town—except for the Bedouin market and the new university, it mostly resembles a vast building site in the desert, but the energy of the university and its students is appealing. Ben-Gurion University has a kind of open, irreverent, pioneering quality. Students razz their professors with an informality I'm told is rarer at the older universities in Jerusalem and Tel Aviv. I found my students in the foreign literature department lively and fun; they challenged me and my writing. Besides my colleagues in the foreign literature department, I met with Ben-Gurion's brilliant writer-in-residence, Amos Oz, and was warmly welcomed by the president, Avishai Braverman, and other professors.

Ben-Gurion is a university that has as deep a commitment to the desert as its namesake did. The botany department boasts the world-famous Professor Yossi Mizrahi, who is experimenting with such desert-growing plants as white sapote, nopolito, and monkey orange from Mexico; pitahaya and apple cactus once farmed by the Aztecs; and argan from Morocco, which gives a fine oil. The idea is to find forgotten plants or wild specimens that can be used for millennial food. Professor Mizrahi walked me through his desert greenhouse and let me taste the succulent desert fruits that he hopes will defeat hunger in the twenty-first century. I've never gotten excited about botany before, but at Ben-Gurion University it seems a living science. The desert landscape, which initially seems barren, is really a cornucopia of fruits and vegetables.

Beersheva—the name means seven wells, and it was named by the patriarch Abraham in biblical times—also shares the changing light and pure air of the desert. Very near the city are the archeological sites of Tel Arad and Avdat, Masada and the Dead Sea. I ventured into the desert one windy afternoon in a broken-down taxicab to see both Avdat and Tel Arad. I was fortunate to be able to wander through these haunted sites almost all alone.

Avdat, a major stop on the Nabatean spice route, was founded in the fourth century B.C.E. It was the point at which the roads branched off to other desert spots and to the Mediterranean. As with all these desert cities, water-collection played a part in its founding. Avdat flourished somewhat later than Petra, becoming most important during the Roman Empire and during the Byzantine period (400s to 700s C.E.). At Avdat, I was able to explore the remains of a Roman villa, sit in the shadow of a ruined Roman watchtower with a keystone arch, and see what was left of a Nabatean pottery workshop that made clay pots valued for their thinness. I stumbled on the remains of a Byzantine wine press, caves used for storage of wine, and the house of a Byzantine wine merchant. The foundations of a Roman bathhouse attested to Avdat's flourishing in Roman times.

But the single best thing I did in Avdat happened in my imagination—I stood atop the observation balcony that lies on the ruins of a Nabatean temple looking down on a range of wild mountains. With the wind flapping my shirttails and hair, surprised that the desert could be so chilly, I imagined a caravan of hundreds of swaying but sure-footed camels crossing the inhospitable Negev. The camels would have been laden with spices from Arabia, silks from China and India, and frankincense—a vegetable gum used as incense on all the sacrificial altars of the ancient world—from Africa. Frankincense was as valuable in the pre-Christian world as gold, and it would have attracted bandits, as would the minerals from the Dead Sea (needed by the ancient Egyptians for embalming mummies). Unless its leaders paid protection to the Nabateans (who patrolled the spice route), my imaginary caravan would never have gotten across the desert. I understood why the books I'd read had told me that spices, frankincense, and minerals from the Dead Sea often increased 600 percent in value on their journey through the desert. The desert was tough duty; only a few caravans actually made it through.

From Avdat, I continued in the same beat-up taxi to the Canaanite city of Arad (inhabited before 2650 B.C.E.) and its surrounding fortresses built by the kings of Judea more than a thousand years later. In Tel Arad I was able to see one of the water cisterns that had made the desert habitable in ancient times. Water was the key to all these desert cities, as it is often the key to Arab-Israeli relations today.

Tel Arad is also barren, windy, and haunted. It takes another feat of imaginative reconstruction to understand that this was a thriving city thousands of years ago. Ben-Gurion's dream of making the desert bloom was really a harking back to ancient times, when elaborate water-engineering made the desert livable. We tend to think of ancient peoples as technologically primitive. But the cities of the desert—Tel Arad, Avdat, Petra, and Masada—all had elaborate systems for catching and preserving water.

For a thousand years (until the Negev was incorporated into the Roman Empire in A.D. 106) the Nabateans were able to build great cities through their water expertise as well as their hegemony over the most valuable products of the ancient world. By controlling access to the rare goods that had to travel through the desert on their way to Mediterranean port cities such as Gaza, the Nabateans became masters of the desert.

At its zenith, the Nabatean empire extended from Damascus to Yemen, from the Sinai desert to present-day Iraq. Though they had started as raiders, the Nabateans eventually discovered that it was more profitable to sell water and protection to the caravans. Their gain from the booty that crossed the Negev came as a result of their being able to exploit their strategic position between East and West—much like the Venetians of a later time. When the trade routes later changed (as a result of the Emperor Trajan's building of a road between ancient Philadelphia—now Amman—and Aqaba on the Red Sea), Palmyra in Syria inherited the trading wealth that had formerly flowed through the desert to Petra.

In its prime, Petra had been so powerful and feared that it evoked biblical curses against its polytheism. In Deuteronomy, Moses says of the Petrans (Edomites): "They sacrificed to demons which were no Gods . . . I will heap evils upon them . . . they shall be wasted with hunger and devoured with heat and poisonous pestilence: I will send the teeth of beasts against them, with venom of crawling things of the dust . . . they are a nation devoid of understanding; if they were wise, they would understand this! . . . For their rock is not as our Rock."

Petra may also have been the city of Job, the biblical land of Uz whose primary deity was the goddess Venus Al-Uzza. Certainly the ancient Israelites with their monotheistic Father-God cannot have approved of the Nabatean habit of creating brother and sister monarchs who viewed themselves—like their Egyptian counterparts—as divine. Nor can they have approved of their worship of many deities, chief among them a powerful female creator-goddess.

When my gig at Ben-Gurion was over, I chartered a single-engine plane to fly to Petra with friends. We flew to Amman and took a dusty three-hour minivan ride down to the no-longer-lost city. I know now that this is hardly the best way to approach Petra, but my day for visiting the city coincided with a Muslim holiday when the border was open only at Amman and I had no choice. I imagine it's more ravishing to travel to Petra from Aqaba, arrive at sundown, stay in one of the new hotels near the site, and see the sunrise over the fantastic Siq gorge and cut-rock tombs in the morning. My trip didn't work out that way, but I'll do it right next time.

Still, flying over the desert from the Israeli to the Jordanian part of the Negev was amazingly beautiful. Our minivan ride from Amman to Petra took a rough and exhausting three hours, during which we dozed. My friends and I were awakened by our arrival at ancient Petra, which one enters through the narrow Siq gorge. There are always plenty of mules and camels available for hire, but we decided to walk so that we could slowly savor the view.

The soaring canyon walls of sandstone are stained various shades of pink, salmon, and terra-cotta by the iron-rich waters that have flowed over them. Flashfloods are an occasional occurrence; French tourists were drowned in the Siq a few years ago. Though I was grateful to visit Petra without being washed away, the stories of floods certainly made our visit more dramatic.

And the ride from Amman to Petra was beautiful. In April the desert was alive with poppies, and there were bits of green visible in the occasional oasis. In Wadi Musa, the canyon above Petra, which is the supposed spot where Moses struck the rock to provide water for the Israelites, there are abundant hotels, restaurants, and a visitors' center providing guides and maps and craft shops. We had met up with our Jordanian guide at the airport in Amman and he had prepared us for Petra on the way, but nothing can really prepare you for Petra.

Petra defies description, so everyone quotes someone else's line: "a rose-red city half as old as time." I had thought it was Christopher Marlowe's, but it is actually from a much lesser known poet, Dean Burgeon, who is not remembered for anything else. In any case, the line is inaccurate. Most of what you see in Petra is the necropolis outside the city, not the city itself, which is represented mostly by its Roman ruins: the Cardo or main street and a vast amphitheater that once seated more than seven thousand people. The soaring caverns (into which invisible waterways are carved), the tombs hewn out of rock cliffs, and the play of changing light make Petra visually unforgettable. Since it was rediscovered by Westerners only in the eighteenth century, it's not yet destroyed by tourism, though I'm told that the days that swarm with visitors can be disappointing. What I really wanted was the silence to contemplate Petra—to try to imagine it as a flourishing city of traders from all over the known world—and I had that in part because I went there on a Muslim holiday.

Ancient Petra was a city of slaves as well as freemen, a city where, if you were invited to a swell dinner party, your feet were washed by slaves before you reclined to dine, a city where practically everything— from people to jewels—could be bought for a price. It was a city that believed in benevolent gods, watchful ancestors, and malevolent jinns. If I ran into a jinn, I would ask to be transported to Nabatean Petra for just one day and given the gift of language. Like the English writer Rose Macauley, I am less aroused by "broken towers and mouldered stones" than by the notion that human life has repeated itself with minor technological differences for thousands of years; "it is less ruin-worship than the worship of a tremendous past."

My most durable reason for traveling is to transport myself into other worlds. I like to be reminded that human nature is constant, that technological innovation modifies it less than we usually think it does, and that the past is prologue to the present. The Negev charms me because in its seeming emptiness, a pageant of ancient history passes before me. If I can't be transported back to the Nabatean world by a jinn, perhaps I'll write a novel set in that world and make my own magic. I became a novelist in part to travel through time. The Negev is a time machine whose lambent light beams you back to ancient days.

Max M. Kampelman

Max M. Kampelman was counselor of the State Department, U.S.
ambassador to the Conference on Security and Cooperation in Europe,
and ambassador and U.S. negotiator with the Soviet Union on Nuclear
and Space Arms. He is now chairman emeritus of Freedom House,
the American Academy of Diplomacy, and the Georgetown University
Institute for the Study of Diplomacy.

ISRAEL: A PERSONAL PERSPECTIVE

For me to explore the role played by Israel in my life, a worthwhile effort, I must examine my childhood. My mother always had a small collection box in our kitchen where we put pennies to help the Jews in Palestine. We lived in a tenement in the Bronx, surrounded by other Jewish families, and we all knew that Palestine was the birthplace of the Jewish people and should again be a homeland where the Jewish people would always be welcome. The Bible taught us that.

My parents were not devout religious observers, but they wanted me to have a Jewish education. My grade school and high school education took place in Jewish schools where half of our long day was spent studying Hebrew as a language and Judaism as a religion, followed by a half day satisfying the New York State requirements for graduation. Here again, the Bible, coupled with Jewish culture and history, involved the role of Palestine. This relationship with Israel was an integral part of our being as Jews. L'shana habaa b'Yerushalayim—next year in Jerusalem—was a recurring theme in my early training, even though I knew nobody among my relatives, friends, and neighbors who had any desire or interest in leaving the United States to live in the Jewish national homeland.

For reasons unclear to me, I never shared the goal of many of my classmates, who thought of themselves as future rabbis. My father and mother were not strict religious observers of the Sabbath, although my mother kept a kosher home and lit the traditional candles on Friday night. All of our family friends were Jewish, but not strict observers. My parents found their way into the retail business and kept their store open on Saturdays. Indeed, as a youngster, I would spend many hours each Saturday as the cashier in our store—definitely not in keeping with Orthodox teaching. The first retail store of ours was a butcher shop in a non-Jewish neighborhood and one that did not sell kosher meat. This exposed me to Christian customers and suppliers. The same was true when my father decided to take the advice of a friend and close his butcher shop to open a retail millinery store in another section of the Bronx, where I also served as a part-time cashier and where the store was also open on Saturdays.

My father had an interest in politics. He had met Ed Flynn, the boss of Tammany Hall, and was particularly proud of a badge given to him by Mr. Flynn. I also recall his enthusiasm for Al Smith and the Democratic Party when I was about eight years old. My horizons stretched, but never at the price of my identification as a Jew, Jewish traditions, and loyalty to Jewish people all over the world, including Palestine.

In reviewing my education and training, what always impressed me was the biblical lesson that all human beings were created by God and are, therefore, brothers and sisters to one another. The "Shemah" is the best-known basic prayer of Judaism: "Hear O Israel, the Lord is our God, the Lord is One." This was a challenge by the early Hebrew tribes to the prevailing view of the period that there were many gods. With only one Father, we are all one family. Here was the religious justification for democracy and liberty for all human beings. These roots remain deep and serve to strengthen my lifelong commitment to a democratic Israel and a democratic world.

My decision to leave the yeshiva at the end of my high school years to transfer to New York University's Bronx campus just a few blocks from my home was not enthusiastically greeted by my mother, my father having died when I was fourteen years of age. At his death, I scrupulously followed the Orthodox Jewish tradition and attended synagogue services every morning and evening for eleven months. My training in prayer impressed the seniors who attended the synagogue regularly, and who had encouraged my mother to believe that I should take an interest in pursuing a rabbinical career. My mother reluctantly respected my strong preference to become a lawyer. I knew we did not have the financial resources for me to attend the university, but I assured her that I would be able to handle it with a combination of scholarships and hard work in outside employment. It turned out that between serving as a clerk in the campus bookstore, being a hatcheck clerk at as many college dances as I could handle, selling subscriptions to the *New York Times*, and representing a business in the rental of tuxedos to the senior class for their prom, plus working every summer in various jobs, I made more money during each year of my college education than I did for a few years thereafter.

During my first year on campus, I learned that there was a society for Jewish students known as the Menorah Society. I joined it. The following year, my fellow students, knowing of my early yeshiva training, elected me to serve as president of the organization. This exposed me to a citywide group of students on various college campuses that was organized by the Jewish chaplain at Columbia University, Rabbi Isidore Hoffman. He was a Reform rabbi, which exposed me to a less rigid expression of Judaism. We became personal friends, a relationship that lasted until his death. He was the rabbi I chose to officiate at my wedding.

Leaving the yeshiva broadened my horizons. Studying the social sciences, my college major, exposed me to issues of social welfare and government. Becoming the president of our campus Menorah Society as a sophomore led me to meet leaders of the various Christian student groups. Meeting Jewish student leaders from other campuses also educated me further about anti-Semitism in our own country. Palestine seemed less of an issue in the face of the apparent growth of anti-Semitism in the United States being championed by Father Charles Coughlin, who communicated weekly on the radio to the American people. And there were Henry Ford, Charles Lindbergh, Senator Burton Wheeler, and others openly critical of Jews.

Palestine was not an issue for me at that time. I do recall reading a statement from Rabbi Judah Magnes, a leader in the Jewish community, who subsequently became the first president of the newly established Hebrew University of Jerusalem. He called for a binational Palestine, a democratic society for Jews and Arabs, and it made sense to me.

Hitler became known to us as a vicious anti-Semite in Germany, but the extent of his brutality and savagery was slow to reach our country and my consciousness. This slowness and lack of sensitivity proved costly and made war inevitable.

What I do recall are the shameful reports that reached our press about British ships and soldiers violently preventing ships of mercy, containing thousands of Jews escaping from Europe, to land in Palestine in an effort to save themselves. This was in spite of the British government's stated commitment in the Balfour Declaration of 1917 that Palestine should be the Jewish national homeland. We later learned that President Roosevelt also refused to open our doors widely for refugees to enter the United States. These decisions by us and the British not only permitted the Jewish population of Europe to be decimated, but deprived our country and the world of the intellectual and human richness that could have enriched and strengthened our country.

My own personal awareness of this brutality did not reach my consciousness until about halfway through the war, when I volunteered to be a human guinea pig in a semistarvation experiment at the University of Minnesota, financed by the Department of Defense and administered by the university and the late Dr. Ancel Keyes, the originator of the K ration. I was authorized to take course work in law and political science at the university while I completed my selective service with the experiment team. It was at the university that I became conscious of the inhuman brutalities of the concentration camps. I vividly recall a cable from the Defense Department to Dr. Keyes asserting the importance of our work and the need for guidance on how best to rehabilitate and feed the concentration camp survivors and prisoners of war being found and released.

My decision to take advantage of my presence at the university by taking graduate courses also proved to be a wise one. It led to an M.A. and later a Ph.D. in political science and an unexpected brief teaching career.

It was a natural development for me to increase my interest in Palestine as the horrors of Europe's treatment of Jews pierced my consciousness. The thought of emigrating, however, never crossed my mind. When the United Nations in 1947 recognized Israel as an independent country, I enthusiastically welcomed the news, and was outraged when the surrounding Arab countries refused to recognize Israel and declared war. I became more of a Zionist, particularly pleased that Israel committed itself to be a democracy. I also became somewhat active with the Minneapolis Jewish community and developed friendships that I continue to maintain.

It did not surprise me when the mayor of Minneapolis, Hubert Humphrey, whom I met and assisted on occasion, was elected U.S. senator in 1948. It did surprise me when, late in 1948 following his election, he telephoned me at Bennington College in Vermont, whose faculty I had just joined, and asked me to spend January and February, a Bennington vacation period, helping him put his new Senate office in shape. I agreed, and was eventually hired myself.

I knew from our various exchanges in Minneapolis that Humphrey looked upon himself correctly as a friend of the Jewish community and as a Zionist of sorts. Israel and its defense became one of Humphrey's goals as a senator. Israeli ambassadors, as well as its presidents and prime ministers, knew they had a friend in him and also in me, and they responded with appreciation as well as with challenges.

The experience exposed me to the reality that there were a number of Jewish organizations in the United States. Their differences in how best to be effective sometimes blinded them to the strength that comes from unity of effort. That is fortunately being overcome. After leaving government service, I joined a number of the Jewish organizations that were becoming more cooperative with one another. Indeed, my participation was helpful in developing a cooperative effort on the part of the Anti-Defamation League, the American Jewish Committee, and the American Jewish Congress, which led to a negotiation with the National Business Council and important legislation that made it illegal for U.S. businesses to cooperate with the Arab boycott of companies doing business with Israel. We successfully won that legislative challenge.

I decided not to involve myself in Israel's internal policies. My guideline was to be helpful where appropriate to whatever administration had been duly elected by the citizens of Israel. After all, I freely chose not to live in Israel. Israeli politics, I continue to believe, belong to those who choose to live in Israel.

Given my early life as a teacher, most of my formal relationships with Israel related to higher education. I served as national chair of the American Friends of the Hebrew University of Jerusalem and as a member of the university's board of governors. I also, at the request of Mayor Teddy Kollek, served as chairman of the Jerusalem Foundation in the United States. I have also received honorary degrees from a number of Israel's universities and continue to be helpful to Israel's ambassador in Washington.

Anti-Semitism is clearly reappearing. Australia's largest synagogue was defaced with anti-Semitic graffiti that read: "Six million more, please, with fries." A recent study showed that at least fourteen other countries recorded anti-Semitic incidents, in addition to the sermons from many mosques around the world that single out Jews for death. A United Nations conference on racism in South Africa quickly became a carnival of attacks on Israel. Missouri senator Christopher Bond recently reported anti-Israel rallies on college campuses here in the United States becoming more popular once again. Natan Sharansky may be correct in his view that "Israel has become the world's Jew, and anti-Zionism is merely a substitute for anti-Semitism."

Today, Israel's survival continues to be at risk from terrorist attacks. The fact that this is associated with growing anti-Semitism in Europe and elsewhere in the world only adds to the need to intensify our dedication to its survival. Two Israeli professors recently were awarded the Nobel Prize in Chemistry. Advanced technology has turned Israel into a world leader in many areas of international business. Israeli citizens have turned deserts into gardens, and Israel's tulips are even exported to Holland. Its hospitals are open to all people, whatever their religion or citizenship. Friends and supporters of Israel have every reason to be proud of its accomplishments and its democracy.

Peace between Israel and its neighbors must now be the objective. The question remains: Is the issue the boundary of Israel, its size, or its very existence? As an American, I am proud of our president's recognition that the friendship between the United States and Israel is an integral part of a joint commitment to one another and to the spread of human dignity and democracy to those people now deprived of those benefits.

Jonathan Kellerman

Jonathan Kellerman is clinical professor of pediatrics at the School of Medicine of the University of Southern California and the founding director of the Psychosocial Program at Children's Hospital of Los Angeles. A worldwide best-selling mystery writer, he is the author of twenty-three novels, three volumes on psychology, two books for children that he wrote and illustrated, and numerous scientific articles and social essays.

BIG LIES AND VICIOUS BLONDS

On November 20, 1970, Israeli Foreign Minister Abba Eban delivered a foreign policy speech in UCLA's Pauley Pavilion. I was a twenty-one-year-old senior, eager to hear what the statesman had to say, and I made my way to the auditorium, along with hundreds of other students and faculty. As we neared the entrance, we were confronted by a small band of anti-Israel demonstrators.

This vociferous bunch, whom I recognized as habitual campus protesters for a variety of "revolutionary" causes, whooped, screamed, chanted, and brandished placards festooned with an especially vulgar hieroglyphic: crudely interlaced swastikas and Stars of David.

The rest of us did our best to ignore the message and the messengers. In those days I wore a yarmulke, and as I neared the entry, one of the gang, a fair-haired, blue-eyed girl around my age, made eye contact and lunged at me, shrieking, "F—ing Nazi!" On cue, her pals took up the chant. Their contempt rang in my ears as I made it inside and edged toward my seat.

Three and a half decades later, I couldn't tell you what Abba Eban said that day. But the memory of that verbal lynching, so grotesquely ironic that it bordered on black comedy, has remained seared into my consciousness.

Here was a prototypical WASP coed—your Woody Allen heroine rendered shrill by fanaticism—laying the other N-word on the Jewish American son of a Jewish American war hero who'd battled Hitler's hordes for three and a half years in Europe and liberated concentration camps.

Here was milk-fed Blondie, who could've modeled for a Third Reich eugenics poster, itching to brand the broken cross into the hide of an undeniably Semitic fellow, several of whose relatives had perished at the hands of the Nazis.

How vicious. How weird.

I've often wondered what would have happened had I been able to take that young harridan aside and question her in a calm manner about the absurdity of her bigotry. Would a speck of self-doubt have surfaced?

I'd like to think so, but I fear not. During the turbulent years that followed the Six-Day War, a certain revisionist worldview had been promulgated by a certain thugocracy that had morphed into a self-styled liberation movement. And that big lie had found a comfortable niche in left-wing political thought: supporters of Israel were the new Nazis. And Jews, whose history of victimization should have taught them to know better, were to be condemned with special vehemence for their alleged persecution of a people labeled "the Palestinians." (Prior to the sixties, "Palestinian" had referred to all residents of the Holy Land, Jews and Arabs alike.)

What permitted those on the radical left who fancied themselves tolerant humanists to feel comfortable affixing a despicable label to a minority group while remaining free of cognitive dissonance was another big lie: Zionism and Judaism had nothing to do with one another.

Judaism, the argument went, was a venerable religion whose theology might be antiquated nonsense but whose emphasis on social justice was praiseworthy. When Jews remained in their rightful place as an oppressed minority, they merited favored-victim status and a warm welcome into the human family.

Zionism, on the other hand, was a racist, neocolonial, land-grabbing, militaristic horror foisted upon innocent, indigenous Arabs.

Thus, when Jews had the temerity to cast off the victim role and assume an assertive stance, they forfeited their humanity.

Psychoanalysts have a word for such conceptual calisthenics in service of the twisted ego: *splitting*. The utility of this particular bifurcation was clear: one could—indeed, *should*—despise Zionists without fear of being labeled anti-Semitic.

In many so-called progressive circles this fantasy maintains currency (though many serious enemies of Israel have begun to abandon the pretense, coming right out and admitting they hate Jews).

Let's set the record straight, once and for all: any attempt to split Israel from Judaism is either deliberate racist mischief or the product of sheer ignorance.

It's not just all those archeological digs in the Holy Land that unearth obvious truths about thousands of years of Jewish residency. (Shards and amulets and scrolls can be powerful stuff when they butt against big lies, and the destruction of the ancient synagogue in Jericho a few years ago by Arab rioters was anything but an impulsive flare-up. The shul's mosaic floor festooned with Jewish iconography was too damn reproachful.)

It's not just the fact that Israel, lambasted as a colonial interloper, represents a *victory* over neocolonialism, a rare instance of a displaced, indigenous people *reclaiming* its land.

Let's go beyond historiography to the crucial issue. Even a surface study of the scriptures with which Jews gifted the world reveals that Israel is an *essential* element of Judaism. The people and the religion and the land are inextricably bound.

Consider this: of the 613 commandments that constitute the behavioral core of Judaism, 300 can be performed only in Israel. Of these, 189 are related to the Temple service on Mount Zion, 61 involve agriculture, and 48 pertain to the role of Jewish government in Israel.

This is not to say that one cannot be a fine Jew in the Diaspora. A *complete* Judaism, however, can be practiced *only* in the land of Israel.

Yes, Israel serves extratheological purposes. The Jewish state remains a post-Holocaust haven for survivors and their descendants. That miracle is precious and profound and, given the rebirth of barely dormant, classically cruel European anti-Semitism bonded to Islamic Jew-hatred, safe sanctuary in a land of strong Jews is oh so relevant.

Yes, Israel remains the sole democracy in a region conspicuously lacking in such. In the post–Cold War era in which the crucial battle has shaped up as a classic struggle of values, the fractious but ultimately *open* parliamentary process that propels Israeli democracy is a slap in the face to those who champion the evils of death-oriented despotism.

Yes, Israeli genius continues to make the desert bloom, and for a tiny nation, Israel's growing position as a brain-trust of technical, scientific, and medical innovation is beyond impressive. That makes the Jewish state a crucial player in a postindustrial age in which information is king.

On a less heady level, Israel is simply a vibrant, beautiful country whose sound track is often a glorious cacophony of prayer and blasphemy. I've lived in Israel, set a novel there. Each time I set foot on Israeli soil, I find my ancestral homeland wondrous and infuriating, endlessly rife with contradiction. Israel can be spiritually intoxicating, yet Israeli society can be curiously single-minded about adopting some of the most vulgar aspects of contemporary Western culture.

Worship in Jerusalem, disco in Tel Aviv.

Left versus right, secular versus religious.

The shul you go to, the one you avoid.

Does Israel have a way to go in its development as a light to the nations? Absolutely. But it's done a fine job for a nation still in its adolescence.

All that's fine and fascinating and provocative and terrific source material for the chattering classes. But it begs the crucial point: *there is no authentic Judaism without Israel.*

I am that Semitic fellow, degraded in my youth by ignorant malevolent hypocrites. I am a Jew who has studied my religion, my heritage, my birthright.

I am a Jew.

Israel is part of me and I am part of Israel.

Rabbi Naamah Kelman

Rabbi Naamah Kelman was the first woman ordained in Israel by the Hebrew Union College Jewish Institute of Religion, where she is currently the director of the Year-in-Israel Program.

Why do I love Israel?

I chose to live in Israel; I was not born here. I was born into the Jewish people, and that already commits me to Israel. That Israel, the Israel of our heritage, our sacred texts, and our history is not the only reason I love Israel. That is what brought me here. The reasons I remain here are different and equally as rich.

Is it the taxi driver who would not take a friend to the hospital emergency room she asked for, claiming that a different hospital was much better, and drove her straight there? Is it the family doctor who paid a house call for my sick daughter on Rosh Hashanah, and then noticing the shofar in my home, decided to blow it so she could fulfill the mitzvah? Having prescribed the remedy for her body, he then moved on to her soul.

Do I love Israel for her incredible assortment of human beings? The human material here never ceases to amaze, inspire, and infuriate. This is a place of such profound contradictions.

On a pouring January afternoon, I go to attend the swearing-in of my son in his army unit. He will receive a rifle and a Bible. Six hundred young men line up to hear their commanders' charge; they talk about responsibility, humility, and compassion. The army rabbi says that while the rifle serves as our physical protection, the Bible remains our moral compass, no less important, perhaps much more important.

He was not only referring to the Book of Joshua; he was telling them that the eternal values of the prophets must ultimately guide us. I am opposed to the Israeli occupation of the West Bank; I pray for the implementation of a two-state solution, speedily. So I am concerned that my son knows the complexities of this war we are in. I pray that he remembers that human beings were created in God's image. I pray that he remains human and humane in the Israel Defense Forces. At the moment he received his rifle and Bible, he heard the message I had hoped for, knowing full well that reality is far more complex.

Sometimes my love for Israel is as simple as clockwork—the clockwork of the seasons. Pomegranates are in full bloom as we approach the New Year; Sukkoth are built in the most usual and often unusual places. I especially love that we decorate them with Christmas decorations, tinsel and colored lights. The lights in the windows and Israeli doughnuts sold everywhere light up the eight days of Chanukah. The almond trees burst into bloom as we approach Tu B'shvat, and Purim is celebrated here for four days! When Passover ends, we break bread with our dear friends who are Israeli Arabs. They get the fresh pita for us. We look out at their olive grove, knowing that each of us has deep historical claims to this land.

And Shabbat in Jerusalem—there is absolutely nothing anywhere in the Jewish world that compares to the sun setting on the walls of Jerusalem every Friday toward dusk. The hustle-bustle of day slowly seeps away. The colors of the city begin to change. The city walls and buildings move from beige to peach to gold. A collective deep breath is taken just before dark falls, and slowly the smells and tastes of freshly cleaned homes and family Shabbat meals rise throughout the city. For one moment, the anticipation that yes, the world can be redeemed, is shared, if only it could be. . . . maybe this Shabbat!

One Passover, the Muslim contractor renovating my home was so upset with the carpenter in Bethlehem because the kitchen cabinets would not be ready in time. So he went to fetch them himself. That was in the heyday of Oslo, when we went in and out of Bethlehem. We could almost touch the prospect of coexistence. Then it vanished.

There are days I live in the Middle East and days I live in the Med-iterranean. Perhaps this is a clumsy rendering of a Yehudah Amichai poem. The sights, smells, cacophony of outdoor markets, seaside cafes, balmy nights—those are my evenings in the Mediterranean. That is when I can attend the National Book Fair in June at the Israel Museum. Behind me is the Shrine of the Book, containing our most ancient remnants of our culture, the oldest pair of tefillin that exists. In front of me is a booth of the distinguished publishing house of our modern Hebrew poetry. I run my hand over the volumes of Amichai, Rabikovitch, Alterman, and Rachel. There is a direct and unending chain from the words in those tefillin, to the words of modern Hebrew verse. One miracle is simply undisputable. The rebirth of the Hebrew language has changed the way we sing, love, fight, and crack jokes. That particular June day, the book fair opened when the city suffered another horrendous bus bombing in Jerusalem. This was my small act of defiance, to remain a stiff-necked people, to go buy books as a response to the horror. I love Israel, because I wasn't alone there that night.

Many, many days we live in the Middle East, war, terror, and humiliation fill the lives of Jew, Christian, and Muslim. Who here does not have a loved one who has paid the ultimate price? For twenty-five years, a group of friends stood in silence around the grave of a dear friend, killed in a senseless army accident. The parents of the young soldier had deemed this to be the fitting memorial. What can you say when you are twenty, burying a vital young man? We said nothing. Each passing year, we stood together at his grave. Then, with his parents gone, twenty-five years had passed; his siblings asked us to speak. The words and tears flowed. I have too many friends who are widowed. Their dignity in the face of horrendous loss is awe-inspiring. Two in particular have not ceased to be committed to mending the world and not hating the enemy.

On the banks of the Kinneret, the Jewish people were reborn. The cemetery is filled with the pioneers who made it possible. Naomi Shemer, the first lady of Israeli song, was buried there recently. She is a row away from the poetess Rachel, and the other visionaries and activists. Heads of state, musicians, and just plain folk attended Shemer's funeral. When the simple and moving funeral was over, hundreds remained to sing her songs for hours. Where else might this happen? Jews of all backgrounds came to her grave to pay respects to her legacy. She gave us what has become for many the alternative to prayer. She wrote wonderful Hebrew songs for all occasions, always set to the backdrop of the landscape; whole families and communities sing them together.

I look out to the sun setting over the cliffs north of Netanya, far out into the sea. Everything feels possible. There is ease outside of Jerusalem that is palatable. Runners sprint along the beach; windsurfers glide toward the horizon. Modern Hebrew slang is spoken here. For many secular Israelis, Judaism was either/or, black or white. You are either totally observant or Israeli. For many, it has become too political and too stifling, too extreme. Over the past twenty years or so, there has been slow and steady flowering of the liberal streams of Judaism. "There are many ways to be Jewish" was a slogan of a joint public relations campaign of the Reform and Conservative movements in Israel a number of years ago.

"Aren't you a Reform rabbi?" one runner along the beach asks me. "I was at a wedding you performed. I didn't know it was possible to have a meaningful ceremony." I like to call these ceremonies: something old, something new, something borrowed, something blue and white. This is our challenge, to create an Israeli-Jewish, East-West, contemporary, yet deeply rooted way of being here; a way that makes space for others, indeed, welcomes others, as well.

I love Israel because it has given me the opportunity to perhaps make a difference. To share in the growth of progressive Judaism has been both exhilarating and depressing. While the Orthodox establishment keeps alternatives suppressed, an ongoing glacial shift is happening. Reform rabbis now perform over six hundred weddings a year, even though they have no legal standing. Our twenty synagogue centers all over the country are bursting with activities—religious, educational, cultural. In addition to providing ritual, we are increasingly becoming a voice not just for pluralism but also for social action and social justice. Egalitarianism is synonymous with Reform, yet we need to go further and really effect change.

In Israel, everyone is family; those visiting and those living here. We meddle, we get involved, and we state opinions without looking over our shoulders, often very loudly. Every Jew has a stake here. There are political talk shows that feel as if we have returned to gladiator contests, throwing one another to the dogs. Where else could a secular member of the Knesset yell at an ultra-Orthodox member, "Even though I don't believe in it, weren't we at Mount Sinai together?"

Mostly I love Israel because it is ours wholly to tend, to fix, to heal, and to renew.

Aviva Kempner

Aviva Kempner is a filmmaker and writer. She produced Partisans of Vilna *and directed and produced* The Life and Times of Hank Greenberg *and* Today I Vote for My Joey. *She is currently working on a documentary on Gertrude Berg and a comedy,* No Good Bagels in Israel.

ISRAEL'S SPRING IS ALWAYS WITH ME

Israel and I have been forever linked from the day I was born in Berlin and my parents anointed me with a beautiful Hebrew name. Although I was born in December, they named me Aviva, which means the season of spring.

My own folklore is that my birth was a breath of springtime air amid a wintry month. And I enjoy joking that my name stemmed from sexist reasoning. My father, Chaim, was a Lithuanian-born American soldier stationed with the U.S. military government in Berlin. Pops used to tease me that he wanted a male child born in postwar Germany so his son's *bris* would be a sign of defiance. It would be visible proof that Jews had survived the Nazi onslaught.

When a daughter was born, however, the Jewish soldier derived great pleasure in writing a Hebrew name on his offspring's birth certificate as a form of cultural revenge. My baby picture ran on the front page of the *Berlin Observer* as "Miss 1947," affirming the appearance of the first American Jewish war baby born in Berlin. My Hebrew identity was living proof that a Jewish bloodline had definitely emerged from the rubble of defeated Germany.

However, I prefer to believe my mother's explanation for my poetic name. My mother, Hanka Ciesla, blond and green-eyed, had passed as a Polish Catholic in a forced labor camp near Stuttgart until she was liberated by Americans. She claims my name was chosen in honor of my grandmother, who loved the ancient language and had perished at Auschwitz along with my grandfather and aunt. My Uncle David, who was the family's sole survivor of Auschwitz, confirmed stories of my grandmother singing Hebrew songs to her children.

Israel is also deeply rooted in my fraternal family's history. When my father's work was complete in Germany, he wanted us to migrate to Israel. Grandfather had conveyed a strong identification with Zionism to his ten children. Aunt Tziporah had been a Zionist pioneer and moved from Lithuania to Israel in 1924. Aunt Mira lived during the 1950s in Israel. Aunt Luba had hosted Golda Meir in Pittsburgh while she was touring the States in the late 1920s to gain support. Uncle Po spent decades involved in the Labor Zionist movement in Detroit. And a distant cousin, Chaim Herzog, became the president of Israel.

But my mother's wish to move to the United States, where her brother already lived, prevailed. So we moved to Michigan in 1950. The rest of my maternal surviving Polish cousins and Aunt Ruja and Uncle Henoch emigrated from Europe to Israel, joining those who had come before the war.

Growing up in the Midwest, I was always hearing stories about Israeli family members whose welfare was constantly in our minds and hearts. Cousins would come visit us in Detroit, leaving strong impressions of being tough pioneers. One American cousin, Judy, moved to Israel in 1949 with her husband, only to return in 1959 when they could not make it financially.

My earliest thoughts about Israel were very romanticized. I possessed a teenage crush on the sabra Ari Ben Canaan character in Leon Uris's novel *Exodus*. Seeing *Hill 24 Doesn't Answer*, the arty black-and-white film about youthful soldiers protecting an outpost during the War of Independence, inspired my first visual surge of Zionism. The actors reaffirmed my images of my brave Israeli clan.

Having a Hebrew name always made me a walking advertisement for the country. Upon hearing my name, people usually stated, "What a pretty name. What does it mean?" So I proudly answered, "It's Hebrew for spring." I always thought having an unusual first name made me a friendlier person because of the immediate conversation that ensued once I stated my name.

Only once in my youth did my lyrical Hebrew name fail me. I was running for office in junior high and evoked the uniqueness of my name in my campaign speech. Stepping up to the podium, I shouted, "Vote for Aviva; it's the same backwards and forwards." Somehow that linguistic trait went right over their adolescent heads. I lost my feeble attempt at Hebraic cleverness.

My first trip to the Holy Land was a Sweet Sixteen present from my Uncle David. Young and impressionable, I was thrilled to meet kind and loving *mishpoche* who were the surviving remnants of my mother's Polish relatives and the pioneers from my father's side. One of my earliest memories was a naive thought; "Imagine, even the cops are Jewish." I viewed the buildings in Jerusalem from the ancient past more as my lineage than the monuments in Washington, D.C.

My crushes on macho Israeli men abounded, certainly a continuation of my Ben Canaan complex. I remember observing how Israeli men certainly carried themselves differently than American men. Surely it was the required military training. But they proved too "fast" for my puritanical American Jewish upbringing.

This adolescent trip was the beginning of a lifetime love affair with Eretz Israel. Since this virgin trip, I have traveled to Israel over fifteen times. My ties with the country grew even more profound through the years as my father finally realized his dream and made aliyah in 1973. How proud he was to finally become an Israeli citizen.

Kibitzing that there were too many Jews living in Tel Aviv, Pops settled in Rehovot, close to my aunt and her family, who had settled in Kfar Bilu in 1933. He was especially proud to be active in an organization of Americans living in Israel and overjoyed to receive a monetary prize for that work. He kidded that it was the first time Israel had ever given money to him, as he had been raising money for the country for years.

I distinctly remember humorous culinary observations from those trips. There were no good bagels to be found in Israel for years. What Israelis called bagels we American Jews called pretzels. My fondest memory of ending eight days of eating Passover matzo was being in Israel, where I devoured delicious oven-baked bread at Aboulafia's in Jaffa. Yet I never recovered from the knowledge that Israelis ate matzo for only seven instead of eight days. It just did not seem fair.

Then I began to think about another inequity. We in the Diaspora had to learn Hebrew for our bar and bat mitzvahs while Israeli thirteen-year-olds already spoke it. I teased Israelis that they should have a coming-of-age ceremony in a non-Hebrew language. Since they had the home advantage of not having to learn the ancient words, I figured they should have to go through the traumatic ritual of singing foreign words.

Bearing a very typical Israeli name made for some mix-ups when I visited Israel. On the beach, I would hear people yelling for "Aviva," and of course turn around. Then I realized they were not calling me but some six-year-old. I also could never figure out why Tel Aviv meant "Hill of Spring," since there really did not seem to be much of a hill there. Certainly not in comparison to the geography found in Jerusalem.

Further confusion arose when Israelis tried speaking Hebrew to me because of my very Israeli name. So, for years now, I always disclaim being able to speak Hebrew when introduced to any Israeli. It does not prevent them from speaking Hebrew rudely in front of me, but at least I am up-front about sadly being Hebrew impaired.

I was shocked to discover that my name in Hebrew was not spelled as a mirror image like it is in English. Much to my disappointment, I realized I no longer had the distinction of having palindromic nomenclature in Israel.

But visiting Israel also brought great personal sadness. My father's retirement life in Israel was fruitful, but much too short, as he passed away suddenly in 1976. He realized for only three short weeks that he had acute leukemia. My brother and I sadly arrived the afternoon of the morning that he died, and suddenly Israel became the burial place of my beloved parent.

The events were even more traumatic, as I was not prepared for the typical Israeli Orthodox ceremony. As the female relative, I was not granted the opportunity to throw dirt into my father's grave. But as an

American Jewish feminist, I ignored the sexist traditions and threw dirt and a memento peace symbol into his grave.

We were grateful that his family allowed him to be buried at the Kfar Bilu cemetery, near where his pioneering sister and brother-in-law were laid to rest. Every subsequent trip to Israel includes a loving trek to their resting places. Especially enlightening were my later professional trips to the Holy Land. My career switch to produce Jewish-themed documentaries in 1979 generated a film on Jews fighting the Nazis. I was proud that half of the survivors in the film were Israelis who were former partisans. Living with my cousin Fanny, whom I considered an aunt, allowed me to experience daily Israeli life. I relished the fruitful time spent in Israel researching and filming the interviews and employing an Israeli crew. And it was equally rewarding to debut *Partisans of Vilna* in Israel, premiering a documentary replete with Hebrew, as well as Yiddish.

Championing Israeli cultural products, especially cinema, has became a cause of mine while living in Washington, D.C., for the past thirty-one years. When I was directing the Washington Jewish Film Festival, I loved attending the world-class Jerusalem Film Festival to choose the latest Israeli and Jewish films for our festival. We made sure to have the Israeli embassy as the cosponsor for the festival and always screened the latest Israeli movies.

I admire the active and talented Israeli film community, especially when their movies bravely examine Israeli society. I am thrilled that through the years their films have captured a more commercial market in the States and in Europe, and demonstrate great vision. When I cannot visit Israel, I attend the annual Israeli Film Festival in New York City to obtain a quick Israeli cultural fix.

My latest trip to Israel, sponsored by the State Department in the spring of 2004, was very rewarding. I screened my baseball movie, *The Life and Times of Hank Greenberg*, at U.S. ambassador Daniel Kurtzer's house in Herzliyya. This screening included many Israeli diplomats I had befriended in Washington, D.C. I could only imagine how special the film's projection right next to the Mediterranean Sea would have been for my father if he were alive to see it. After all, he was the one who first taught me about the game of baseball. Pops used to tease that the only two things he regretted leaving in the United States were baseball and his children. And my brother and I were never sure which he missed more.

Loving Israel, as in any amorous relationship, is not all roses or wonderful memories. It's a love affair always fraught with worry. Watching the news, especially during wartime, Scud attacks, and the intifada, has often been extremely painful. Many mornings I wake up with troublesome thoughts about my Israeli friends and relatives. I immediately click on CNN to see if there have been any bombings in Israel.

The difficulty is compounded by my personal feelings of guilt for not living in Israel, and feeling restricted by being a distant supporter. I often ponder if I should have followed in my father's footsteps and made aliyah. But with my inability to learn languages, especially Hebrew, such a move is inconceivable to me. Also, I am just not brave enough to make the leap of living out the Zionist dream.

Although I remain living in the States, my strongest friendships are with people who share my concern for Israel. Among my closest friends are either Americans who came back from living there or Israeli-Americans who have mentally never left their country. We call one another constantly to digest and interpret the latest news. Proudly wearing Naot shoes, we entertain Israeli visitors.

My family's tradition of using Hebrew names continues in the next generation. Many of my American cousins sport Israeli first names. I am proud that my brother Jonathan named his oldest daughter Aliza. I hope to accompany her and her two sisters when they make their first visits to Israel. I will especially enjoy seeing Aliza's amazed face when someone calls her name on the beach, only to find they are calling another child with the same name.

Year after year, forever the cockeyed optimistic American Jew, I make the same prayer. Every time I lift up my glass to toast at a Jewish holiday or blow out my birthday candles, I wish for peace between Israel and her neighbors. I fantasize about Israel having healthy and fruitful relations with a peaceful, democratic Palestinian state.

Toward that end, I write my yearly contributions to Friends of Peace Now and New Israel Fund. I marvel how friends, Dennis Ross and Aaron Miller, past peace negotiators for the United States, continue to devote their lives to establishing peace in the region.

And I am always dreaming about my next trip to Israel. For years, I have pledged to myself, "Next year I will return to Israel to make another film there." But this movie will be a hilarious comedy, titled *No Good Bagels in Israel*. Since I always tease those I love, why should Israel be an exception?

Larry King

Larry King is the Emmy Award–winning host of CNN's Larry King Live *and the recipient of the George Foster Peabody Award for Excellence in Broadcasting. He has written several books, including* Remember Me When I'm Gone: The Rich and Famous Write Their Own Epitaphs and Obituaries.

There is something uplifting and breathtaking about the way Israel was born. Out of the tragedy and despair of the Holocaust, Jews and others from around the world, both openly and secretly, with the help of friends and despite the opposition of many others, established a place where Jews would be at home in their own land, no longer under the control of others. Israel was the answer and antidote to thousands of years of wandering and the most horrific acts that the world has ever known.

Visionary Zionists had been working for a Jewish state for some sixty years before Israel's birth. What they could not have envisioned when they first started working to create a Jewish state was Hitler and Nazism. The pogroms and other atrocities that Jews endured throughout the centuries were a pale precursor to the pure evil that spread across Europe in the 1930s and 1940s. For the first time in human history, somebody tried to wipe out an entire people—and might even have succeeded, had Hitler confined himself to that and refrained from aggression against more powerful countries.

As Jews, we are taught never to forget what happened during the Holocaust. My purpose here is not to go over the details of Nazi atrocities, but to point out and indeed celebrate the inspiring contrast between what happened to the Jews and what they did next. The establishment of the state of Israel was an awesome historical event.

From what may be the lowest, most dismal point any ethnic or religious group has ever been in, Jews rose up and surprised the world. Israel shows that no matter how overwhelming the adversary—or the adversity—we can not only overcome it, but make something great from that tragedy. Israel isn't a symbol. Israel is the practical manifestation of hope, freedom, and self-determination.

I've never been a particularly observant Jew, but when I look upon Israel's achievements, its strength and its vibrant democracy, I feel tremendous pride to be a Jew.

Morton Klein

Morton Klein is the national president of the Zionist Organization of America, the oldest pro-Israel group in the United States, and a member of the Executive Committee of the American Israel Public Affairs Committee. A child of Holocaust survivors, he is also an economist who served in the Nixon, Ford, and Carter administrations, and is considered one of the leading Jewish activists in the United States.

WHAT ISRAEL MEANS TO ME—AS AN AMERICAN, AS A JEW, AND AS A CHILD OF SURVIVORS

As an American, I take pride in the words inscribed on the Statue of Liberty, inviting to these shores the tired, the poor, and all those yearning to be free. Throughout our country's history, the spirit of that message has offered hope to the world's downtrodden, and it was they, the refugees from the four corners of the globe—including my own parents—who built this country and made it what it is today. Only one other country has served as a sanctuary for refugees of every culture and background: Israel. We Americans correctly see much of our own country's spirit in the people of Israel.

Americans have not just admired Israel's miracles from afar. We have contributed to its triumphs in many important ways. We have contributed financial aid, to help Israel build a modern and self-sufficient economy. We have contributed military aid, so that Israel can defend itself against those who attack it. We have contributed thousands of idealistic men and women who have made Israel their new home and who have shared with Israel the benefits of their experience growing up in the United States, including two distinguished prime ministers, Golda Meir and Benjamin Netanyahu.

I am equally proud that the relationship goes both ways—that Israel is a constant source of help to the United States. This is particularly important in the context of America's greatest contemporary challenge, the war against terrorism. Israel is one of America's few real allies in the war against terrorism. Israel has fully and consistently supported U.S. efforts against the Taliban regime in Afghanistan, the Saddam Hussein regime in Iraq, Osama bin Laden, and other terrorists and their sponsors.

Israel has always shared with the United States its experience and expertise in confronting terrorists. For example, New York City police investigators were sent to Israel in May 2002 to receive training in detecting and investigating suicide bombers. The Israeli Defense Ministry helped the U.S. Federal Aviation Administration develop a blast-resistant container for cargo flown aboard passenger aircraft. Many of the most serious terrorist attacks over the years, such as the bombing of the Pan Am flight over Lockerbie, Scotland, were the result of bombs planted in cargo containers. The American forces fighting terrorists in Afghanistan are using an Israeli-manufactured airborne targeting pod. The U.S. Air Force used the Israeli-made AGM-142 air-to-ground missile in its attacks on bin Laden strongholds in Afghanistan.

I note with pride that nearly 85 percent of U.S. aid to Israel is spent by Israel in the United States, on American goods and services. Thus U.S. aid to Israel helps the American economy and generates jobs for Americans. Among the products Israel purchases from the United States are military systems. Israeli military experts often improve the quality of these systems, and then share the new technology with the United States, thus saving the United States billions of dollars in research and development costs. Israel imports more, per capita, than other allies of the United States. During the 1990s, Israel imported $732 per capita worth of U.S. goods, compared to $443 by Great Britain, $242 by France, and $236 by Germany.

The ongoing strategic cooperation between Israel and the United States gives the United States access to Israeli technology and intelligence. Israel and the United States frequently conduct joint military exercises and undertake exchange programs for senior military officers. Twice each year, U.S. Marine Corps units travel to Israel for crucial desert warfare training. During the 1970s and 1980s, this alliance gave the United States access to crucial information from Soviet-made weapons systems that Israel had captured from the Arabs. In more recent years, the strategic alliance between the United States and Israel has meant opportunities for the United States to benefit from Israel's experiences fighting against Islamic terror.

As Americans, we take special pride in the fact that Israel and the United States are democracies, with free elections. By contrast, the Arab regimes are dictatorships, in which "elections" have just one candidate. Israel and the United States have freedom of religion. In Arab countries, Islam is the official state religion. Israel and the United States protect the rights of women and minorities. In Arab countries, women are treated like men's property, and religious and ethnic minorities are systematically persecuted.

To me as a Jew, Israel's creation and history seem to be an almost miraculous fulfillment of the Torah's prophecies. After two thousand years of exile, pogroms, Crusades, and gas chambers, a Jewish state was reborn from the ashes of Auschwitz and, exactly as the Torah foretold, ingathered millions of exiles to forge a modern nation.

On the day Israel was established, its population numbered some 650,000. During the next four years, the infant Jewish state took in nearly 700,000 new immigrants—penniless refugees, Holocaust survivors from Europe whose property had been stolen or destroyed by the Nazis, Jews who were expelled en masse from Arab countries with just the shirts on their backs, their homes and property having been seized by the Arab governments.

Amazingly, Israel was not overwhelmed by the burden of the newcomers. It treated the burden as a blessing. Secular and religious worked side by side to build their new country. They did so at a time when Israel was being invaded by five Arab armies. Despite the strains of mass immigration and the hardships of defending against Arab assaults, Israel developed one of the world's most vibrant democracies.

Israel's extraordinary scientific, medical, and cultural achievements are too numerous to mention, except to note that this, too, is part of what Israel means to us—Israel serving as a "light unto the nations" in so many ways. From science and medicine to art and literature, Israelis not only have excelled in every imaginable field but have generously shared their achievements with the international community.

In recent years, the miracles have continued. In 1967, the heartland of the Jewish national home was finally liberated—Judea, Samaria, and Gaza returned to Israel. Jerusalem was reunited after centuries of Arab neglect and desecration of Jewish holy places and neighborhoods. The Temple Mount in Jerusalem, the Tomb of the Patriarchs in Hebron, the Tomb of Rachel in Bethlehem, the Tomb of Joseph in Shechem (Nablus)—all finally returned to their rightful owners.

That was not all. Israel rescued tens of thousands of Jews from starvation and civil strife in Ethiopia. While other nations cheered from the sidelines as the Soviet Union collapsed, Israel took in hundreds of thousands of Soviet refugees—at a time when Iraqi Scud missiles were raining down on Tel Aviv.

To me as a Jew, what could be more meaningful?

For me as the child of Holocaust survivors, who lost dozens of family members in Hitler's genocide, and who was born in a displaced persons camp in Gunzberg, Germany, Israel has another special meaning. The existence of a powerful, sovereign, Jewish state is our insurance that we Jews will never again find ourselves trapped by our enemies, with no place to flee. We cannot prevent violent anti-Semitism from erupting again, perhaps even on a mass scale. We cannot prevent the international community from once again abandoning the Jews. But now there is a home to which Jews can come, and which will always protect us.

For those of us whose lives have been permanently scarred by the Holocaust, there is especially profound meaning in the reality that Israel rose from the ashes of Europe's murdered millions—that precisely when the Jewish people had suffered more than at any time in our collective three-thousand-year-existence, Jewish fighters in the land of Israel rose in revolt against the British occupation forces and brought about the creation of a Jewish state. Israel is the answer to Auschwitz. Jewish statehood is the answer to Jewish powerlessness.

.   .   .

But as an American, as a Jew and a Zionist, and as the child of Holocaust survivors, I am deeply worried for Israel's future. Today, I see a Jewish state making extraordinarily risky concessions in order to achieve "peace" treaties—only to see the Arabs flagrantly violate every provision of those treaties. I see Israel subjected to merciless international pressure to make even more one-sided concessions. I see deeply alienated Israeli intellectuals rejecting their Jewishness and the most basic precepts of Zionism. I see Diaspora Jews growing weary of defending Israel, and becoming numb to the constant torrent of terrorist attacks.

Israel has given meaning to our lives as Jews. That is too precious a thing to risk losing. But the reality in today's bleak situation is that unless Jews the world over actively protect and assist Israel in every way possible—politically, financially, personally—its very existence may be jeopardized.

Edward Koch

Edward Koch is a former mayor of New York City. He now practices law; writes books and articles, including a weekly column for Newsday; and is a commentator for Bloomberg Television.

Why is the security of the state of Israel so important to Jews throughout the world and particularly so to the American Jewish community?

Most American Jews will never leave the United States to resettle in Israel on aliyah. Most of us believe that the time we are living through in the United States will someday be known as the Golden Age for Jews in America. In the last century, we have risen from the American ghettos we inhabited as new immigrants on the basis of individual merit. Anti-Semitism is at a minimum and rejected by all political leaders. We are viewed by our fellow citizens as friends and neighbors, and we have assimilated to a degree that some consider alarming.

For me personally, the United States has been a glorious place. After serving as a combat infantryman in Europe during World War II, I went to a fine law school and then entered politics. I have successfully held the public offices of city councilman, member of Congress, and mayor of the city of New York, having been elected mayor for three terms with the overwhelming number of votes coming from non-Jews. I am equally proud of the fact that since leaving the mayoralty fifteen years ago, I continue to be relevant in New York City's public affairs.

So why am I concerned about the security of Israel? The reason is simple. I go to bed every evening without fear. Yet I know that somewhere in the world there are Jewish communities fearful of what will happen to them and their children during the night or the following morning. Two countries that come to mind immediately are France and Argentina, where anti-Semitism is growing and virulent.

Should it become necessary, I know that under the Law of Return, the Jews of those countries will be able to find sanctuary in Israel without limitation in number and regardless of their physical or economic condition. Before World War II, Adolf Hitler challenged the world, saying he would allow the German Jews to leave Germany if any country would take them. No country was willing to accept more than a token number, and for many German Jews, the doors to freedom were slammed shut. They and more than five million European Jews living in countries conquered by the Nazis were murdered in the ghettos and the concentration camps to which they were shipped. Had Israel been in existence at the time, every Jew allowed to leave Germany and ultimately subjugated countries of Europe would have been welcomed and allowed to live in that Jewish state. Regrettably, Israel has had to fulfill that same role of providing sanctuary for Middle Eastern and Ethiopian Jews many times since it came into being in 1948.

There are those who seek to taunt Jews with the charge of dual loyalty, because we are concerned with the fate of our fellow coreligionists and ethnic brothers and sisters. Such concern exists for all of our ethnic communities in the United States. In the United States, we are entreated by our traditions and government to never forget our own history and from whose loins we sprang. By observing our obligations to one another and defending and carrying out our country's tradition of honoring and caring for one's extended family, we are better citizens. On one occasion, commenting on the charge of dual loyalty, I said as I raised my right hand before the audience, "If Israel ever invades the U.S., I shall stand with the U.S."

Melvin Konner

Melvin Konner is the author of Unsettled: An Anthropology of the Jews. *He teaches anthropology, behavioral biology, and Jewish studies at Emory University.*

TRADITION, PRIDE, REFUGE

The last, best refuge of the most oppressed people in the world . . .

Not where Jews will all end up, and not the safest place right now. Nor are we *currently* the most oppressed people. But Jews think in millennia, and Israel is our millennial refuge. The Bible aside, archaeology places us there *continuously* for 3,500 years. There was ample Egyptian oppression, but no scientific evidence of the Exodus; many wars, but no great conquest from outside. Hebrew culture evolved *there*, where the people had always been. There they first heard the Ten Commandments, called out to their invisible God, and resisted Egyptian tyrants who had brutalized them, taxed them into starvation, and yes, carried some of them into slavery.

Overthrowing the Egyptian yoke—their kingdom tiny, a buffer between empires—they found the powers of the weak: writing, a moral code, abstract thought, God. Dragged to Babylon, their faith intensified; they returned as the people of the book, of laws, arguments, resistance, the people who would not bow down to any earthly thing. To most Greeks, they were atheists, but to a student of Aristotle's, "philosophers by race." Forced out again by Romans, they took their faith everywhere. Debates continued, becoming rabbinical Judaism. "Your laws were like hymns to me," sang the psalmist, "wherever I wandered."

Trickling back for two millennia, they braved all risks to feel the land with their feet, scrape their hands and lips on the broken wall. "My heart is in the East," mourned Judah Halevi a millennium after the Temple fell. Seven centuries later, Judith Montefiore wrote of Jerusalem that, like "the home of our youth, were it leveled with the earth . . . the same thoughts would arise in our hearts as if the building was still before us." Carved over her marriage bed: "If I forget thee O Jerusalem . . ."

They remembered. The devout prayed toward Jerusalem three times a day—east in Granada, west in Bombay, south in Ankara, north in Addis Ababa—longing for return. Murdered in York, Mainz, Cordoba, Mecca, they inwardly dwelt in one place. Some had never left. Muslim conquerors, Crusaders, Christian clerics all found Jews there. In the 1170s, a Prague rabbi visited Jewish communities in the Galilee, Tiberias, Acre, and Jerusalem. In 1603, a visitor to Tsfat found 300 rabbis, 18 yeshivas, and 22 prayer houses. In 1839, the British consul in Jerusalem wrote that the Jews spoke "entirely in Hebrew."

The trickle grew. Tens of thousands settled in Israel. Jews worldwide became Zionists. Anti-Semitism of race and blood, not just religion and culture, grew in Europe and infected the Arab world with its pogroms. Israel was rough—malaria and Arab attacks were common—but more Jews came, bought land, built settlements, defended themselves. Finally, genocide sent many survivors to Israel.

The UN proposed two states, but six Arab countries invaded the Jewish one. The Arab League's secretary general said, "This will be a war of extermination." The spiritual leader of Palestine's Muslims said, "I declare a Holy War, my Muslim brothers! Murder the Jews! Murder them all!" Jews repelled their armies, gaining a more defensible territory. Arabs who fled were refused reentry, like hundreds of thousands of Jewish refugees from Arab lands fleeing to Israel, leaving everything behind.

In 1967, another attack loomed. Egypt's president said, "Our basic objective will be the destruction of Israel." Iraq's said, "Our goal is clear—to wipe Israel off the map." Israel won in six days, occupying the Sinai, the Golan Heights, the West Bank, and Gaza. In 1973 another invasion was turned back. When Egypt and Israel made peace, Israel left the Sinai, removing Jewish settlements by force.

In the late 1980s, violent Palestinian protests led to talks and the Oslo Agreement. Much of the West Bank and Gaza were governed by Palestinians. Both sides broke the accords, but President Clinton brokered negotiations. Israel's initial offer of more than 95 percent of the territories was summarily rejected. A second, bloodier intifada began. Palestinians blew themselves up in Israel, murdering many civilians, and were celebrated as martyrs. In Europe, a new anti-Semitism spread as synagogues and other Jewish targets were attacked. As ever, Diaspora Jews took refuge in Israel. Israel built a wall, painful for Palestinians but effective against bombings, and withdrew from Gaza and part of the West Bank—for many Jews a source of hope.

That is what Israel means to me as a member of the tribe, heir to a dismal history of persecution. But what does it mean to me as a person, a Jew?

In 1985, on my first trip to Israel, riding the bus from the airport through Tel Aviv on December 25, seeing late-afternoon shopping in the bustling streets, not a Christmas decoration in sight; swaying with an unaccustomed prayer book in hand (shades of my Orthodox childhood), hearing a friend say, "There's Mel Konner again, praying to the God he doesn't believe in;" slogging up Masada on a warm winter morning, hearing the roar of a fighter jet, feeling a twinge of fear, looking up to see the Star of David on its wings, glinting in the desert sun; responding to a lovely colleague's question (why did I look upset?), "This is the greatest adventure in Jewish history and I am not a part of it"; and for months after, waking every day with a pain like unrequited love, asking, *"Why aren't I there?"*

In 1990, at Kibbutz Bar Am, a stone's throw from the Lebanese border, meeting people who, for generations, hid their children in holes in the ground, picked up their rifles, and held the line against a hostile army; and at the Wall with my children for the first time, two reciting the Shema, while the youngest—at age three roaming the plaza oblivious of gender—stopped, surveyed the worshipers, and sang, *"Ma nishtana halayla hazeh mikol haleylot . . ."*

In 1991, on the Golan Heights, looking down through the gunslit of a Syrian bunker at the kibbutz playground into which they lobbed shells as long as they held that high ground; hearing Natan Sharansky recount his prison ordeal and the Russian Jews' flight to the last place they expected to go; and visiting a West Bank settlement, hearing Gush Emunim—Block of the Faithful—leaders say they would stay, no matter what.

In 1985 and 1991, meeting Ethiopian Jews just airlifted out of millennial persecution—the first time whites took blacks out of Africa to free them—strangers in a strange land that now belonged, if not to them, then at least to the dazzled children pressing their faces into their mothers' skirts around their tired feet.

In 1999, three years after her mother's death, taking Sarah on a bat mitzvah trip—bodysurfing in the Mediterranean, horseback riding in Galilee, windsurfing on the Kinneret, poking through the forest at Tel Dan, climbing Masada, and praying at the Wall, seeing through her young eyes this country that I loved.

In 2000, sitting in a rental car with Susanna, who had just spent a semester in Palestine—on the road to Ramallah, blocked by Palestinian boys burning tires, both of us crying over our bitter argument about the Palestinian plight, on a trip that deepened my view forever; hearing my new friend, Walid, scion of an old Jerusalem family, condemn Palestinian leaders as strongly as he condemned "the Israelian aliens"; seeing in an Amman apartment a map of "Palestine"—without Tel Aviv, without Haifa, without any Israeli town, as if they had never existed, or had been destroyed.

In 2001, deplaning at Ben-Gurion, needling a gruff Israeli-American, hearing his sleepy, growly singsong: "What will happen? The sun will be shining, people will be happy, you will be happy. Are you Jewish?" Me nodding, him saying crisply, "This is the only land you will ever have, believe me," passing the Dolphinarium, a hip club by the sea where twenty Jewish teens had just been murdered while waiting on line to dance, and where a mosque across the street had been unjustly trashed by a Jewish mob the following day; drinking beer with an old friend on the beach at Caesarea, under an endless stretch of stars, hearing her proudly tell how her father, a pioneer-turned-banker, had used his old Palmach pistol to end his Parkinson's disease; seeing her son, seventeen, glow as he told of his triumph in a weekend-long competition—four chosen out of hundreds—for "The Unit"—the only name it needed, the most renowned commandos in the world.

In 2002, with his father, a helicopter pilot in the 1973 war—a perilous combat role—still mourning Yitzhak Rabin's murder by a Jew—and hearing a Zionist heresy: You can't understand Israel without the Holocaust; and hearing a surgeon who pioneered a new operation for liver cancer talk of weeks with his infantry unit, just another soldier, concerned for the Palestinians but bent on surviving, trying to pacify Tulkarm.

In 2004, on an Israel-bound plane, watching an old man with a purple number on his forearm pray to the God he did believe in, one of hundreds of thousands who escaped to find refuge in their ancient land; seeing Adam and Sarah, now grown, embrace at the source of the Jordan; sitting atop Har Hatzfakhot with Adam, gazing down at Israel, Jordan, Saudi Arabia, the Red Sea, and the rocky Sinai range where, the Torah says, God gave the Jews his laws.

Anti-Semitism takes a different form in every generation, and virulent anti-Zionism is the anti-Semitism of our time. Of course criticism of Israel is legitimate—it is Israel's national pastime. But why so out of proportion to its sins?

Sudan, with its Arab genocide against Africans, gets less attention; so did the 1994 Rwanda genocide, which resulted in 800,000 deaths. Communist China smashes dissent with an iron fist. Many Islamic countries treat women in ways that grossly violate UN human rights standards. Government violence killed up to 500 followers of a dissident cleric in Yemen in September 2004 and hundreds of citizens in Côte d'Ivoire in November. Indonesian soldiers have perpetrated what Amnesty International calls "grave human rights violations" for decades, killing and torturing civilians. The Nepalese army engineers civilian "disappearances" and executions that AI calls "a slide towards a human rights catastrophe."

None of these countries has been subject to a fraction of the criticism leveled by the UN against Israel. Special committees, information centers, and sessions at international conferences are devoted to Israel, little or none to these atrocities. Why rule out anti-Semitism as part of the explanation? Explicit and classic anti-Semitic libels (for example, Jews make matzoh from Christian children's blood) have been leveled in speeches at UN events, without official reaction.

The world let Jews be murdered for millennia, culminating in history's greatest genocide. From remorse, it created Israel, but soon hardened its heart again against this hapless people, cutting it little slack in its effort to survive. Israel is vulnerable whatever it does, but it will stand and fight. The world, through millennial abandonment, has lost its right to criticize Jews for defending themselves.

It is not just Jews who can claim that land, but we do have a claim—more legitimate by far than, say, the United States, Australia, and all Latin American countries have to their lands. There will be a Palestinian state, but also a Jewish one—a homeland, a refuge. For that I will always be grateful.

Israelis are Jews with teeth. They have made me, in my safe American haven, very proud. Do they make mistakes? Of course. Do they harm others? Sometimes. "Never again" does not mean, "Never again except if we become a flawed country," "Never again except if the world condemns us," or "Never again except if we have to kill and die to prevent it." Tragically, it does not even mean, "Never again except if, inadvertently, we sometimes have to harm innocent people." No nation hinges its survival on contingencies. It means, while Jews have breath to say it and hands to raise in their own defense, quite plainly and simply, *Never again.*

Rabbi Harold Kushner

Rabbi Harold Kushner is the rabbi laureate of Temple Israel in Natick, Massachusetts, and the author of When Bad Things Happen to Good People, Who Needs God, *and* How Good Do We Have to Be?

One of the fundamental conceptual differences between Judaism and Christianity stems from the fact that Christianity was a faith before it had a people, whereas the Jews were a people before they had a faith. When Christianity begins, there are no Christians. There is only an idea, a theological premise about the nature and role of Jesus. People who were persuaded by that idea committed themselves to it and were bound to each other by their shared theology. Judaism, on the other hand, started with a people, the descendants of Abraham, Isaac, and Jacob, sharing the experiences of enslavement and exodus and fashioning a faith to articulate the insights those shared experiences gave them. As a result, theology is basic to Christianity; peoplehood is basic to Judaism. One can be an agnostic or atheist Jew and still be a Jew by virtue of one's commitment to the Jewish people in a way that one cannot be an agnostic or atheist Baptist or Lutheran. Similarly, a person who accepts the divine origin of the Torah but feels no kinship with the Jewish people may be a fine, God-fearing individual but is not a Jew.

That is why Israel means so much to me and to every Jew. A theology can live in the pages of a book. It can disappear for a generation and be rediscovered and flourish. But a people has to live somewhere in the real world. Israel represents the central point of a circle, so that people of differing ideologies can be connected to one another by virtue of their shared connection to that center point. Jews cannot live

Jewishly as individuals any more than one of my limbs can function on its own, detached from my body.

The story is told that when Chaim Weizmann was lobbying the British government for support of Zionism, an effort that would result in the Balfour Declaration, one skeptical member of the House of Lords challenged him: "Why do you Jews insist on Palestine when there are so many undeveloped parts of the world where you could settle with less controversy?" Weizmann replied, "That's like my asking you: why did you drive ten miles to visit your mother last Sunday when there are so many old ladies living on your street?"

A second dimension of Israel's importance to me, and I am sorry that it has to play as prominent a role in my thinking as it does: in the wake of the Holocaust, Israel has become the symbol of the world's willingness to let the Jewish people live, not just as individuals but as a recognized, legitimate corporate entity. It is unfair and outrageous that we have to justify our right to exist, but alas, that is the case.

Why does Israel mean so much to me and to so many other Jews? Many American Jews, visiting Israel for the first time, are astonished to discover how much it means to them that everyone they meet is Jewish—the policeman, the hotel clerk, the shopkeeper, the television newscaster. We have lived in the Diaspora for so long that we have developed a Diaspora mentality, constantly aware of the fact that we are no more than a tolerated minority. And if we ever did forget it, the television schedule every December would come along to remind us. Israel is the cure for that feeling. I remember, when I was a graduate student in Jerusalem in the winter of 1957–1958, seeing the stores decorated for Chanukah in mid-December while in a corner of the Jerusalem YMCA stood a forlorn little Christmas tree struggling to remind Jerusalem's Christians that a holiday was coming.

And finally, I dream of a day when survival will no longer be an overriding concern for Israel and it can come to play another role in my life and the lives of Jews everywhere, a day when Israel will be free to explore what a Jewish educational system, a Jewish health care system, a Jewish system of taxation might look like. For out of Zion will come Torah, to apply Jewish values to twenty-first-century issues.

May that day come speedily and soon, in my lifetime and yours.

Rabbi Lawrence Kushner

Rabbi Lawrence Kushner is the Emanu-El Scholar at Congregation Emanu-El of San Francisco and visiting professor of Jewish Spirituality at the Graduate Theological Union in Berkeley. He is the best-selling author of Honey from the Rock: An Introduction to Jewish Mysticism, The Book of Letters: A Mystical Hebrew Alphabet, *and* The Way into Jewish Mystical Traditions.

Like Jews everywhere, I am furious, livid, that Israel is routinely held by the world press to a higher standard of political ethics. What for any other nation-state would be just another ho-hum, business-as-usual blunder, misjudgment, or indiscretion, for Israel is front page news. But the truth is, like many Jews, I suspect, I also secretly love it. In much the same way, I want my kids held to a higher standard, and I hope to be judged by one myself. I have no desire to be like everyone else. Something in me wants the entry of the Jewish people into world politics to be judged by the highest conceivable measure. Indeed, that may be what is both so inspiring and confounding about the existence of Israel.

I am reminded of a story told by Rabbi Richard Hirsch, one of the *gedolim* of the Reform movement in Israel. He was in a taxicab on his way to Kennedy back in the days when the airport was still called Idlewild. When the cab driver, whose name was Motke Goldstein, found out that his fare was a rabbi on his way to Israel, he waxed eloquent about how wonderful Israel was and how he would love to live there.

"If it's so good," said Hirsch, "then why don't you make aliyah?"

"Oh, I could never do that," replied the cabbie. "There they have Jewish thieves, conmen, prostitutes, criminals . . ."

"Nu?" said Hirsch. "They don't have Jewish thieves, conmen, prostitutes, and criminals in New York City?"

"Here I can stand it," replied the cabbie, "but in Israel, it would kill me."

The great Hasidic master Rabbi Levi Yitzhak of Berditchev, who had certainly never been to the land of Israel and who died 139 years before the founding of the state, offers a similar teaching. It appears in his *Kedushat Levi* and has been masterfully translated by Norman Lamm in his *The Religious Thought of Hasidism*. The teaching, like so many of this genre, is based on a deliberate misreading of a biblical passage, in this case, Numbers 13:2 (*parasha Shelakh lekah*), where God directs Moses to "send out men who will scout out the land of Canaan which I am giving to the children of Israel."

Levi Yitzhak suggests that the verse can also be read as meaning not to send out men, but even before entering the land, to send away the corporeal part of themselves that is so easily seduced by owning things. Their task was not to spy it out physically (God forbid, says Levi Yitzhak), but "to make a spiritual impression in the land" by how they would serve God there. And to do this they would have to commit themselves to the highest standard of morality. The goal, says the Berditchever, is that they would make such an impression that "the land itself would long for the children of Abraham, Isaac, and Jacob."

Yes, I do understand that such talk comes from the ethical luxury of two thousand years of political powerlessness. And I am painfully aware that people like myself, who have chosen not to become citizens of Israel, do not have much right to moralize about it to those who are. Nevertheless, for all this inconsistency, that is still what Israel means to me.

Stan Lee

Stan Lee is the creator of many legendary Marvel comic superheroes, including Spider-Man, the Incredible Hulk, and the X-Men.

Almost all my adult life I've written stories about superheroes, noble characters who battle insurmountable odds in the name of justice and righteousness. Perhaps that's why I'm such a fan of the tiny, valiant nation of Israel and of the indomitable spirit of its people.

Eternally vulnerable, surrounded by much larger, hostile nations whose most fervent desire is its complete and total destruction, the postage-stamp nation of Israel stands like a shining beacon of courage and progress whose light has never flickered.

Just as my fictional tales of mighty superheroes inevitably have happy endings, I pray the courageous sacrifices of this embattled little nation will also have a happy ending—an ending in which Jew and Arab will finally come together in peace and friendship and, working side by side, make the Middle East a land of brotherhood, peace, and plenty.

Rabbi Michael Lerner

Rabbi Michael Lerner is the editor of Tikkun *magazine, cochair of the Tikkun Community, rabbi of Beyt Tikkun Synagogue in San Francisco, and the author of nine books, including* Jewish Renewal: A Path to Healing and Transformation *and* Spirit Matters: Global Healing and the Wisdom of the Soul.

Loving Israel, and Being Betrayed by Israel

My earliest memory is standing in front of a neighborhood bank with a JNF box singing "Hatikvah" and collecting money for the Zionist movement just before the creation of the state of Israel. I couldn't wait to go there, passionately loved Israel from afar, and deepened my love while working on Kibbutz Eyn HaShofet. When people at Berkeley, where I was doing my Ph.D. in philosophy, criticized Israel's takeover of the West Bank and Gaza, I joined with fellow activist Mario Savio and together we created an organization that affirmed Israel and the right of the Jewish people to national self-determination in our ancient homeland.

I wanted to give my own son that same love for Israel, so I took him out of school in the United States, and for half a year before his bar mitzvah we lived in Jerusalem—*ulpan* for him, while I was teaching and doing research on the psychodynamics of Israeli society. It was that year, 1984, that I first began to meet Israeli peaceniks, and then Palestinians, who told me a history I had never heard—the story of the Palestinian people and of their expulsion from their homes.

Growing up in a Zionist home, I had heard the story of people being encouraged by their own leaders to momentarily flee in hopes that the Jewish people would be wiped out. No one had ever told me what I learned from a new breed of Israeli historians whose access to

Israeli archives had revealed an ugly and immoral reality: that tens of thousands of people had been force-marched from their homes at gunpoint by Israeli soldiers, that there had been a conscious plan by the terrorist organizations Lehi and Etzel (led by future Israeli prime ministers Menachem Begin and Yitzhak Shamir) to terrorize Palestinian civilians and noncombatants and that is why they murdered hundreds of people at Deir Yassin, precisely because it was a village that had not joined in the Palestinian revolt against the Jewish community (the Yishuv) and thus the massacre there could convey the message to Palestinians that none of them would be safe.

At first I rejected this information, thought it was the exaggeration of zealots who for some bizarre reason had turned against the Jewish people. But then, meeting Palestinians on the West Bank, I had another Zionist stereotype destroyed for me: that all Arabs wanted to drive the Jews into the sea. Instead, I met dozens of Muslims who spoke to me of a desire to return to their homes but who simultaneously wanted to live in peace with Israel and hoped that Israelis would eventually turn to the highest values of their religious tradition and take seriously the Torah injunction to "love the stranger." I witnessed firsthand the horrible conditions that existed in Gaza for many refugees and was astounded to see that Israel had not used the occupation as an opportunity to show generosity to the Palestinian people and lift them out of poverty, but instead had thrown roadblocks to development and used the Palestinians as a market for Israeli goods and as a source of cheap labor inside Israel. Yet when I reported these encounters to my friends in the Orthodox shuls where I davened in Jerusalem, many responded with racist slurs that reminded me of the racist language that had once been used against Jews. What was most striking to me was that many of these fellow Jews were people who were gentle and caring to each other, and very supportive to me as a single father trying to raise his child with a love for Israel.

I had watched with dismay as a significant part of the leadership of the American Jewish community began to move to the right in the Reagan years; and to provide an alternative voice, I had decided to start *Tikkun* magazine as the voice of liberal and progressive Jews who wanted to reclaim the peace-oriented and social justice–oriented elements of Judaism. Yet as rooted as I was in the United States, I felt myself drawn to live half of each year in Israel, and there to create a voice for peace-oriented religious Jews—the Beyt Midrash l'Shalom. We hired a group of teachers including Moshe Halbertal, Uri Simon, Avi Ravitsky, Yishayahu Leibowitz, and many other peace-oriented scholars of Judaism and began to offer courses on the deep roots of peace, respecting the other, and the values of tolerance and compromise in Jewish thought.

Then came the first intifada and suddenly the private concerns I had about the treatment of Palestinians became a major public issue. Members of *Tikkun*'s editorial board, among them some of the most respected liberal leaders of the Reform and Conservative movements in Judaism, accurately predicted to me that the great initial success of *Tikkun* as a voice of American Jewish liberalism would be quickly undermined if *Tikkun* became critical of Israeli policy in anything but the most abstract terms. I could, they warned me, talk about peace and justice, but I should not apply those categories to criticizing the occupation of the West Bank and Gaza or to publicizing the horrible conditions that existed for many Palestinians.

I did not take their advice. *Tikkun* began to publish the analyses of the Israeli peace movement and to become the place in which American Jews were first exposed to the voices of Israelis who felt that the occupation was not only immoral but incredibly self-destructive. And *Tikkun* published the new historians, most notably Benjamin Morris, who told a different story about the creation of Israel than that taught in the Jewish mainstream.

There was no way for an impartial observer to hear these as anti-Israel voices—these were people who continued to serve in *milu'im* (the IDF reserves that required a month of service every year till age forty-five) and who passionately believed in the Zionist vision. Yet very quickly the American Jewish press, controlled largely by the UJA-Federation world with its need to raise money by promoting itself as the way to help Israel, began to denounce *Tikkun* as a voice of "self-hating Jews."

At first I dismissed this as too ludicrous to be worthy of attention. Unlike many of those who were using this language to denounce the peace movement as "self-hating," I was not a secular Jew but a religious Jew who prayed daily for the rebuilding of Jerusalem. But as the blessing after the meal put it, we praised God who rebuilds Jerusalem with *rachamim* (compassion), and yet that compassion seemed increasingly absent in Israel and in the official organs of the American Jewish community.

I had seen *Tikkun* as a vehicle to bring young Jews closer to God, Torah, and Israel; but now I found that Torah ideals were being increasingly scorned, as a new language of justification through armed power began to dominate in the Jewish world. And the more it did so, the harder it became to convince younger idealistic Jews that they could find a place for themselves in the Jewish world. So *Tikkun* began to lose subscribers and supporters: on the one hand, from establishment-oriented Jews who thought that any criticism of Israeli policy was the same thing as not loving Israel and betraying Jewish interests; and on the other hand, liberal and progressive younger Jews who felt so upset with what Israel was doing that they wanted nothing to do with the (till this very day in 2006) still strongly supportive of the original Zionist dream *Tikkun* magazine. Self-interest dictated that we moderate our stance, follow the path of magazines like *Moment* or *Reform Judaism* that barely addressed the issue except to defend Israel, or the path of the *Nation* or *Mother Jones* or Pacifica Radio, which only could find fault with Israel and thus could appeal to the growing lefty antagonism to the whole Zionist enterprise. Maintaining a middle path was losing support for *Tikkun* from both directions.

To me, the highest cause was to remain a witness to God in the world, which translated directly into remaining a voice that would root itself in the prophetic tradition and speak for the possibility of a world based on love of the powerless and the demeaned Other, to believe that all people (not just Jews) are really created in the image of God and that it would be a sin to treat them otherwise, to insist that our people treat the Torah injunction to love the stranger not as a quaint and outdated dictum but as a central part of what it meant to be Jewish. I was repeatedly disappointed not only that the Orthodox people with whom I davened were not really believing in God's message of love and generosity of spirit, but that even the Reform Jews, supposedly committed to social action, justice, and *tikkun olam* (healing of the world) were unwilling to apply these when it came to Israel itself.

Because *Tikkun* had a Politics of Meaning agenda—calling for liberals and progressives to recognize the deep hunger for values and for a spiritual path that could transcend the selfishness and materialism of the competitive marketplace, and to recognize that many people were drifting to the right because it was only in right-wing religious communities that they were hearing these needs being explicitly addressed—*Tikkun* became an important voice in shaping the thoughts of Bill and Hillary Clinton from 1988 to 1992. So when Hillary gave her first major speech in 1993 calling on the country to develop a Politics of Meaning, and then invited me to the White House to confer and quoted my ideas to journalists doing interviews, the pro-occupation forces in the Jewish world became alarmed. Led by Jews affiliated with the American Israel Public Affairs Committee, they orchestrated a campaign of vilification against Hillary and against me, claiming that the idea of a world based on love and generosity and peace was the soft-minded thinking of New Agey mush, and warning Hillary that she would become anathema in the Jewish world if she let me influence her thinking. Hillary had told me privately that she and Bill fully believed in *Tikkun's* perspective on Israel, but as the assault intensified, she backed away not only from the affiliation with *Tikkun*, but also from the peace perspective on Israel. She was "being used by the left," she was told by some of her AIPAC supporters; self-interest dictated distancing.

But there was a deeper issue at stake: the millennial struggle between cynical realism and the belief in God. For the cynical realists, the world is filled with self-interested self-aggrandizing others who will dominate and control you unless you dominate and control them first. Believers in God do not deny this tendency (what we call in Jewish tradition *yetzer ha'ra*) but insist that there is a countertendency in human beings, a tendency toward love, compassion, generosity, and caring for others that is rooted in the fact of being created in the image of God and having the potential to be partners with God in *tikkun*, the healing of the world. To the extent that societal energy flows toward pessimism and despair, more and more people give primary focus to the cynical realist voice—and I watched as that happened to the Clintons. The more they adopted the advice of the cynical realists, the more people began to think that "if these Clintons who preached a Politics of Meaning are now acting from the standpoint of what is in their own narrow self-interest, taking polls to find out what is popular rather than being guided by their own inner moral compass, then why should I pay higher taxes or health care benefits to take care of others—after all, if everyone is out for themselves, maybe I should be also, so why not vote for Gingrich and the Republicans who make no pretense of hiding their self-interest." Cynicism begets cynicism. And I also watched as these same dynamics intensified in the context of Israeli politics.

Even the signing of the Oslo Accords didn't change that deepening cynicism in Israel. I met with Yitzhak Rabin at the celebration in Washington, D.C., following the White House signing of the Accords, to which I had been invited by the Clintons. I urged Rabin to tell his fellow Israelis to use this moment to create a new dynamic of openness, compassion, and friendship for the Palestinian people, to encourage Israelis to learn Arabic and to make friends with Palestinian families as a patriotic duty, and to build a new atmosphere of trust. I sent a similar message to Arafat, urging him to use that moment to build a new attitude toward the Israeli people among his Palestinian followers. Neither side listened.

Rabin, instead of urging a new spirit of reconciliation, told Israelis not to worry because he didn't trust the Palestinians and he wouldn't let them "use" the peace treaty to take advantage. Instead of fostering a new discourse of mutual reconciliation, Rabin thought he would play to the cynical realists on the right, showing them that even though he was for peace he would be "tough." He introduced checkpoints throughout the West Bank that made travel from one city to another extremely time-consuming and filled with humiliating searches by the Israeli army, and he did not dismantle Israeli settlements. Though his attitude did not stop Israeli rightists from calling him a traitor and eventually leading one of them to murder him, it did undermine the voice of Palestinian moderates who had hoped to use the peace treaty to build a new attitude or reconciliation that would offset and isolate Hamas and extremist factions within the PLO. Nor did it help that Arafat, while talking a language of peace in English, continued to talk about "holy struggle," or jihad in Arabic (claiming that he meant nonviolent struggle, but being heard by many of his listeners as affirming the need to continue the struggle till not only was the West Bank liberated but also the rest of Palestine).

I remained hopeful for peace, and even gave the written permission (required by the IDF for only children serving in combat units) for my son to serve in the Israeli paratroopers. Living in Israel once again, praying for my son's safety each week and then laundering his clothes and trying to give him physical and spiritual nurturance each weekend, I yearned for peace not only as a Jewish ideal but as a matter of personal and familial necessity. And once again, I was struck by the deepening cynicism in Israel, even while there was supposedly a peace process going on. The peace forces talked about the economic benefits for Israel of peace, but few were willing to talk about the humanity of the Palestinian people or to challenge the deep racist assumptions about Arabs. They were all "Amalek" (the tribe that the Torah had supposedly ordered us to kill off as retribution for their unprovoked attacks on us some three thousand years ago), and all they had in their hearts was a longing to destroy us!

After Rabin's death, the misery of the Palestinian people increased. By 2000, when Israeli Prime Minister Ehud Barak convinced President Clinton to invite Arafat to Camp David, the supposed "peace process" that was going to produce a Palestinian state in the West Bank and Gaza in five years (by 1998) had instead led to a doubling of the number of Jewish settlers in the West Bank and to an intensification of Palestinian suffering. Hardened by Israel's failure to live up to the terms of the Oslo Accords, Arafat had made only the faintest efforts to restrain people in his own organization and in Hamas who adopted the same attitude toward Israelis that had governed Israeli policy toward Palestinians: "Those Others only understand violence." In turn, the use of terror by Palestinians was used by Israeli rightists to justify further acts of repression and delays in implementing every agreement Israel signed with the Palestinians.

There were as many reports of what happened at Camp David as there were people in attendance. But when agreement was not reached, both Clinton and Israeli prime minister Barak proclaimed that Arafat had rejected the most generous offer that the Palestinians could ever possibly expect. Not so, said Yossi Beilin, Barak's minister of justice, who had been the principal negotiator of the Oslo Accords. In Oslo, the Palestinians had been convinced to give up claims on 78 percent of pre-1948 Palestine in exchange for a Palestinian state on the 22 percent of Palestine that was on the other side of the 1949 armistice line (the "Green Line," as it became known).

Now, in 2000, Barak was trying to convince Arafat that he was being generous to offer a large part of that 22 percent that Beilin had, as the representative of Yitzhak Rabin, offered totally to the Palestinian people in return for the recognition of Israel that Arafat and the PLO gave (publicly altering their infamous and hateful charter to do so). But what was most extraordinary about the allegedly "generous offer" was that it had no specific plan to provide compensation for the three million Palestinian refugees, many of them living in horrific conditions in Gaza and Lebanon. This had always been a central part of the problem, yet Barak offered nothing, and instead insisted that the agreement he was offering must include a clause in which Arafat and the Palestinian Authority, speaking on behalf of the entire Palestinian nation worldwide, would renounce any further claims on Israel and agree to Barak's terms as the "final settlement agreement."

We at *Tikkun* joined with Yossi Beilin in arguing that the negotiations should continue, but that there was nothing "generous" about an agreement that did not include anything concrete in the way of compensation for refugees. For this, we were once again labeled as self-hating Jews. And when Ariel Sharon, accompanied by hundreds of Israeli police, made a provocative appearance at the Islamic mosques atop the Temple Mount in Jerusalem and managed to provoke the very violence that would lead to deeper despair and to his own election as prime minister, *Tikkun* went into strong opposition, calling for Israel to return to the peace process that Sharon had completely rejected.

It has been a terrible time for me and for *Tikkun* ever since. We've condemned unequivocally Palestinian acts of terror. We've repeatedly pointed out that the occupation, no matter how oppressive, the bulldozing of Palestinian homes as part of a slow but palpable process of ethnic cleansing, the torture of Palestinians held without charges in Israeli jails and compounds and documented fully by the Israeli human rights organization B'Tselem (www.Btselem.org), the violation of international standards of decency and human rights, including the building of a wall through the middle of the West Bank (officially declared illegal by the International Court of Justice in the Hague)— none of this is justification for a Palestinian to place a bomb in a bus or a nightclub or a restaurant or a synagogue where innocent Israeli civilians gather. Terror is always wrong.

Yet in the Jewish world, I've faced increasing vilification and weekly death threats from Jews who claim that I am a hater of the Jewish people. The Jewish media simply refuse to quote us or any of the other peace voices, except in ways that are out of context and that make us seem one-sidedly anti-Israel. Deaths of Palestinians, we are told, are not "morally equivalent" to the deaths of Israeli civilians (supposedly because the three times as many Palestinians killed are merely by-products of enforcing the occupation, not a policy aimed at killing Palestinians, while the death of Israelis is meant to be targeted against civilians). I say, "Of course there is no moral equivalence, because there cannot ever be moral equivalence between any one human being killed unnecessarily and any other human being killed unnecessarily, since each human being is precious in God's eyes, so the very notion of moral equivalence in reference to human lives is an abomination."

On the other hand, *Tikkun* and I have increasingly been denounced in the left media and by lefties as being one-sidedly pro-Israel. And the fact is that we are pro-Israel. I totally reject the attempt to portray Israel as a colonial power, or as instituting apartheid, or as oppressing Palestinians purely for racist or religious chauvinist reasons. I know that many of those who vote for the right in Israel do so out of a justifiable fear of Palestinian terrorists, and an unjustifiable conclusion that the best way to protect Jewish lives is to ignore the needs of the Palestinian people.

I have been outspoken in critiquing those who move from legitimate criticism of Israeli policies to illegitimate or anti-Semitic critique. For example, when the leading organization creating anti-Iraq war demonstrations used those mass marches to single out Israel for vilification, I publicly denounced them for so doing, and was rewarded by being barred from speaking at their demonstrations.

Tikkun has created a new interfaith organization called the Tikkun Community that seeks to educate the public to a two-state solution, and equally important, to a "progressive middle path" that is both pro-Israel and pro-Palestine. How can you be both? Because the well-being of Israel and the well-being of the Palestinian people are intrinsically linked. And this is a lesson that we preach to Palestinians as well. We insist that the Palestinian movement give up violence not only momentarily, but as a principled commitment to nonviolence. We tell them that the only way to convince Israelis that they can be safe with a Palestinian state is if Palestinians begin to act and talk in ways that reassure Israelis that they recognize the humanity and fundamental decency of the Jewish people, and our right to our own state in our ancient homeland. Conversely, we tell Israelis that it is *not* enough to come up with a two-state solution (we support the Geneva Accord), but that Israel, as the more militarily powerful force, must be the first to exemplify a new spirit of generosity, open-heartedness, repentance, and atonement in the style and way that Israel deals with the Palestinian people. It is only by touching the heart of the other that peace will be anything but an empty agreement on a piece of paper.

One place to start is to open our hearts to the stories and perceptions of the other side. In my books *Healing Israel/Palestine* and *The Geneva Accord and Other Strategies for Middle East Peace*, I tell the story of both peoples, starting from 1880 and going through 2004 in a way that you can understand how each side had a justifiable case, and how each side systematically accepted the worst possible interpretation of the intentions and desires of the other side, interpretations that became self-fulfilling. It is only with this kind of a discourse, a discourse based on compassion and a willingness to believe in the possibility that neither side is the "righteous victim" and neither side is the "evil oppressor," that one can build a path to peace.

But this remains a difficult and problematic task. Students seeking to create the Tikkun Campus Network on college and university campuses around the United States have often been vilified as either anti-Israel (by the pro-occupation crowd that dominates most Hillel Foundations on campus) or as apologists for Israeli human rights violations (by lefties who call themselves pro-Palestinian). Synagogues routinely turn down our requests to send speakers to present our "Progressive Middle Path," Jewish media reject our op-eds, and lefty media marginalize us as being too pro-Zionist.

Each year the Tikkun Community brings hundreds of people to Washington, D.C., to speak to policy makers and public opinion shapers to try to convince them that the best interests of Israel and the United States would be served by a middle path that provides for an economically and politically viable Palestinian state and compensation for Palestinian refugees, but also provides for a mutual security pact for Israel with the United States so that Israel can be protected from all its potential enemies. Often we are told that the Congress members really agree with us but are afraid to say so publicly lest they be branded "anti-Israel" by AIPAC or other Jewish establishment groups. We in Tikkun fear deeply that someday this imposition of Jewish "political correctness" is going to backfire against Israel and against the Jewish people worldwide.

Yet for me, the greatest sadness comes in the reactions I get from young people who come to my Shabbat or High Holy Day services in Beyt Tikkun synagogue, but who do not want to hear anything about Israel. Often they tell me that it is only because they know that I support the Israeli peace movement that they are willing to come into a synagogue at all. Many others refuse to come—and tell me that they've seen Israel as the embodiment of Judaism, and have come to feel that Judaism has no moral legitimacy if it condones the violence of the Israeli occupation. I try to explain to them that Israeli policy, far from being a manifestation of the essence of Torah, is actually a rejection of God and Torah. The Israelis and their supporters in the American Jewish establishment who give Ariel Sharon and his successors a blank check are actually people who do not believe in the God of Jewish tradition—the God who, according to our tradition, silenced the angels when they sang praises when our enemies the Egyptians were drowning in the sea with the following admonition: "My children are sinking in the sea, and you dare offer songs of celebration?!"

It is the absence of this voice of compassion for the other that has transformed too many areas of Israeli and Jewish culture into a mean-spirited, power-worshiping, cynical voice that is directly the opposite of what Judaism had mostly been. True, there have always been voices of cynicism and despair, what I call in my book *Jewish Renewal* a "settler Judaism" mentality that sought to destroy the other. But the major voice was another one—the voice that talked of a God of compassion and love. The irony today of hearing that that is a Christian conception, when in fact it is deeply routed in Torah, is just one of the many markers of how far the official Judaism of our time has strayed from its foundations and been distorted by its attempts to cheerlead for the policies of a particular government.

This is how Israel has betrayed the Jewish people—by allowing the inevitably flawed and distorted policies of a particular state and its government to become identified with the essence of our Judaism, to insist that to be Jewish is to be loyal to that particular government or state; in short, to promote a new form of idolatry.

I still love Israel, the land, its people, and its promise. I love it so much that I continue to be willing to face death threats; to have my magazine be economically in trouble when it could be flourishing if only we stopped critiquing Israel or embraced whatever scheme the Israeli government put forward as its latest attempt to hold on to much of the West Bank while claiming to be in pursuit of peace; to have my synagogue vilified by the proponents of the Jewish status quo. I love Israel so much that I will not be silenced until it becomes true that from Zion will come forth Torah—not the Torah of hate and anger and fear, but the Torah of love, kindness, generosity, social justice, and peace. I love Israel, and will not allow the cheerleaders to offer praises to its current mistaken direction because they care more about how they are perceived by their fellow Jews or by the Jewish establishment than about the long-term survivability of a Jewish state. I love Israel, and for its sake I will tell the deepest truth: Israel's salvation lies not in alliances with the United States or in military power, but in building a global reality of peace, justice, and ecological sanity in which all peoples are flourishing, that our well-being as Jews depends on the well-being of everyone else alive on the planet and the well-being of the planet itself, that there is no particularistic solution for Jews that is not also a solution and a salvation for all people on the planet, and that therefore our own self-interest is to promote the well-being of everyone. Developing this new spiritual consciousness is the task of the Jewish people, and when Israel becomes the embodiment of that consciousness, it will finally be able to play the role intended for it as a light unto the nations.

Norman Liss

Norman Liss is an attorney and a member of the executive committee of the American Jewish Congress, an organization that advocates on behalf of Jewish causes at home and abroad, and (in the words of its mission statement) works to advance the security and prosperity of the state of Israel and its democratic institutions, and to support Israel's search for peaceful relations with its neighbors in the region.

As a young child, I remember seeing the American Jewish Congress magazine on a shelf in the kitchen. It was addressed to my father, Morris. I was very young and paid little attention to it.

Until I was a little older, I could not understand, nor was I interested in, my father's background. But I recall when I was nine years old, during World War II, listening to his conversations with uncles and aunts and my mom. He had left his birthplace in Tarnow, Poland, in 1919 as a young man and had emigrated with a group of young men and women to Palestine. He remained there for four years, living in Petach-Tikvah and the Galilee areas, helping to build roads. His parents and the family rabbi had tried to convince him not to leave Poland. At that time, Palestine was an undeveloped, barren land, with continual daily dangers to the Jewish population from Arab threats and raids. My father related his mixed feelings about how the challenge of Palestine excited him, while the difficulty of leaving his family was a source of trauma.

He remained in Israel until 1923 before immigrating to the United States, building a new life, marrying my mother, and leading an active life with a Zionist commitment. He joined the American Jewish Congress. He visited Poland in 1932 and returned with family pictures of his father, mother, brother Dave, and sisters Helen and Rose and their children. Upon his return, the mail came regularly until 1939 and then ended. His family was never heard from again.

I recall my father talking about visiting the Red Cross at the end of World War II, looking for information about his family. He was unsuccessful in locating any information concerning them. From indications and the stories of friends, he determined that they died in the Nazi camps, possibly Auschwitz. This was never discussed in my family, with my older brother or me, but there was an ever-present sadness whenever such things were alluded to in a general sense. Although he never articulated it, I guess that my father always had a feeling of guilt for having gone to Israel and left his family to eventually perish.

I have always felt that had there been a Jewish state of Israel instead of an undeveloped land of Palestine, his family, like others, would have left Poland with its growing anti-Semitism and the impending German invasion.

And so, Israel has been a meaningful and important component of my life. My wife, Sandra, and I visit regularly and contribute to it in so many ways. It is the essence of our being Jewish. Its very existence provides a sense of security for Jewish people around the world and is an answer to the possible danger from a potential future holocaust.

I am now on the executive committee of my father's organization, the American Jewish Congress. The American Jewish Congress magazine is now addressed to me.

David Mamet

David Mamet is the Pulitzer Prize–winning playwright of Glengarry
Glen Ross. *He has written over two dozen screenplays and stage plays
and is the author of* Jafsie and John Henry, *a book of short essays that
includes a reflection on anti-Semitism.*

Noam Chomsky was interviewed in the summer 2004 issue of *Heeb* magazine.

Q. What about recent incidents in Europe and the Arab world? It would seem to involve pretty acrobatic leaps of logic to say that those are not anti-Semitic.

Chomsky: In Europe there's a large Muslim population, and much of it has been driven to fundamentalist Islam. They display hatred toward Jews that is a reflection of Israeli practices. I mean, if you carry out a brutal and vicious military occupation for 35 years . . . it has consequences. Sometimes the consequences can be quite ugly, and, among them, is the burning of synagogues in France. Yes, it's anti-Semitism, but Israel insists on it. Remember Israel does not call itself the state of its citizens. The high court in Israel declared over 40 years ago that Israel is the sovereign state of the Jewish People, in Israel and the Diaspora.

In effect, as the Jewish state has proclaimed itself the home of all Jews, within its borders in the Diaspora, for the Diaspora Jews to do other than renounce this as a usurpation of their personal rights, of their rights as undifferentiated citizens, is tantamount to their endorsement of that which Mr. Chomsky sees as a criminal enterprise (the state of Israel). Mr. Chomsky, a Jew, does not recognize the Jewish state's right to existence; he *does*, however, recognize as somehow morally binding the pronouncements of this phantom state. Upon whom are they binding? Upon members of that state's predominant religious group.

These Diaspora Jews, we will note, reside in countries whose right to existence, presumably, Mr. Chomsky *does* recognize. For example, France.

France, as a sovereign nation, then, has the right, as Israel does not, to protect its citizens. The right, however, does not, in Mr. Chomsky's view, extend to French Jews—their right to live unmolested and in peace has, alone among French citizens, been somehow abrogated by the actions of another state.

Various Muslim countries, Syria, and so on, and the Palestinians, have, as a matter of both religious and political doctrine, expressed their intention of destruction of Israeli Jews. This intent is not an adjunct of a territorial dispute, but an essential component of their polity—this hatred cannot be mitigated by concession, by negotiation, even by capitulation; it can only be assuaged through blood.

Mr. Chomsky does not seem to object to this incitement to geno-cide, neither does he extend the same standard for extraterritorial guilt to Diaspora Muslims.

The United States, in the aftermath of September 11, has taken care (it may be insufficient, but it is a matter of national policy) to pro-tect the rights of Arab Americans, on guard lest an ignorant and fright-ened populace turn on the guiltless because of mere ties of race or religion to the criminal.

This would seem to be the most basic operation of human justice—to endorse a vendetta against the innocent based on race or religion is here seen, and simply seen, as obscene criminality. Mr. Chomsky, how-ever, sees fit to understand and applaud such actions, as long as they are carried out against the Jews.

This is anti-Semitism—it is race hatred and incitement to murder.

That Mr. Chomsky wears the mantle of respect, that he occupies the position of "intellectual," and that he continues to confuse and debauch the young with his filth is a shame. To abide this shame is part of the price of living in a free society.

Israel is a free society. The rights of the minority, of the oppressed, indeed, of the criminally foolish are protected. Mr. Chomsky would be as free in Israel to pronounce this nonsense as he is in the United States.

Were he to move to the Arab world, he would be persecuted as a Jew (as, indeed, he might be in France).

And were he, God forbid, persecuted, Israel would offer him a home, under the Right of Return.

That is what Israel means to me.

Daniel S. Mariaschin

Daniel S. Mariaschin is the executive vice president of B'nai B'rith International and a lifelong Jewish activist for Jewish rights. Through his work on behalf of international Jewish organizations, he has met with many world leaders, including Lech Walesa, Margaret Thatcher, King Hussein of Jordan, Helmut Kohl, and King Hassan II of Morocco.

THROUGH A PRISM, A STORY OF ISRAEL

My first memory of Israel was a small photo on our mantelpiece. It was a picture of the Arad family: Shmuel, Chia, Dalia, Amatzia, Shlomo, and Boaz.

Chia was my mother's first cousin. A Zionist activist as a youth in Lithuania, she arrived in Palestine in 1934, at the age of twenty. Soon after, she married Shmuel Arad, himself an immigrant—from Bulgaria—and settled in Kibbutz Beit Zera, in the Jordan Valley, fulfilling their dream of being able to make the (Jewish) desert bloom.

Chia and Shmuel raised four children. Though the photo on the mantelpiece was in black and white, you could see that the sun was shining; no doubt, their skin was bronzed as a result. The photo was probably taken about 1954, and, notwithstanding all the difficulties Israel had already endured during its first years of independence, there is a look of optimism on each of the six faces.

My mother and Chia at that point had never met, but they corresponded, in Yiddish, on a regular basis. They didn't phone each other. Instead it was letters from my mother on the blue aerogrammes of the U.S. Post Office, and green ones, from Chia, mailed in the other direction.

I was five or six years old when my mother displayed the photo in that central place in our living room. I probably glanced at my cousins several times a day as a result. In 1956, when I was seven, I recall my parents discussing the Sinai Campaign, not understanding exactly what was happening in Egypt, connected somehow because of my relatives, the Arads. I used to go to school bragging that "I have cousins in Israel."

Just before my bar mitzvah, we received a package from the kibbutz. In it were a *tallit*, a picture book about Israel, and a miniature View-Master with little wheels of photos of historic sites of Israel. There was also a tape recording of Chia and the family wishing me and our family well. We didn't have a tape recorder then, so we borrowed one. So after all the letters, it was the first time I heard the voices of real Israelis. And I was actually *related* to them!

By mail, we followed the family's progress. Dalia, the eldest Arad child, was married to Shimon Dekel, a Romanian immigrant. Shimon, in his own right, looked the quintessential kibbutznik: tanned, hardworking, and personable. Sent to Central America as an agricultural adviser in early 1967, he dropped his farming implements when war broke out in June and flew home immediately to join his unit. That story became legend in our family. At the time, I was a senior in high school, and my pride in Israel's lightning victory had become personal because of Shimon's part in it.

Five years later, I made my first trip to Israel, as part of a graduate school summer program. On Friday afternoons, I took off to see my relatives (in the intervening years we had discovered another cousin and his family). The mantelpiece photo had come to life: Dalia and Shimon took me touring one weekend to Binyamina and the beautiful park at Gan Shelosha. My trip to the kibbutz to see Chia and Shmuel by bus, which near the end of its route in Tiberias wends its way around the Kinneret (Sea of Galilee), introduced me to the communal dining room, the bicycles and blue work shirts of the *kibbutznikim*, and the children's communal nursery.

The Arad bungalow was typical: surrounded by the shade of date palms and the constant cooing of doves, the rooms were tiny and neat, with every available space filled by bookshelves—the perfect Zionist convergence of the land and the book.

My trip back to Jerusalem, going back around the shores of the Kinneret, passed kibbutz after kibbutz, neatly cultivated fields of fruits and vegetables, and small kiosks selling sodas and ice cream. In those years, the burst of pride and optimism that followed the Six-Day War seemed to keep the sky always blue and tomorrow a better day.

I returned to Israel every summer after that. In July 1973, I was back. I wanted to visit Safed to see the synagogue of the Ari and other historical sites. Chia offered to take me, but insisted first—I couldn't figure out why—on seeing the military cemetery in the city. We walked the rows of headstones, stopping here and there to read the names. "This one, you see," said Chia, "was from Morocco. Twenty years old. And that one, from Poland, he was twenty-two." I was moved and found it interesting, and could only conclude that she had taken me there for an up-close lesson to learn that the Zionist dream was achieved through great sacrifice.

In late October 1973, my father, my mother, and I returned home from synagogue to find, in the mailbox, one of Chia's green aero-grammes. I had an apprehensive feeling about this one. Israel was still in a fight for its life since the outbreak of war on Yom Kippur, and I knew that Boaz, Chia's youngest, had been serving in the Israel Defense Forces.

Before handing it to my mother, I opened the letter, and though I couldn't read the Yiddish, I could make out the Roman numerals "X, IX." My heart dropped. My mother, still standing outside the door of our house, read Chia's words aloud: Boaz had been killed in action on the Golan Heights, on October 9. He was twenty-two. We were crushed.

The next summer, I made the trip to Israel again, going to the kibbutz to see Chia and Shmuel. Shmuel took me to the military cemetery in Nahariya, on the cliffs high above the Mediterranean shore. We visited Boaz's grave. Shmuel patted the soil around the headstone. But mostly he stood silent, deep in thought. When it came time to leave, Shmuel said, barely above a whisper, "Boaz, *shalom l'cha.*" My heart cried not only for a relative, but for a simple parent mourning his son.

In 1975, Shmuel's heart condition worsened and we had heard that he was admitted to Tel Hashomer Hospital in Tel Aviv. His father in the hospital, Shlomo, the middle son, who had been doing reserve duty in the Sinai, hitched a ride home on a transport plane so he could visit his dad. He never made it. The plane crashed into a mountain in the Sinai, with all lives lost. Shlomo, an aspiring composer and musician, was twenty-nine.

I'm told that Amatzia, the eldest son, went to the hospital to break the news to Shmuel. When Amatzia walked into the room, Shmuel looked at his face and said, "It's Shlomo, isn't it?" Shortly after, Shmuel died, surely of a heart already broken. He and Shlomo were buried side by side, the same day, on the kibbutz.

To me, Chia embodied the classic Israeli. Had she been born or lived in the United States, she'd have been a professor or writer. She was highly cultured; literature, music, and art were important to her. She was fourteen years younger than my mother; the two were like sisters. Indeed, she and my mother were the only real family tree experts in our family.

I visited Chia on what became my twice-yearly trips to Israel. She insisted on speaking Hebrew to me (though her English was quite good), forcing me to use my limited capability.

Though she appeared stoic, the loss of her two sons in the military and a husband to whom she was so devoted took a heavy toll. Chia traveled once or twice to Europe on kibbutz-sponsored excursions, but she never made the longer trek to the United States to see the relatives here, though we encouraged her to do so many times.

She poured herself into her work in the kibbutz library, and was doted on by her remaining children, grandchildren, and great-grandchildren. My trips to Beit Zera became fewer, and my phone calls to her became somewhat inhibited by my deficient Hebrew. Small in stature, like my mother, she was otherwise a giant—my Zionist conscience and frame of reference.

After the deaths of Shmuel and Shlomo, Amatzia, who had moved with his family to Kibbutz Elot (neat Eilat), in the south of Israel, returned to Beit Zera to be near his mother. With his beard, broad shoulders, and ever present sandals, he was yet another quintessential kibbutznik. At Elot, he cultivated the kibbutz's date palms, producing some of Israel's tastiest of this ancient fruit.

Amatzia's English was better than my Hebrew, but we really couldn't converse very well without an interpreter at hand. But I so admired his boundless enthusiasm for Israel and the Jewish people, later played out when he went on *shlichut* to work with Jewish communities in the former Soviet Union.

Though barely into his sixties, Amatzia had suffered from some serious health problems in recent years. He died suddenly in 2004, a year or so after Chia's passing.

I have always been closest to Dalia, the eldest Arad child. The mother of four and grandmother of thirteen, she's a combination of both her parents. Cultured and well-read, a concerned mother and doting grandmother, Dalia exudes the self-confidence that is a hallmark of a generation of Israelis that remembers the British administration and occupation and everything that followed. She has seen it all. She and Shimon live near Tel Aviv, and I try to see her every time I'm in the country.

Dalia is the last of the six Arads in the mantelpiece photo. She has seen two of her brothers taken from her while in the service of her country, seen another brother go prematurely, and lost her parents under the burden of the tragedies they endured.

Like other Israelis in her lifetime, she's seen the birth of Israel, its proverbial desert bloom, its wars and terrorism, its hopes for peace raised and dashed, in what continues to be a "dangerous neighborhood." There's a certain stoicism about such people; I've often thought that if every incident that occurred on a daily basis were to be taken to heart, they'd never make it.

The Arad family is unique in one way but universal in another. Most Israeli families have been affected by the political storms and the triumphs and tragedies of the past fifty-six years. In that sense, the Arad story is *Israel's* story.

My perspective on Israel has broadened over the years. I am married to an Israeli, and one of my sisters moved to Israel and has raised a family there. In recent years, dozens of our cousins have moved from the former Soviet Union to Israel, many of whom we have yet to meet.

But my first window on Israel's world was largely shaped by the family in the photo on the mantelpiece. We have taken pride in their individual accomplishments and have grieved with, and for, them in their days of sorrow.

A new generation of Arads is now taking shape. I don't have a recent photo of the family, as it has grown and prospered. I'd like to put one in a prominent place in our living room. I know that when I get one from Dalia, the sun will be shining, and the faces will, despite everything, be bronzed and smiling.

Laraine Newman

Laraine Newman is an actress who was part of the original cast of
Saturday Night Live. *In addition to her on-camera roles in movies*
(The Flintstones *and* The Coneheads, *among others), she is heard as*
the voice of a panoply of animated film characters (Jimmy Neutron,
Monsters, Inc., The Wild Thornberrys Movie) *and on television*
(Rugrats, Grim and Evil).

I srael represents a nation of "tough Jews." The common stereotype of the mild-mannered accountant (I won't mention lawyers, because they're tough Jews) or the scholarly professor (nothing to be ashamed of) is blown out of the water when one considers someone like Moshe Dayan with his eye patch, holding a tommy gun on top of a jeep. I checked out a Web site to get some background on some of the military leaders of Israel. I Googled Moshe Dayan, and the first thing I clicked on was a laundry list of devastating and seemingly unprovoked attacks on surrounding Arab lands. I could feel the blood sinking to my lower extremities. I realized I'd stumbled on probably the more subtle of hate sites. It was veiled as "history," but even a mere actress like myself without a college education could surmise that no nation would invade or impose a curfew anywhere without good reason.

When I first learned of the Holocaust as a kid, my reaction was that I would have done anything to try to pass as a non-Jew. Shameful and cowardly as that is, it's the truth. And speaking of "passing," let's talk about Hollywood; the great dichotomy. A business created by Jews who wanted assimilation more than anything in the world. So much so that, for lack of a better term, they identified with the enemy. There were very few images of Jews on screen in Hollywood. People changed their names, dyed their hair, got nose jobs. Maybe you think what I'm talking about couldn't possibly still be going on. Don't kid yourself. Most played down their observance or had none at all. This was the Judaism I grew up with.

My father, however, was a tough Jew. He was raised in Arizona; they were pretty much cowboys. His grandfather was a cattle merchant and his dad owned holding corrals for auctions. Dad had a horse, the whole shootin' match. My dad told a story of walking down the street at age seven, when one of the locals said, "Hello, Arnold, you little sheeny." My dad asked his dad what a sheeny was. Grandpa Harry went over and popped that guy right in the jaw.

I've just given three reasons why Israel is so important to me. There must be a nation of Jews. A nation of "tough Jews." Although I'm a Democrat, Rudy Giuliani's speech at the 2004 Republican convention had a comment that summed it all up for me: the Arab countries have policies that aren't successful. They are failing their people, and instead of trying to remedy it or take responsibility for it, they blame Israel and the United States. Israel means Jews are no longer victims. War and conflict are never just or sensible. Neither is prejudice and blind hatred. Our people have been survivors for centuries because we value learning, family, and giving. I am proud of those values and proud to be a Jew, and I support the survival of Israel.

Michael B. Oren

Michael B. Oren is the author of the New York Times *best seller* Six Days of War. *A former paratrooper in the Israeli army and advisor to the government under Yitzhak Rabin, he is a senior fellow at the Shalem Center in Jerusalem.*

I srael, for me, is about responsibility. For nearly two thousand years before the creation of their state in 1948, Jews could not bear responsibility for themselves as a nation. Though they developed a highly refined system of law and a finely tuned sense of morality, and while they often cared for one another's welfare as individuals, they rarely would—or could—build a city or establish civil laws. Seldom could they make the most basic decision of all, namely, to defend themselves as a people. Israel means just that: Jews assuming responsibility not only for their defense but for their prison and sanitation systems, for hospitals, highways, and airports. They take responsibility for their policies, foreign and domestic, and for justifying them before the nations of the world. For Jews—indeed, for any people—there can be no weightier burden.

Yet, it is precisely this burden that I have always cherished. Though born, raised, and educated in the United States, the son of Conservative Jewish parents who, though they supported Israel fervidly, never for a moment considered moving there, I was always something of an anomaly: a natural-born Zionist. As far back as I can remember, I was aware of the recent massacre of one out of every three Jews in the world, and cognizant of the responsibility of the surviving two-thirds to ensure that Jewish life could never again be taken with impunity. But my attraction to the Jewish sovereignty was not only negative. I was ecstatic over Israel's triumph in the 1967 Six-Day War, with the notion that Jews could overcome the threat of a second Holocaust, defeat vastly superior enemies, and reunite with the holiest places of their ancient homeland. I was fascinated by the transition of Jews from victims to victors, and drawn to the obligations they incurred en route.

Though I was always an admirer of Theodore Herzl, the founder of modern political Zionism, my Zionism was less Herzlian than it was Schwartzian. The reference is to Delmore Schwartz, a Beat poet of the 1950s and 1960s, one of my favorites. If Herzl said, "If you will it, it is no dream," Schwartz rejoined, "In dreams begin responsibilities." I longed to bear the responsibilities of which generations of Jews could only dream.

So, as soon as I could, I moved to Israel. Receiving citizenship immediately upon landing in the country, I thrilled at the sense of assuming responsibilities. I felt their weight the first time I voted in a national election, the first time (of a great many) that I paid my taxes, and the first time I laced up my paratrooper boots. As a soldier in the Israel Defense Forces, fighting in a war, I learned the ultimate meaning of responsibility, and not only toward my buddies. There was also the responsibility I had to show toward civilians, and even toward my enemies, once they became my prisoners. The IDF teaches its troops that carrying a gun, wielding the ability to take a human life, is both a terrible onus and a sacred right. I tried to bear them both—the duty and the privilege—proudly.

Responsibility did not, of course, end with my army service. On the contrary, it merely began. Israeli life is rife with responsibility. One has to decide, for example, whether to build a security fence between us and the Palestinians that may help protect us against terrorist attacks, but that is liable to deepen Israel's isolation in the so-called international community. One has to decide between supporting Israel's withdrawal from areas of the West Bank and Gaza, and by doing so, giving the terrorists a sense of victory, or remaining in all of the territories and undermining the Jewish majority on which the state is predicated. One has to decide whether the IDF should pull its forces out of the major Palestinian cities and take a risk for progress toward peace, or increase the likelihood of suicide bombers reaching our municipal buses—between reducing the danger to my eldest son, who is currently patrolling those cities, and enhancing that of my two younger kids, who ride those buses to school.

None of this comes easily to us as Jews. For nearly two millennia, since the destruction of the Second Temple, Jews developed a tradition of repugnance to the very notion of accepting responsibility for themselves, for sovereignty. Regularly abused by non-Jewish rulers, Jewish communities concluded that power itself was bad and, whenever possible, was best avoided. "May God bless and keep the Czar," Reb Tevye prayed, "far away from us!" In Israel, though, there can be no escape from the requisites of power. We must be the policemen and the soldiers, the judges and the jailers. Many Israelis wish it were otherwise. Some dream of the creation of a new Middle East in which Israel would blend into an Eastern version of the European Union, and others of establishing a theocracy in which rabbis—and through them, God—make every decision. Either vision involves a total abdication of responsibility, a return to the powerlessness of *mahallahs* and ghettos.

This is the challenge confronting all Israelis today, to deal with the consequences of our successes and our failures, our setbacks as well as our achievements. I feel blessed and privileged to live in an age when Jews can make their own sovereign decisions and address their ramifications. Having the ability to shape our lives as Jews, to defend them and fulfill them, that is what Israel means to me.

Norm Ornstein

Norm Ornstein is a political commentator and regular contributor to Roll Call, *the* New York Times, *and the* Washington Post. *He is currently a resident scholar at the American Enterprise Institute for Public Policy Research, a Washington, D.C., think tank.*

F rom the time I was young, I felt linked to Israel—by birthday. I was born in 1948, so every memorable or landmark birthday for me—ten, thirteen, twenty-five, fifty—was a memorable or landmark birthday for Israel. We shared bar mitzvah years, and middle age (although, of course, middle age for a person is not exactly middle age for a country).

While I was not deeply religious, my Judaism was a central element of my adolescent life, particularly in the years around my bar mitzvah when I lived in a smaller community in Canada—Moncton, New Brunswick. Our Jewish community was small but vibrant, and our social lives revolved in considerable measure around the only temple in the extended area, an Orthodox one. Many of my school classmates had never met a Jew before they met me.

Still, my sense of Jewish identity, which included a deep involvement in AZA (Aleph Zadik Aleph, the young men's order of B'nai B'rith youth organization), was not really one I thought through in any profound or philosophical way. I was Jewish, not many of the people around me were, my New Brunswick tribe was close-knit and an extended family, Israel was a Jewish state born the same year as me—but that was as far as it went. My Hebrew school education, which was fairly intense, made no particular impact on me. I did not have any mystical tie to Israel and had no relatives in the country—in fact, I don't remember meeting an Israeli until I was an adult. Israel was more an abstraction than a reality.

As with so many other young Jews, that changed for me with the 1967 war. Suddenly, my people were under attack, a tiny, brave country facing huge and menacing enemies that surrounded it. I followed the war intensely, and my feelings about Israel changed in my core—it was no longer an abstraction, but a real country filled with real people tied inextricably to me. They could easily suffer the same fate that Jews in Europe, including many of my forebears, had suffered in the Holocaust. Israel to me was the face and voice of Abba Eban—erudite, sophisticated, warm; I could almost envision him as my British-Israeli uncle.

From that point on, I viewed Israel in a different light. I followed Middle East politics in a way I hadn't before. I began to see more clearly the contrast between Israel's democracy and the autocracies, or worse, in the other countries in the region. The Yom Kippur War again roused my emotional attachment to Israel, as yet again its neighbors attacked the country to eradicate it. And Entebbe, in 1976, left me ecstatic as Israel responded brilliantly and courageously against vicious terrorists—showing again its ability to fight back and humiliate its evil adversaries.

My relationship to Israel changed yet again, and fundamentally, when I visited it for the first time in the late 1970s. I traveled with my wife through a large swath of the country, through the desert to Masada, Haifa, Tel Aviv, and Jerusalem. I met with policy makers, politicians, academics, and businesspeople. We went to Bethlehem and Jericho and up to the al-Aqsa mosque, seeing the confluence of three great religions all born in the same small spot. Fortunately for us, we visited at a time when one could travel freely and easily anywhere in the West Bank. The magic of Israel's culture and history, the vibrancy of its press, the rough-and-tumble of its democracy in action—all things that I knew from reading, but that resonated in a different and deeper way by being there. With any country, there is no substitute for seeing, feeling, smelling, and experiencing things firsthand. That is doubly true of Israel.

My first visit was magical for another reason. That year, 1977, had brought a different dynamic to the region, when Anwar Sadat went to Israel and single-handedly changed the world. The Camp David Accords a year later seemed to signal an inexorable path to peace or at least stability. Sadat's assassination in 1981 shattered that illusion.

As with many other Jews, my attitudes took a turn in a different direction in 1982 with Lebanon. Israel's invasion of Lebanon, whatever the motives, need, and provocation, was an aggressive move, and some of the things that followed shook my faith in its purity. The Sabra and Shatila debacle that followed was even more shocking and hard to absorb.

In some ways, my shock at Israel in Lebanon was a maturing experience—like a child who believes his father is perfect seeing him do something bad for the first time, and ultimately realizing that he is human like everyone else. But I remained uneasy as I saw the Lebanon occupation fester and put Israel regularly into difficult situations that resulted in more violence and that changed both the reality on the ground and the rhetorical dynamic in the region. I continued to believe in the magic of the state of Israel, its creation against the odds, and its ability to survive against repeated efforts by its neighbors to wipe it out. But I had a less idealistic vision of its purity.

The difficult years that followed left me frequently torn and often frustrated at Israel's policies, particularly the expansion of settlements. As the 1980s turned to the 1990s, and as Israel's relationship with Palestinians in the territories grew more complicated, I found my feelings toward Israel growing more complicated and ambivalent. I read about the confiscation of Palestinian lands and the roadblocks that seemed often designed more to inconvenience people than to reinforce security.

But I grew at least modestly hopeful during the Clinton years that agreements with Syria and the Palestinians could be achieved, through the artful efforts of American negotiators Dennis Ross and Aaron Miller, the skillful work of Israel's ambassador to the United States Itamar Rabinovitch, Israel's top expert on Syria, and the drive of both President Clinton and Prime Minister Barak. It was not to be, and what has followed has been dismaying and disheartening.

The intifada has been heartbreaking on many fronts. The rise of suicide bombers and the devastation of innocent life in Israel is sickening. There is no satisfaction to be derived from the related destruction of the Palestinian economy and disruption in the lives of average Palestinians, driven by their corrupt and awful leadership. Israel's response to terrorist acts, I am convinced, is little different from what Americans' or Europeans' would be if they confronted regular attacks of comparable magnitude, but that provides scant satisfaction.

Another visit gave me a deeper appreciation for the reality of life in contemporary Israel. On this trip, I was able to take the fabled helicopter tour of the country that Texas governor George W. Bush took with General Ariel Sharon, which shaped Bush's whole view of Israel and the Middle East. I had an Israeli army colonel as my guide. Our helicopter went from Tel Aviv up to the border with Lebanon, where we saw Hezbollah missiles aimed at the heart of Israel; over to the Golan Heights, where we could see how vulnerable the country would be to bombardment or invasion if it were in the hands of an enemy; down along the Jordan River to Masada, seeing along the way how close West Bank villages are to Israeli towns and cities, how many settlements are basically closed-in suburbs of Jerusalem; and back to Tel Aviv—all in about four and a half hours. No one can take that trip without understanding how unique Israel is—how distances in that country are so different from ours or most others, how the territories in dispute are in many cases the equivalent of Chevy Chase and Bethesda in relation to downtown Washington, D.C. And no one with any objectivity can take that trip without understanding the unique security concerns and needs of Israel.

My third visit to Israel came during the summer of 2004. My wife and I went to a bar mitzvah at the Western Wall, and we traveled by car from one end of the country to the other. A cousin of my wife's drove us from Tel Aviv past the Sea of Galilee, up into the Golan Heights, then over to the Lebanon border, and back to Tel Aviv. By car, this trip took a full day—which meant traversing the entire northern half of the country in one day—but it again underscored the teeny size of Israel, while also showing me in a deeper way its beauty.

This trip had other impact. Our first night, in Jerusalem, we went to a lovely restaurant in the German quarter. The immediate sign of change from our initial trip was the guard at the restaurant entrance checking us for weapons or any malign intent. We sat in the outdoor garden and had a lovely meal—and learned the next day that the previous week, a putative suicide bomber had been dropped off a half-block away from that restaurant intending to blow himself up in another eatery. He had had second thoughts and returned to the West Bank, where he was killed just before we arrived in the country.

To us and the other throngs eating in the many restaurants in the area, there was no hint of danger or sign of stress. And that was true throughout our trip. The State Department had issued a travel warning to Americans that was published the day we arrived in Israel—in effect, do not travel there, and if you are there, get out. But what we saw were Israelis everywhere, determined to live normal lives, to defy the danger all around them. Suicide bombers and other terrorist attacks were simply not going to faze them. The malls, restaurants, and beaches were full of resilient Israelis.

When I travel around the world, I meet Europeans and Asians who have wholly different views of Israel and Palestinians. They see Israelis as aggressors and colonialists, and Palestinians as noble victims of occupation. They usually have seen Yassir Arafat as a hero, trying only to free his imprisoned people. They are unable or unwilling to look at history—at 1948, 1967, 1973, the concerted and coordinated efforts by Arab countries to destroy Israel by naked aggression; at the concerted terrorist attacks over decades aimed at innocent civilians; at the unwillingness over decades of the PLO to eliminate its credo calling for the destruction of Israel; at the failure of Arafat to opt for peace and a two-state solution when he had the chance. They are blind to the fact that Israel, for all its warts, is a vibrant democracy where governments and leaders fall, where a press regularly eviscerates people in power, where overreach by the military and corruption by civilian officials is punished—and that the countries and officials they lionize are dominated by autocracy and corruption.

I see it differently. I recognize full well Israel's faults and problems, and am unhappy with many of the government's policies. I am frustrated by a political system that has built in hyperproportional representation and made the ultrareligious Jewish community a superpower outside of all proportion to their population. This community has done its best to make non–ultrareligious Jews who are Reform or Conservative feel less worthy. In a curious way, a visit to Israel does not make me feel that I am with "my" people. Most Israelis are not like me—they don't look like me, they don't sound like me; they are clearly Middle Eastern while I am very much American. But I see a people whose basic desire is to live in peace with its neighbors, working its way through its own differences and disputes. I also believe that most Palestinians, and most other Arabs, have the same desires—but they have been saddled with regimes and leaders they cannot change or influence.

Unfortunately, I also see something else. The virulently anti-Israel attitudes expressed throughout Europe, including in publications like the British newspaper the *Independent*, also reflect a rise of a new form of anti-Semitism, something seen in a more vicious way in the frequent attacks on Jews in France. It is also reflected in the moves being made by the Russian leader Vladimir Putin in his selective attacks on oligarchs—with all of those under siege seeming to be Jewish. It is seen in the attacks on Jewish facilities, including schools, in Argentina and Venezuela, and in the moves on many American campuses to force universities to divest themselves of interests in companies doing business with Israel—but not those interacting with the Palestinian Authority.

I am an American, through and through. Every day I thank God that I was born an American, and have been able to succeed beyond my and my parents' wildest imaginings in this country. Neither I nor my children have ever suffered in any way from being Jewish. The same was true of my years in Canada. To be sure, Europe is in no way like it was in the 1920s and the 1930s. But around the world, the veneer of acceptability for Jews remains thinner than it should be. Old patterns can reemerge, even anti-Semitism without Jews. Every time I am reminded of that fact, I appreciate Israel even more for what it is and how it arose. And I pray even more for an eventual reconciliation with its neighbors that can at least bring a measure of regularity to the daily life of Israelis.

I happened to be with President Clinton immediately after the Camp David talks broke down, as we both traveled to Little Rock for a memorial service for a mutual friend. His disappointment (and exhaustion) was etched on his face, especially a disillusionment with Yassir Arafat's unwillingness or inability to pull the trigger on a settlement that would have spared the world the bloodshed and heartache of the past several years. Now, with Arafat gone, a new chance exists, over time, to heal the breach. It will not come easily and will require both leaps of faith on both sides and a willingness to take on Jewish and Arab absolutists. I applaud the courage and foresight of Prime Minister Sharon, who has transcended his own history and worldview to take a leap for the long-run security of his country and his people. If peace, even a cold peace, ever comes, it will not bring Nirvana, any more than the end of the forty-year journey by Moses and his people brought a placid and perfect life. Israel will be a rollicking, disputatious, difficult democracy, with huge internal economic, social, religious, and other problems. Jews will battle with Jews, and the disputes will often be rancorous and bitter. I'll take it.

Judea Pearl

Judea Pearl is a professor of computer science at UCLA and president of the Daniel Pearl Foundation, founded in memory of his son, the journalist Daniel Pearl, to further the ideals that inspired his life and work.

Israel is the crucible where the most noble aspirations of mankind have been brought together to develop and cross-pollinate side by side.

I was born in Tel Aviv in 1936, and quite naturally, my feelings toward Israel are suffused with the love, pride, memories, music, and aromas that nourish and sustain all natives of any country. Yet, remarkably, as the years pass, I discover that these same feelings toward Israel are echoed by people everywhere, including many who have never set foot in that country.

My family love affair with Israel began in 1924, when my grandfather, a textile merchant and devout Hasid in the town of Ostrowietz, Poland, decided to realize his life dream and immigrate to the land of the Bible. Family lore has it that my grandfather was assaulted one day by a Polish peasant with an iron bar shouting, "Dirty Jew!" My grandfather crawled home then, wiped off his blood, and announced to his wife and four children, "Start packing! We are going home!" In the weeks that followed, he sold all his possessions and, teaming with twenty-five other families, bought a piece of sandy land about seven kilometers to the northeast of Jaffa. That land was near an Arab village called Ibn Abrak, described by the newspaper *Haaretz* in July 1924 as "a few mud-walled huts surrounded by a few scattered trees."

The Arab real estate broker in Jaffa had probably no inkling why a group of seemingly educated Jews, some with business experience, would pay so dearly for a piece of arid land, situated far from any water source, which even the hardy residents of Ibn Abrak found to be uninhabitable.

But the twenty-six Hasidic families knew exactly what they were buying—Ibn Abrak was the site of the ancient city of Bnai-Brak, well known in the biblical and rabbinic days, the town where Rabbi Akiva made his home and established his great yeshiva. The sages say that it was to Bnai-Brak that Rabbi Akiva applies the famous verse: "Justice, justice shalt thou pursue" (Sanhedrin, 32b).

The vision of reviving the spirit of that ancient site of learning was well worth the exorbitant price the broker demanded, the dusty winds, the merciless sun, the lack of water, and all the daily hardships that pioneering agricultural life entailed.

My father was fourteen when his family arrived at Bnai-Brak in 1924 and, whenever he reminisced about that early period of hardship, he always referred to it as the "rebuilding of Bnai-Brak," as if he and my grandfather had been there before, with Poland and the whole saga of the Jewish Diaspora merely an unpleasant nightmare.

We, the children who grew up in Bnai-Brak, had not the slightest doubt that we had been there before. Every Passover, when our family's reading of the Haggadah reached the well-known story of the five rabbis who were sitting in Bnai-Brak, reciting the story of the Exodus, my grandfather would stop the reading, look everyone in the eye, issue one of his rare mysterious smiles, and continue with emphasis: *"She'hayu mesubin b'Bnai-Brak."* The message was clear: "We never really left home!"

A short distance from our school, there were two steep hills that almost touched each other. The older boys told us that the two hills once were one, and got separated when Bar Kochva—the heroic figure who led a futile Jewish rebellion against Rome in the second century A.D.—rode through them on his famous lion, causing the gully between. We had no doubt that it was only a matter of time before we would find Bar Kochva's burial place; we needed only to dig deep enough into these hills—which we did enthusiastically for hours and hours. It was only a matter of time, we thought, before the earth all over Israel would ooze and unravel the mysteries of our historic infancy. It was this cultural incubator that shaped my childhood—an intoxicating enthusiasm of homecoming and nation rebuilding.

Those who say that this sort of culture no longer inspires youth in our generation are mistaken. Seventy-eight years after my grandfather first set foot in Bnai-Brak, in a desolate shed in Karachi, Pakistan, his great-grandson, Daniel Pearl, stood before his captors-murderers and said, "My father is Jewish, my mother is Jewish, I am Jewish." Then, looking straight at the eye of evil, he added one last sentence: "Back in the town of Bnai-Brak there is a street named after my great-grandfather, Chayim Pearl, who was one of the founders of the town." Was a page of history ever chanted with a greater pride? Was a more gentle love song ever sung to a homebound founder of a new town?

My mother's story was different, yet still driven by the same forces of history. A native of Keltz, Poland, she applied for immigration in 1935, when anti-Semitic intimidation reached unbearable proportions. Hitler had delivered his Kristallnacht sermon two years earlier, his threats were broadcast all over Europe, the handwriting was on the wall, and masses of Polish Jews applied for immigration to their biblical homeland—Palestine. Ironically, the Brits were bending to Arab pressure to stop Jewish immigration, and my mother's hopes of leaving Poland before the storm were at the mercy of a political controversy that has not been settled to this very day.

I recently read the argument the Arabs used in that debate, as published in the Arabic newspaper *Carmel:* "We know that Jewish immigration can proceed without dispossessing a single Arab from his land. This is obvious. And this is precisely what we object to. We simply do not want to peacefully turn into a minority, and European Jews should understand why." The counterargument of the Jewish leadership was equally compelling: "This sort of morality is morality of cannibalism, not one of the civilized world, for it dictates that the homeless must forever remain homeless; we beg merely for a small fraction of this vast piece of land." (Paraphrased from Zev Jabotinsky, "Medinah Ivrit," Tel Aviv, 1937, p. 79.)

But the British sided with the stronger, allowing a trickle of only 15,000 immigration certificates per year. My mother could not wait, so she paid a huge sum to a cousin who had an immigration certificate to arrange a fictitious marriage that would later be annulled. Fortunately, her father intervened and she found a better prospect—my father—a suntanned young Palestinian in a summer suit, who was searching the towns of Poland for a refined European bride. My mother's parents, her brother, and her sister were not so lucky. Stranded by the British-Arab blockade, they all perished in the Holocaust with six million other victims.

I once asked my mother how she felt when she arrived. "I came to Israel on the eve of Chanukah, 1935," she said. "The first day after my arrival, I went up to the roof and I could not believe my eyes— how deeply blue the sky was, compared with the gray sky that I left behind in Poland. I was breathless!

"Then I met a neighbor, a teacher who invited me to visit her kindergarten. There I experienced one of the happiest days in my life. Scores of children were standing there loudly singing Chanukah songs, in Hebrew, as if this was the most natural thing to do, as if they were singing those songs for hundreds of years."

"Why the wonder?" I asked. "Didn't your family celebrate Chanukah in Poland?"

"Not exactly," she said. "Yes, we lit the candles, but it was in a dark corner, with my father whispering the blessing and mumbling 'Maoz Tzur' quietly. You see, the neighbors were goyim, and he did not feel comfortable advertising that we celebrated a Jewish holiday. And here I come and suddenly find these toddlers singing 'Maccabee-Gibbor!' in full volume, and in the open courtyard."

Just a few months ago, as I was preparing for a Muslim-Jewish dialogue, I read that the Palestinians have decided to view themselves as descendants of the Canaanite tribes conquered by Joshua. I couldn't help but imagine how lonely it must be for a Palestinian boy not to be able to sing "Canaanite-Gibbor" in the language of his ancestors, not to have Canaanite role models after which to name songs, towns, and holidays and, more lonely yet, to be taught by teachers who had never heard of his Canaanite ancestors when they went to kindergarten. Without dismissing any claims that Palestinians may lay to the land of the Bible, justice must acknowledge the historical reality of those children in Bnai-Brak, singing "Maccabee-Gibbor" before my ecstatic mother.

The relation between Jews and the land of Israel is an issue that has surfaced quite often in my recent dialogues with Muslims and, admittedly, it evokes some fundamental questions that I have not seen answered with sufficient clarity.

Muslims find it almost impossible to understand why American Jews, the foremost champions against the politicization of religion, identify so strongly with a specific political entity other than one's own country, that is, the state of Israel. A Pakistani journalist who attended a memorial service for my son in a Jewish school in Maryland commented that he could not possibly imagine a school in Pakistan where students would salute the Saudi flag the way students in that Jewish school saluted the Israeli flag.

One immediate explanation for this emotional connection is, of course, that Jews are concerned for the safety and physical survival of the beleaguered five and a half million Jews now living in Israel, many of whom are directly related to American Jews. Another, less obvious answer lies in the latent insecurity that Jews everywhere feel in the Diaspora, for whom the knowledge of Israel's sovereignty provides a psychological security blanket.

Still, these answers do not explain how an emotional identification with a political entity could become so embedded in the spiritual life of synagogues, prayers, and day schools half a world away. The answer here touches on the distinct nature of the Jewish identity and escapes the standard measures by which other religions are defined.

Jewishness, owing to its unique and turbulent history, is more than just a religion. For a Jew, ancestry, religion, history, country, culture, tradition, nationhood, and ethnicity are inseparably interrelated.

Historical narratives and the ancient landscape in which they unfolded are as much part of the Jewish experience as are any specific beliefs in a deity or the hereafter.

This meta-religious characterization of Jews entails an unparalleled intellectual connection to the Holy Land, the birthplace of Jewish history. While this connection bears some resemblance to that which Muslims feel toward Mecca and Christians toward Jerusalem, it is more intensified by national ties because, unlike Islam and Christianity, the Jewish religion was not written with the intention of being transported to other nations or other lands. (Proselytizing is discouraged in Judaism.) It was written exclusively for the Jewish nation and meant to be practiced specifically in the land where this nation was born and shaped.

For example, a third of the Mishna makes sense only in the context of the land of the Bible. Establishing a residence in that land is said to be "equivalent to all other Mitzvoth in the Torah put together" (Sifri 53). The daily prayers, likewise, have reminded Jews three times each day, for two millennia, of their inevitable return, as a sovereign nation, to that biblical land.

As a result, the collective memories and aspirations of the Jewish people today are expressed in language and imagery that are utterly dependent on this one land. To take away that land from the consciousness of a Jew would be like taking away one of the five books of Moses, or ripping away the story of Bnai-Brak from my grandfather's Haggadah—the landscape has become *the* scripture. (These arguments merely explain the intimate historical, cultural, and spiritual connection of Jews to the land of Israel. Clearly, the ties, sentiments, and aspirations of other people in the region must be accommodated.)

A related question arises from the claim for "Israel's right to exist as a Jewish state." "Why Jewish?" ask Israel's antagonists. "Isn't the notion of a religious state anachronistic in modern times? Do you really mean to shape Israel after theocracies like Iran or Pakistan that favor members of one faith over others?"

Of course not! It is unthinkable that Israel, one of the most secular societies in the world, would aspire to religious exclusiveness. The confusion arises from the coarseness of language and the failure of the word "Jewish" to distinguish the various aspects of Jewish identity. One might more aptly say that Israel does not seek to be a "religious-Jewish state" but, rather, a "national-Jewish state," with a "national-Jew" being an individual who, by choice, identifies with the collective history and destiny of a group of individuals who call themselves "Jews." (According to this definition, Neturey Karta, the small sect of anti-Zionist ultra-Orthodox Jews in Jerusalem and New York, would not qualify for a national-Jewish status, because they choose not to share destiny with the rest of the Jewish collective. A Christian-born, unconverted immigrant to Israel, on the other hand, one who proclaims his identity as "Jewish," should qualify for a "national-Jew" title by virtue of the Jewish education his or her children are getting, and their commitment to serve in the army and become part of the Jewish society in Israel.)

In contrast to the religious interpretation of "Jewish state," the status of Israel as a "national-Jewish state" is perfectly compatible with modern standards, no different, for example, from the status of Spain as a national-Spanish state, where holidays and textbooks commemorate milestones of Spanish, not Portuguese, history, and where streets are named after Spanish, not French, writers. (While the official Israeli definition of nationality is currently based on religious considerations, in accordance with rabbinical laws, it is only a matter of time, in my opinion, before the determination is based on more refined progressive criteria.)

Indeed, when early Zionists talked about Judenstaat, they had in mind a state for "national-Jews," not "religious-Jews." It is highly important to recall that Theodore Herzl was a secular Jew, as were the majority of the delegates to the Zionist congresses. Moreover, so are the majority of Israelis today who define their Jewishness as a national affiliation—a commitment to shared history and shared destiny—not as a matter of religious faith. (See the essays by A. B. Yehoshua, Amos Oz, and David Grossman in *I Am Jewish: Personal Reflections Inspired by the Last Words of Daniel Pearl*, Judea and Ruth Pearl, eds., Jewish Lights Publishing, 2004.)

. . .

Yes, Israel is a land of paradoxes, redefinitions or, more precisely, a land of dynamic contrasts.

My hometown of Bnai-Brak, now a bustling replica of an extremely Orthodox Eastern European shtetl, is situated among totally secular neighborhoods, in which May 1, International Workers Day, is celebrated with school ceremonies and marching bands. At the same time, it is not uncommon to find youth groups in Marxist-leaning kibbutzim engaging in a nightlong trance of Hasidic melodies.

This marvelous blending of an intense clinging to the past with an innovative, indeed revolutionary and optimistic outlook to the future, is the essence of what Israel means to me.

The optimists among us say that the world will never abandon Israel, because civilization cannot afford to dispose of such an innovative project, one where the noblest aspirations of mankind have been brought together to develop and cross-pollinate side by side. Pessimists tell us that the fate of Israel is the fate of civilization itself, and the latter does not look very promising.

As a proud descendant of a stubborn tribe of survivors, I take the optimistic side. True, the world may not fully appreciate the importance of noble projects, and it may appear to belittle the miracle of creating a vibrant democracy and a center of arts and science from the few mud-walled huts that my grandfather found eighty years ago. But I am nevertheless convinced that, deep below all the criticism and the rhetoric, it is the heroic example of Israel's struggle and progress that currently fuels the will of civilization to survive.

And with Israel as a role model, and civilization as Israel's guardian, the symbiosis is invincible.

Natalie Portman

Natalie Portman is an actress who has starred in many films, including Anywhere but Here, Where the Heart Is, Closer, and the Star Wars prequels. She made her Broadway debut playing the title role in The Diary of Anne Frank. She was born in Jerusalem, speaks fluent Hebrew, and graduated from Harvard University.

ISRAEL IS . . .

Where I was born. Where I ate my first Popsicle and used a proper toilet for the first time. Where some of my eighteen-year-old friends spend their nights in bunkers sleeping with their helmets on. Where security guards are the only jobs in surplus. Where deserts bloom and pioneer stories are sentimentalized. Where a thorny, sweet cactus is the symbol of the ideal Israeli. Where immigrating to Israel is called "ascending" and emigrating from Israel is called "descending." Where my grandparents were not born, but where they were saved.

Where the year passes with the season of olives, of almonds, of dates. Where the transgressive pig or shrimp dish speaks defiantly from a Jerusalem menu. Where, despite substantial exception, secularism is the rule. Where wine is religiously sweet. Where "Arabic homes" is a positive real estate term with no sense of irony. Where there is endless material for dark humor. Where there are countless words for "to bother," but no single one yet for "to pleasure." Where laughter is the currency, jokes the religion. Where political parties multiply more quickly than do people. Where to become religious is described as "returning to an answer" and becoming secular "returning to a question."

Where six citizens have won Nobel prizes in fifty years. Where the first one earned an Olympic gold in 2004 for sailing (an Israeli also won the bronze for judo). Where there is snow two hours north and desert *hamsin* (desert wind) two hours south. Where Moses never was allowed to walk, but whose streets we litter. Where the language in which Abraham spoke to Isaac before he was to sacrifice him has been resuscitated to include the words for "sweatshirt" and "schadenfreude" and "chemical warfare" and "press conference." Where the muezzin chants, and the church bells sound, and the shofars cry freely at the Wall. Where the shopkeepers bargain. Where the politicians bargain. Where there will one day be peace, but never quiet.

Where I was born; where my insides refuse to abandon.

David Raab

David Raab, who in 1970 was held hostage by Palestinian hijackers for three weeks, is now a management consultant who lives in Raanana, Israel, with his wife. He formerly headed a pro-Israel PAC in northern New Jersey.

THAT'S WHY!

As countries go, Israel leaves much to be desired. Its democracy is flawed, lacking checks and balances, true representation, and ultimately, accountability. Its government is bloated, bureaucratic, and at times corrupt. Israel's educational and health care systems are second-rate and deteriorating. Its economy is small, overcontrolled, and over-taxed, limiting opportunities. Its citizens are often aggressive, impatient, judgmental, insensitive, and parochial, yet self-certain.

Nor is Israel the safe haven for Jews that Herzl intended it to be. Quite the contrary. It has been a lightning rod for terrorism ever since it was founded. I would know. I was held hostage by the Popular Front for the Liberation of Palestine in Jordan for three weeks in September 1970 after being hijacked on my return home to the United States following a summer in Israel. Today, Israel is the only country where Jews are killed regularly simply for being Jewish. It continues to live among neighbors who are unreconciled to its very existence and who seem prepared only for a cool peace.

So why indeed is Israel so central in my life? Why is it such a driving force that during the 1990s I devoted days and nights to pro-Israel activity in the United States and, in 1999, picked up my family, gave up a wonderful career, community, and country, and moved here?

Why do I stay here despite my need to commute back and forth to the United States to earn a living? Why do I love this country so?

It is because Israel represents the potential for achieving ultimate Jewish fulfillment in terms of spirituality and observance, physical rooting, and peoplehood. The first two are straightforward; the last is the main challenge.

I love Israel because it is easy to be Jewish here. (Being Israeli is the hard part.) Jewish observance is not an overlay on a Christian, Moslem, or other culture. The rhythm of the country is Jewish. The week is built around the Jewish day of rest. Shabbat is Shabbat; holidays, holidays. No need to explain to colleagues why I have to get home before sunset on Friday afternoon—in fact, few work Friday afternoon—or what kosher is. Jewish observance is as natural here as eating and sleeping. The nonobservant celebrate the Jewish holidays, too, even if in negation. Jewish learning is more widespread and intense here than ever and anywhere in Jewish history. The spoken language is the language of the prophets. Spirituality is almost a by-product, not an independent goal.

I love Israel because the land beckons me. This is the land that God promised my people. This is where my forefathers walked, where my religion grew and blossomed, where my forebears built societies. This is where my ancestors yearned and strove to return to as they were being persecuted for two thousand years in Europe, Russia, and Arab lands. And this is where one great-grandfather came from Hungary in the late 1880s to farm the land and found Petach-Tikva and another was a sixth-generation Jerusalemite. I cannot explain it, but I feel chemically linked to the land. My body harmonizes with it; it resonates in me. I feel that I am home.

I love Israel because this is where the Jewish people have the potential to blossom and shine as a people. Over the past centuries, Jews have contributed immeasurably to civilization. But it has typically been as individuals or relatively small groups. As a people, we have been downtrodden, far from an inspiration to others, far from being a light unto the nations, as the prophets envisioned.

The state of Israel is a cosmic test for the Jewish people, I believe.

After almost two thousand years of an exile brought on by internal strife and gratuitous hatred, God is granting us a historic opportunity to demonstrate that we have learned to be a people, to love and care for one other, to work with one another, and to cherish our Jewishness. I am not convinced yet that we are passing our test. The Knesset floor alone shows that we have not learned to speak civilly to one another and respect others' opinions. Israeli society is extremely divisive, confrontational, and even spiteful and, unfortunately, comes together only in time of crisis.

In truth, I am more concerned about our internal relations—how we deal with one another—than about our external threat. Many times I wonder whether this country will make it. I pray that we will learn to get along with ourselves, but, for now, it is the hardest part of living in Israel. It makes me question often why I moved here.

But then I see a nonobservant woman reflexively touch her hand to the mezuzah when she enters a room, or I am wished *Shabbat shalom* by the checkout clerk at the supermarket, or I hear a Talmudic idiom inserted into a totally secular conversation on the radio. Or, I am attending a mid-December business conference in Tel Aviv when suddenly the proceedings are halted to light Chanukah candles and the entire audience joins in for a rousing rendition of "Maoz Tzur." And then I remind myself: that's why I moved here and that's why I am so full of hope.

Pat Robertson

Pat Robertson is the founder and chairman of the Christian Broadcast-
ing Network, Operation Blessing International Relief and Develop-
ment Corporation, and a number of other organizations and broadcast
entities. He was awarded the Defender of Israel Award from the Chris-
tians' Israel Public Action Campaign, as well as the State of Israel
Friendship Award by the Chicago chapter of the Zionist Organization
of America.

WHY EVANGELICAL CHRISTIANS SUPPORT ISRAEL

One day in the nineteenth century, Queen Victoria of England
reportedly asked her prime minister, Benjamin Disraeli, this question:
"Mr. Prime Minister, what evidence can you give me of the existence
of God?"

Disraeli thought for a moment and then replied, "The Jew, your
majesty."

Think of it: according to Disraeli, the primary evidence that God
exists is the existence of the Jewish people, a people who in 586 B.C.
were deported to Babylon, yet returned after seventy years to rebuild
a nation; who were again brutally massacred and dispersed by the
Romans in A.D. 70; yet after countless centuries of Diaspora, expul-
sions, pogroms, ghettos, and attempts at genocidal extermination, have
clung to their faith, their customs, and now, after some 2,500 years of
wandering, have returned to the land promised by God to their ancestors. A new nation began in that land in 1948 named after their
ancestor Jacob, whose divinely appointed name "Israel" means
"Prince with God." And to fulfill another ancient prophecy, God
moved on the heart of Eliezer Ben-Yehuda, whose son Ehud told me
that while his father was living in Eastern Europe, he heard a voice and

This essay is excerpted from Mr. Robertson's address to the Herzliya Conference
in December 2003.

saw a light directing him to bring forth for the Jewish people a pure language—Hebrew—the language of the Torah and of the ancient prophets.

Yes, the survival of the Jewish people is a miracle of God. The return of the Jewish people to the land promised to Abraham, Isaac, and Jacob is a miracle of God. The remarkable victories of Jewish armies against overwhelming odds in successive battles in 1948, and 1967, and 1973 are clearly miracles of God. The technological marvels of Israeli industry, the military prowess, the bounty of Israeli agriculture, the fruits and flowers and abundance of the land are a testimony to God's watchful care over this new nation and the genius of this people.

Yet what has happened was clearly foretold by the ancient prophet Ezekiel, who, writing at the time of the Babylonian captivity, declared this message for the Jewish people concerning latter days:

> For I will take you out of the nations; I will gather you from all the countries and bring you back to your own land.... I will give you a new heart and put a new spirit in you . . . to follow my decrees and be careful to keep my laws. You will live in the land I gave your forefathers; you will be my people and I will be your God. I will save you from all your uncleanness.
>
> I will call for the grain and make it plentiful . . . I will increase the fruit of the trees and the crops of the field, so that you will no longer suffer disgrace among the nations because of famine. . . .
>
> This is what the Sovereign Jehovah says: "On the day I cleanse you from all your sins, I will resettle your towns, and the ruins will be rebuilt. The desolate land will be cultivated instead of lying desolate in the sight of all who pass through it. They will say, 'This land that was laid waste has become like the garden of Eden; the cities that were lying in ruins, desolate and destroyed, are now fortified and inhabited.'
>
> "Then the nations around you that remain will know that I, Jehovah, have rebuilt what was destroyed and have replanted what was desolate. I, Jehovah, have spoken, and I will do it." Ezekiel 36:24 ff.

Ladies and gentlemen, evangelical Christians support Israel because we believe that the words of Moses and the ancient prophets of Israel were inspired by God. We believe that the emergence of a

Jewish state in the land promised by God to Abraham, Isaac, and Jacob was ordained by God.

We believe that God has a plan for this nation that He intends to be a blessing to all the nations of the earth.

Of course, we, like all right-thinking people, support Israel because Israel is an island of democracy, an island of individual freedom, an island of the rule of law, and an island of modernity in the midst of a sea of dictatorial regimes, the suppression of individual liberty, and a fanatical religion intent on returning to the feudalism of eighth century Arabia.

These facts about modern-day Israel are all true. But mere political rhetoric does not account for the profound devotion to Israel that exists in the hearts of tens of millions of evangelical Christians.

You must realize that the God who spoke to Moses on Mount Sinai is our God. Abraham, Isaac, and Jacob are our spiritual patriarchs. Jeremiah, Ezekiel, and Daniel are our prophets. King David, a man after God's own heart, is our hero. The holy city of Jerusalem is our spiritual capital. And the continuation of Jewish sovereignty over the Holy Land is a further bulwark to us that the God of the Bible exists and that His Word is true.

And we should clearly take note that evangelical Christians serve a Jew who we believe was the divine Messiah of Israel, spoken of by the ancient prophets, to whom He entrusted the worldwide dissemination of His message to twelve Jewish apostles.

To our Jewish friends, we say: We are with you in your struggle. We are with you as a wave of anti-Semitism is engulfing the earth. We are with you despite the pressure of the Quartet and the incredibly hostile resolutions of the United Nations. We are with you despite the threats and ravings of Wahhabi jihadists, Hezbollah thugs, and Hamas assassins. We are with you despite oil embargos, loss of allies, and terrorist attacks on our cities.

We evangelical Christians merely say to our Israeli friends: Let us serve our God together by opposing the virulent poison of anti-Semitism and anti-Zionism that is rapidly engulfing the world.

Having affirmed our support, I would humbly make two requests of our Israeli friends:

First, please don't commit national suicide. It is very hard for your friends to support you if you make a conscious decision to destroy yourselves.

The slogan "land for peace" is a cruel chimera. The Sinai was given up. Did that bring lasting peace? No. Southern Lebanon was given up. Did that bring lasting peace? No. Instead, Hezbollah rode tanks to the border of Israel, shouting, "On to Jerusalem!" Now, as many as ten thousand rockets aimed at Metulla, Qiryat Shemona, and all of northern Israel have been put in place throughout southern Lebanon.

Arafat was brought up at the knees of the man who yearned to finish the work of Adolf Hitler. How could any realist truly believe that this killer and his associates would have become trusted partners for peace?

I am aware of the deep feelings of many Israelis who yearn for peace, who long to be free from the terror of the suicide bombers of the intifada.

Second, the world's Christians ask that you do not give away the treasured symbols of your spiritual patrimony.

I read in the *Wall Street Journal* an article written by an American Jewish commentator who remarked that the Temple Mount and what is termed the "Wailing Wall" are "sacred stones and sites," but hardly worth bloodshed.

Just think: the place where the patriarch Abraham took Isaac to offer him to God; the place bought by King David from Araunah where the Angel of the Lord stood with drawn sword; the place of Solomon's temple; the place of the Holy of Holies; the place where Jesus Christ walked and taught; the very spiritual center of the Jewish worship of the one true God—nothing but a pile of sacred stones— unworthy of sacrifice? What an incredible assertion!

Make no mistake: the entire world is being convulsed by a religious struggle. The fight is not about money or territory; it is not about poverty versus wealth; it is not about ancient customs versus modernity. No, the struggle is whether Hubal, the Moon God of Mecca, known as Allah, is supreme, or whether the Judeo-Christian Jehovah God of the Bible is supreme.

If God's chosen people turn over to Allah control of their most sacred sites; if they surrender to Muslim vandals the tombs of Rachel, of Joseph, of the patriarchs, of the ancient prophets; if they believe their claim to the Holy Land comes only from Lord Balfour of England and the ever fickle United Nations rather than the promises of Almighty God—then in that event, Islam will have won the battle. Throughout the Muslim world the message will go forth: "Allah is greater than Jehovah. The promises of Jehovah to the Jews are meaningless. We can now, in the name of Allah, move to crush the Jews and drive them out of the land that belongs to Allah."

In short, those political initiatives that some have asserted will guarantee peace, will in truth guarantee unending struggle and ultimate failure. Those political leaders who only understand the secular dimension of Israel's existence and who cavalierly dismiss the spiritual dimension will find that they receive the mess of potage of Esau rather than the inheritance of Jacob.

On Christmas Day in 1974, I had the privilege of interviewing Prime Minister Yitzhak Rabin for my television program, *The 700 Club*. Rabin lamented the fact that after Israeli military victories, the nation had been stopped from achieving a peace treaty.

That was over thirty years ago. Israel seemed as isolated and alone then as it does today. As I concluded my interview, I asked Prime Minister Rabin a final question: "What would you want the United States to do now for Israel?"

He replied without hesitation, "Be strong! Be strong!"

That evening I joined for dinner a group of several hundred people who had accompanied me from the United States. We were meeting in the large dining room of the InterContinental Hotel on the Mount of Olives in Jerusalem, whose floor-to-ceiling windows gave a stunning view of the illuminated Temple Mount. As I related to the group the substance of my meeting, I began to recall the feeling of sadness that had come from the prime minister—the sense of the isolation of his nation. That evening, I made a solemn vow to God that, despite whatever might happen in the future, I and the organizations I headed would stand in support of Israel and the Jewish people. I am proud to say that I have kept that vow each year since 1974.

In closing, I would deliver to Israel the message Yitzhak Rabin delivered to the United States on Christmas Day in 1974, for you are the living witnesses that the promises of the Sovereign Lord are true. "Be strong! Be strong!"

He will be with you and so will your evangelical friends.

Thank you, and God bless you!

Anne Roiphe

Anne Roiphe is the author of seven novels, including the best-sellers Up the Sandbox *and* Fruitful. *She also writes a column for the* New York Observer.

I was twelve years old in 1948, and the founding of the state of Israel meant to me what it meant to almost every American Jewish child: redemption after the Shoah—hope for our own lives and the lives of our grandchildren. It meant that while you might destroy Jews by the millions, the Jewish nation itself was indestructible. I believed that Israel would rise from the ashes and that the new state would shower blessings on its people and all the people of the world. It was bittersweet, this birth of a Jewish state. It had come too late, this nation that would have protected Jewish life, taken in Jewish refugees. But now it was there, small, surrounded by enemies, but there. It was a great victory, and my young mind leapt to the conclusion that good would always triumph over evil in the end. America had demolished Hitler. Haman, whatever name he called himself, would hang upside down like Mussolini. Only years later did I realize that history doesn't pause to admire its accomplishments and "in the end" is never the end but only a period between sentences.

Then I was enormously proud of the Haganah and the Palmach. They had saved the country from the Arab invaders. I thought the Irgun and the Stern gang were akin to the resistance fighters in the Warsaw ghetto and had forced the hand of an indifferent world. I was fiercely proud that Jews had taken up arms, and I felt in my New York City bed safer, stronger. My assimilated Jewish family had no intention of leaving their comfortable life. My mother was not a pioneer. My father was attached to his athletic club. I sent money for a tree, and then another tree, and then my interest turned to boys.

When I was eighteen years old and about to go off to Smith College, I spent the summer in New York City's Metropolitan Museum of Art walking about the galleries. I had thought that an Israeli soldier home to visit his mother might be in the museum, meet me, fall in love with me, and take me to Israel to live ever after. Anyone who doesn't understand why I didn't simply go to Israel myself doesn't understand what it meant to be a girl in 1953 who had never been out for the evening unless a boy came to the door and picked her up. I wanted to go to Israel and nurse tomatoes on a kibbutz, but I knew no one who had gone, no one who would greet me there, no one to explain how to change your world by yourself, no one to tell me how to start the motor of a tractor. Of course, I lacked courage and independence: my misfortune. On the other hand, my absence may have spared some kibbutzniks grief: due to circumstances beyond my control, I had not yet made my own bed, literally.

I became in college an existentialist. It is easier to explain what I wore than what exactly that meant to my spinning brain. My daily outfit consisted of a black leotard and sandals and a blue beret. I believed in meaninglessness. I went to Paris upon graduation and married for art's sake and eventually divorced for sanity's sake. I had not completely forgotten my love of Israel, and my heart was in my mouth in 1967. I followed the news with fear during the Yom Kippur War and in 1976 rejoiced at Entebbe. The fate of Israel was never far from my thoughts even when other matters took precedence. I found myself returning to my Jewish identity in midlife.

I then went to Israel and discovered a normal state, a state like any other, just as Herzl had wished. It was bustling with commerce and eager to sell and buy and create and wheel and deal, and was made up of good and bad and fanatics and businessmen and poets and farmers, and was alive in every corner with argument and language and clashing visions of how to do anything at all and beautiful in its flowers and its trees and its drip irrigation and its flowering fields in the Negev and its lakes in the north. It gave me, that first visit, a fierce love of every stone and every hill and every leaf. There at the Kotel, or there where the Romans had built their palaces, or there where the fighting on the road to Jerusalem had claimed Jewish lives, or there in the olive groves and in the pink light on the Jerusalem stone, there in the black-coated figures bending in prayer, there in the dark Ethiopian eyes and the sound of Russian in the streets and the stores with mezuzahs and menorahs and blue and white flags, or there in the hills where I saw the white stones and donkeys and terraced groves, and there in Tel Aviv where I saw vendors and buses and cafes and hotels and blocks and blocks of apartment houses, white buildings lining avenues where once empty land had waited for our return—there I felt not religious exhilaration but a sweet buzz of constant irrational joy. Whatever it was that Jean-Paul Sartre had said, I knew, beyond any doubt, that life had meaning and history had a place for me.

When I swam at the beach in front of the Tel Aviv Hilton, I felt that I was in my water, elbow to elbow with my people, in our genius state. It wasn't all romance. I saw development towns and poverty and the difference between those who enrolled at the Technion and those who drove trucks. I saw that the kibbutz dream had not brought about a perfect world and that men and women with the best of intentions had trouble creating a viable life of equality and mutual respect, even in the promised land. It was clear that Ashkenazim thought they were better than Sefardim and everyone had some other group to dislike. This did not surprise me, but it was disappointing nevertheless.

I saw that the people without a land had found a land, but it was not a land without a people. So the real Israel, not the romantic Israel, found its way into my life, not as a banner that should be waved, not simply as the potential refuge for my kin, but as it is, as it is now, a Jewish homeland with a terrible and potentially fatal problem of Arab enemies who would destroy it on the outside, and fundamentalists on the inside who would pull down the walls they love as they insist on biblical claims.

Israel is not a monolithic entity. Years ago at a press conference in Jerusalem, I heard Meir Kahane ranting about eventual transfer of Arabs and saw his supporters wearing guns, and one of them pushed me brutally against a wall as he forbade me to take notes. I walked in sections of Jerusalem and saw the anger in men's eyes as they turned their heads away from me, a secular female. I know that the balance between secular and traditional in Israel is a battle that lies ahead, and that theocracy may in the end triumph over democracy and that an Israel that does not respect the rights of all will never see the Messiah. I know that some Israelis are planning to retake the Dome of the Rock. I know that others have lost patience with the suicide bombers and now think all Arabs are enemies and peace is a lost and hopeless dream. Some use this argument as if it were a cover of night to build more settlements, more facts on the ground. If those who have given up all hope of peace are right, we might just as well sit down and mourn today. We know how. We already have our lamentations burnished to perfection.

Over the years in Israel, I have met with writers at the university and stood with the Women in Black as the cars swirled around the plaza. There are Israelis who believe in Oslo and those who don't. It is not anti-Semitic or anti-Israel to agree with many citizens of the state that compromise is necessary and that a two-state solution is the only way to preserve democracy and human decency. I am not so sentimental as to believe that one should be kind to those who would destroy you, but at the same time it seems to me a perversion to give in to violence and allow bloodshed to become the means to an ever disappearing end. It is not anti-Israel to feel sorrow for the Palestinians whose leaders have turned their backs on realistic solutions and sensible compromises. It is not anti-Israel to feel that domination and suppression of one group by another cannot in the end lead to a confident, democratic, flourishing land, at least not in the twenty-first century. It is not sentimental sympathy for those who would destroy us to hope that the fence will harm as few Palestinians as possible and one day will be torn down. It is reasonable to be proud of the Israeli court that voiced an opinion that supports the dignity even of those who might not support ours.

It is true that as America became a powerful nation, without any qualms we took the land from the native tribes and killed them and exiled them, leaving remnants to struggle for generations in cultural and economic disaster. For our sins, we in America simply became stronger and greater. We could wish that Israel, too, might emerge victorious from a purge of Arab populations, but America handed out smallpox blankets in an age before the camera, the instant photo that shakes the world. That was at a time when moral response could only be expressed a century or so later. Today Israel cannot, like nineteenth-century America, simply take what has not been freely given. So caring for Israel as a state means accepting some border limits, and accepting that a way will have to be found to ease the hatreds that now breed on all sides. There is no use making claims that Arab venom is more venomous than our venom. This may be true, but it doesn't move us forward. There is no hope in continually saying that we have no partner to talk to. Common sense tells us that many Palestinians also want their children to grow up in peace and go to the university and improve their material lot. Common sense tells us that there is a way out of this, no matter that the Arabs started it by invading in 1948. By now everyone has been humiliated by sufficient death. Holding on to hope for peace is essential, especially for those of us in America who believe that Israel must continue to exist and must serve as the thriving center of Jewish life for the eons to come.

How hard it must be for Israelis to live under the threat of suicide bombers, attack, biological terror, and daily fear for their children as they leave for school or return in the afternoon. It is heartbreaking to think of the families of the murdered living on with such grief. It does make one hate the Arab enemy and it does make one frightened for the country itself. I saw in Rachel's tomb the wedding dress of a girl who was slaughtered on the day before her marriage. Its white silk shimmered on the wall and it was terrible to see. The political side in Israel that is mine has been defeated in the elections over and over again. This is bitter, very bitter. Many in the Labor Party and others to their left along with their American supporters predicted this endless inflammation years ago. This is of no comfort at all. The assassination of Rabin, the worship at a shrine of Baruch Goldstein, the call for Sharon's murder, nightmarish acts all, are cancers that grow inside the state. I hope that Israel will never be overcome by these distortions of all-too-human thought.

With a little historical imagination, we can see catastrophe on the horizon. Israel loses its democratic nature and dominates an increasingly large noncitizen population. Israel, hated by the world (hate heated by the fuel of anti-Semitism), becomes overwhelmed, ostracized, taken over by the fundamentalists within; universities deteriorate, the people lose confidence and many immigrate, and finally all are exiled by an Arab victory that becomes nuclear and causes millions on both sides to die and destroys the land for a thousand years after. The only alternative to that vision is the continued fight for peace, for a return to a reasonable plan for both Israelis and Palestinians. Therefore, despair is itself our enemy.

Some question the right of an American Jew to comment on Israeli policy since our own lives are not on the line and our children do not serve in the army. But we in the Diaspora are not of another nation. We are simply living for now in a far-off place. What happens to Israel, whether it can survive the hostility of its neighbors and the enmity of the Western world, is of enormous significance to our lives. As a serious illness in a beloved spouse affects the life of the mate, so what happens to Israel affects us. Israel is the heart of the Jewish people, and if it dies, our own vulnerability will be obvious. But it is not simply self-interest that binds us to the ground of Israel. Its geography remains at the center of our imaginative life, the stage on which our best and most basic narratives were played, where our people met with catastrophe and learned how to survive without their temple or their priests, and if we can find a way toward peace we will demonstrate the human potential. We will show that it is possible to master the double terrors of zealotry and uncompromising nationalism and the horrors these always bring in their wake.

There are religious reasons that Israel must survive as a Jewish state. Those reasons echo in even secular minds and surely influence our passions on the subject. We also have practical reasons to care that the state does not implode. Israel served as the redemption after the Shoah, and we need to feel that all is not lost, not again. Israel, small but fierce, besieged but powerful, should walk proudly among the peoples of the world, and we will be made safe by its army and its air force. We know the Law of Return will if necessary sweep us into the nation, wherever we may be, whatever passports we may hold. All of us say at our Seders, "Next year in Jerusalem," and while most of us mean this metaphorically, poetically, we hear it also as a call to fold ourselves into our people's future; and Israel is the center, the source, the spring from which we come and which will ensure our collective place in the history of mankind.

Our history is long and has its sorrows. But we have always created new ideas and good laws and made progress in science and commerce, and we have always or almost always held the moral high ground against the savagery of strangers. The role Israel performs in the grand scheme of things, that so many should die for its continued existence, is one that we can only dimly perceive and hardly argue with sound logic, but we know that our people have a special purpose. We believe that our story will form a significant thread in the human tapestry as the eons pass. We do have a contribution to make, and to do that we must hold on to our identity, to our place, to our Jewish souls from generation to generation. Israel is where the story began, and we need Israel, the central pillar of our house now.

My anxious hope is that the fanatics among us, the overly aggressive, those who are deaf to any story but their own, those dancing to the beat of irrational inspiration will not pull it down about our heads, and that our fear of the Arab will not blind us to the opportunity (if the opportunity should come) to end the cycle of destruction that has caught both sides for so many years.

I have been fortunate. I have loved a good man and have children who bring me pleasure in so many ways, including grandchildren. I have had work that interested me that would only have been possible in the English language, my mother tongue. But now that I am nearing the end of my life, sometimes it occurs to me that I should have been an Israeli. I believe that my family would have been stronger if they had become a part of the state, served in the army, explored the wadis, lived with fewer American consumer pleasures, and stiffened their resolve with more purpose and sense of pride in country and people. But even as I say this, I know that the idea is romantic folly. In Israel people are beset by the same doubts, drugs, insomnia, bitterness, lovelessness, joblessness, and fear of death that exist everywhere and will continue to do so until the end of days. Achieving a measure of human contentment is not a matter of where one lives, but how. Nevertheless, that said, I will always know that a shadow life waited for me in Israel and I did not have the personal integrity to pursue it. How many American Jews of my generation share this rueful thought?

Donna Rosenthal

Donna Rosenthal is an educator and lecturer and the author of The
Israelis: Ordinary People in an Extraordinary Land. *An award-winning journalist, she was a news producer at Israel Television and a
reporter for Israel Radio, and she taught at the Hebrew University.*

I srael is an archaeological, historical, and spiritual mother lode, but
it's much more than ancient sites. To me, Israel means the Israelis.
Not the politicians or generals, or the guests you see on CNN, but
ordinary Israelis. There are only 6.8 million Israelis—about the population of the San Francisco Bay Area—all crammed into a country
about twenty times smaller than California. Although Israel, with
more international reporters per capita than any other country,
captures more media attention than China, India, and all of Africa
combined, I'm discovering how little people know about contemporary Israelis. When one of my former journalism students got a job at
CNN, he asked me, "Our viewers are confused. We have footage of
Jews who look like Arabs. Arabs who look like Jews. Black Jews.
Bearded sixteenth-century Jews in black hats. And sexy girls in tight
jeans. Who are these people?" I decided to take him beyond mislead-
ing headlines and confusing thirty-second sound bites and write *The
Israelis: Ordinary People in an Extraordinary Land*. In it, Israelis smash
stereotypes in their own words.

For five years, an intriguing mix of fervently modern and devoutly
traditional Israeli Jews, Muslims, Christians, and Druze welcomed me
into their colliding worlds. I visited their boardrooms, barracks, and
basketball courts, and met Israelis with a rich sense of fun and irrever-
ence. Some order Big Macs in the language of the Ten Command-

ments, others believe waiting in line is for sissies or light up under NO SMOKING signs. Israeli kids, the world's biggest MTV fans, took me into their bedrooms decorated with Brad Pitt posters. We surfed the Internet and chat rooms where they discuss teen heartthrobs and Hamas. I met religious Ethiopian newcomers shocked to see strange, nearly naked white Jews wearing "dental floss" bikinis on the beach, and the teenage third wife of a fifty-six-year-old Bedouin who watches *Oprah*. Then there was the exhausted religious emergency worker. He no longer can eat anything red—watermelon, tomatoes, or cherries.

I'm fascinated by the Israeli zest for life. Despite the traumas of the second intifada, Israelis fill symphony halls, dance in discos, and argue in cafes—most of which do not explode. Expert at living with a level of terrorism no other people have endured for so long, Israelis have all-night trance parties on the Red Sea, picnic at the Sea of Galilee, and turn out for Tel Aviv's Love March, which resembles carnival in Rio. And each fall, thousands of Israelis gather near the ruins of Meggido (Armageddon of the Christian Bible) to observe Rosh Hashanah, the Jewish New Year, Woodstock-style—with Bibles and bands.

In certain neighborhoods, ultra-Orthodox Jewish men on "modesty patrols" make certain women bus passengers are "properly" dressed and sitting apart from males; yet they live in the only country that drafts (non-Orthodox Jewish) women. Israeli women wear army helmets and wigs and veils. Young Israelis also wear baseball caps backward and wires that dangle from their ears, connected to Sony Walkmen or iPods. When I ask them who their heroes are, they say the entrepreneurs who have turned Israel into the world's second Silicon Valley, not veteran kibbutzniks (few Israelis pick oranges, and most agricultural workers are Thai). The Israeli digital generation is busily beating swords into stock shares, transforming the ancient land of prophets into the modern land of profits. These Israelis created the Pentium and Centrino chips and major components of the cell phone. Only the United States has more high-tech and biotech start-ups or more companies on the New York stock exchanges.

When I speak to American Jewish audiences, almost all are Ashkenazim whose families originated in Europe. But not Israeli Jews. Over half are Mizrahim whose families fled the Islamic countries of the Middle East, Central Asia, and North Africa. In 1949, there were fifty-six synagogues in Baghdad, which was one-quarter Jewish; now there are no Jews. Israeli Jews came from Afghanistan, Morocco, Lebanon, Yemen, and Egypt. The president of Israel was born in Iran, the foreign minister in Tunisia. In today's Israel, a "mixed" marriage is when couscous meets gefilte fish. No longer are these marriages rare.

I was surprised to learn that the most popular name for a new Israeli baby boy is Muhammed. About one in five Israelis is an Arab Muslim. Young Israeli Muslims learn the Koran and often know better Hebrew and more about Judaism than most Jews of the Diaspora. A Muslim Israeli filmmaker expressed the feelings of many Israeli Muslims when he said, "We're Israeli, but Jews treat us with distrust. We're Arabs, but Palestinians treat us with distrust." He went on to describe the conflicting identities of the 1.2 million Muslim Israelis. The ones I interviewed call themselves various names: Israelis, Arab Israelis, Palestinian Israelis, Palestinian citizens of Israel, Palestinians who live in Israel, Palestinians with Israeli passports, and the "stand-tall generation." The names they choose reflect their ages and/or political attitudes. In Israel's largest all-Muslim town, Um al-Fahm, a hotbed of Islamic fundamentalism, I met a housewife who rarely misses daily prayers—or an episode of *The Young and the Restless*. Then there's the secular Muslim doctor who saves lives of Jews and Arabs. He broke into tears when he told me a Hamas suicide bomber killed one of his Jewish patients.

Along with Muslims, ultra-Orthodox Jews are the fastest-growing group of Israelis. The vast majority of Israeli Jews are non-Orthodox, but over 98 percent of synagogues are either ultra-Orthodox or Orthodox. I heard many Jews complain that the Orthodox rabbinate has a monopoly on whom and how Israeli Jews can marry and if they can divorce, and where Jews can be buried. I'll never forget the story of a twenty-two-year-old sergeant killed in Lebanon. He was an Israeli citizen, but the Orthodox rabbinate refused to allow him to be buried in a Jewish military cemetery. Under Jewish law, he wasn't Jewish because his mother wasn't Jewish. In Russia, he was taunted for being a "Yid"; in Israel, he was labeled a "goy." Like him, over a million

Soviets have immigrated to Israel since the 1990s—the equivalent of the United States absorbing the population of France. They're a tremendous "brain gain": today Israel has the world's highest number of doctors, lawyers, engineers, scientists, and musicians per capita. Parts of Israel feel like Moscow on the Mediterranean, with churches, Christmas trees, and butchers selling pork. About half the newcomers aren't Jewish.

Many Christian visitors walk Jerusalem's Twelve Stations of the Cross but rarely meet Israeli Arab Christians—who I learned are the most educated and affluent of all Israelis per capita. Israel is the only country in the Middle East with a growing Christian population, but not in Nazareth, Jesus's turbulent boyhood town. Near the imposing Basilica of the Annunciation, I lunched with two Arab Christian women who publish a daring Arabic language magazine—a cross between *Cosmopolitan, People,* and *National Catholic Reporter.* It's filled with articles about pedicures, dieting, dating, polygamy—and "honor" killings. In Jerusalem, near the site where many believe Jesus was crucified, clerics from six Christian denominations run the Church of the Holy Sepulchre. But I discovered they squabble so much—sometimes violently—that for centuries, one Muslim family has kept the keys to the sacred church.

Some of the most devout Israeli Jews are Ethiopians. For centuries, they prayed in grass hut synagogues to return to the Promised Land. While reporting in Jewish villages in Ethiopia's craggy highlands for Israel Radio, I met a boy who'd never seen running water or electricity. He became my adopted brother and the first Ethiopian in the Israeli Air Force. In 1991, he helped lead a James Bond–type operation that secretly brought 22,000 Ethiopian Jews to Israel in thirty-six hours. Children who arrived on the world's largest human airlift today wear knit *kippot* (yarmulkes) and sing hip-hop in Hebrew. Many barely speak Amharic. Like good sabras, they park in front of NO PARKING signs and argue politics passionately. The photo of a stunning Ethiopian woman on the cover of *The Israelis* reminds me of her family drama. Her parents hate the guy she's dating—not because he's a WASP (a White Ashkenazi Sabra with Protexia), but because he isn't religious enough.

Amnon Rubinstein

Amnon Rubinstein is the founder of the Shinnui political party and a former member of the Knesset, the parliament of Israel. He is the author of From Herzl to Rabin: The Changing Image of Zionism.

I srael means to me different things; first, it means home. Only in Israel—and more specifically, in Tel Aviv—do I feel entirely at home. I may, and I do, enjoy other venues, but I feel unremittingly at home only in my home country.

The rub is that my home country has been in a state of war for its very existence ever since its inception, and that it is a much-maligned country among many enlightened circles. Therefore, one needs a more specific clarification with which to elucidate not only the meaning of Israel, but also why it is worth fighting for, and occasionally even dying for.

But let me introduce myself: I am a nonreligious, nonnationalist Jew. Indeed, I am Jewish in the existentialist meaning of the word. I have fought for separation of the state of Israel from the coercive Orthodox establishment, as well as for a compromise, painful though it may be, with the Palestinians. I am Jewish in the sense that I want Jewish civilization to persist, that I want the Jewish state to put an end to Jewish helplessness, and that I want to remain Jewish and wish that my descendants will continue to belong to our abused and proud tribe.

Though not religious, I express my affinity to Jewish tradition, somewhat irrationally, by adhering to a few selective practices; and I have evolved my own Jewish philosophy: all things Jewish are not foreign to me, but nothing Jewish obliges me to follow it if it clashes with universal values pertaining to human rights, tolerance, and equality. That's why I enjoy so much Yom Kippur in Israel. It is indeed a unique experience: in a nonstop country, everything suddenly grinds to a complete halt. The buzz of Tel Aviv is replaced by the silence of totally trafficless, empty streets and by the sight of families—including those who do not ordinarily frequent a synagogue—making their way "to hear Kol Nidre"; and all this is done voluntarily, without the law decreeing cessation of traffic. Yom Kippur in Israel is a collective expression of Israeli Jews' determination to remain Jewish and to continue a manifold manifestation, not necessarily Orthodox, of Jewish civilization.

But cannot one give such expression to this credo in a Jewish community outside Israel in the Diaspora? The answer is "yes, but." Yes—Jewish civilization can thrive in the Diaspora, as indeed it has done for hundreds of years; and furthermore, in some respects, Jews outside Israel are rid of the curse of Orthodox coercion that mars Jewish life in the Jewish state. The "but" stems mainly from the fact that only in Israel can you be completely, remorselessly Jewish. Only in Israel can you be rid of being self-conscious about being Jewish. Only in Israel can you be wholly Jewish without caring about what others think of your Jewishness. You do not have to be self-conscious about your behavior; or about your voice being too loud or what the salesman thinks unspokenly about your attitude; or whether you have made a good impression and "shaped up at dinner"; or whether the snub you have incurred was directed at you personally, or at you as a Jew; or whether the indifference shown toward recent anti-Semitic outbursts stems from mere decadence, or from deeper, more frightening aspects.

I do not have Jewish complexes about the gentiles, nor do I share bouts of Jewish paranoia; I do not believe that the Holocaust is repeatable, nor have I ever believed in the rumored existence of car stickers proclaiming "Burn Jews, not oil." But I am not content with that. I insist on being Jewish, and doing it my way, without feeling different. That is to me the crux of what Israel is all about.

But Israel means more than that. The Israeli experience is unique in a wider sense. And it is this uniqueness that means so much to Israeli Jews and that makes life outside Israel less meaningful to Israelis.

Israel embodies, in the most dramatic way, the Jewish paradox. Why should people who are so different from one another and who are so similar to non-Jews want to stick together and retain their identity despite all odds?

When Evelyn Waugh, the famous English author and satirist, landed in Haifa in the 1930s, he was amazed to see a plethora of different faces and races—all Jewish. He wrote to his friend, Nancy Mitford, about this discovery: that in Palestine, a Jew was anyone who decided that he is Jewish. This must be inherently true, regardless of what the Israeli "Who's a Jew?" laws state. When you take a good look at Israeli Jews, who come in all shapes and colors, you must concur with Waugh. Israeli Jews, despite the wide societal gaps that still exist, have merged into one another and have formed a distinct, recognizable society.

Thus the Jews of Israel have avoided the dilemma of Diaspora Jews: whether to remain apart or assimilate into non-Jewish society. The Jews of Israel, as any visitor can attest, have succeeded in practicing a twin assimilation: into one another and into the outside, Western, democratic world. This double assimilation goes a long way to explain Israel's strength as well as its idiosyncrasies.

Finally, there is that feature of Israel that is hardest to convey: the congested compilation of history, land, scenery, memories, and people—all compressed into a tiny land, hardly noticeable on the globe but full of significant contrasts.

Perhaps the best way to perceive this uniqueness is to travel from Tel Aviv to the Dead Sea—a drive that traverses different climate zones and straddles history in an unparalleled way.

You enter your car on a hot, steamy summer day in Tel Aviv's humid and sticky center and you make your slow way out of the bustling, nonstop tumult, amid crowded streets and seedy neighborhoods. Traffic jams, exacerbated by nerve-racking hooting, make your journey unbearable. The street peddlers and the noise level remind you that you are in the East. Finally, you have extricated yourself from the bottleneck and find yourself in the suburbs—the unwholesome remains of the housing developments of the 1950s and 1960s, when hastily constructed apartments were built to house the Jewish refugees from Europe and from the Arab states.

The road widens and you cross Mikveh-Israel, the first agricultural school established in Palestine over a hundred years ago. Here, for the first time after a millennium of absence, Jews began to till the abandoned land. Here, near the old palm trees, stood Theodore Herzl, tropical hat in hand, beseeching the helmeted, horse-riding German kaiser to support his impossible dream: a state for the Jews in Palestine. Not far from here took place one of the most brutal Arab massacres of Jews in the War of Independence—hours before Ben-Gurion announced Israel's birth on May 15, 1948.

Now the road makes its way through fertile, orchard-filled land, but occasionally you can still see remnants of pre-state Palestine: sabra fences, weather-beaten cypresses, a solitary fig tree.

You identify a big army base, Zriffin, inherited from the British, by the clusters of soldier-hitchhikers waiting for a lift on both sides of the road. From afar they look like two big blobs of khaki, but as you get closer, you discern the human mélange making up these blobs: older and younger men, girls and boys, black, brown, and white—all carrying their self-defense rifles. You can tell the reservists not only by their age, but also by their tattered overalls, resembling partisans more than regular-army soldiers.

Now you reach Ramlé. Here, for a time, was Palestine's capital, under Arab rule. Here took place decisive battles between Baldwin, crusader king of Jerusalem, and the Muslim armies entering the Holy Land from Egypt. This was, up to 1948, the Arab Palestinian town from which Jewish convoys were attacked, and from which, after its conquest by the fledgling Israeli army, thousands of Arab dwellers fled and were deported. Here, not far away, in Lydda, the last hopeless rebellion of Jews against the might of Rome took place. Its suppression signaled the end of Jewish national life in Zion. Fifteen hundred years later, the return to Zion began. For centuries, rabbis, pilgrims, and pioneers crossed this junction on their way to

Jerusalem. Nowadays, billboards proclaiming a coming rock concert cover the walls, and next to the old Ottoman tower, sun heaters bloom on the roofs of modern houses.

You see the mountains—or more correctly, the hills—of Judea. A curve in the road, and the full panorama of the valley of Ayalon opens toward you. Here, in desperate battle against the Jordanian Arab Legion, the fledgling state suffered one of its most painful defeats; here, new immigrants, survivors from the camps, who had reached British Palestine illegally only to be deported to Cyprus, died namelessly in the battle for Latrun. They died for their homeland without having lived in it. Here the Maccabeans descended at dawn from their mountain hideouts to defeat the Greek battalions seeking to suppress the rebellious Jews. Here still stands the British-built police station. Scarred by war, it now serves as a museum of the armored corps. Right next to it is "Mini-Israel," a miniature reproduction of a miniature country. Now you reach Bab-el-wad, the valley's gate, where the road begins its steep climb to Jerusalem. Here in 1948, Jewish convoys tried in vain to break through Arab strongholds in order to relieve the siege of Jewish Jerusalem. Young Israelis still sing sad songs about these battles and their dead.

Here, in the old Ottoman guest house, Christian pilgrims, tourists from all corners of the globe, had an overnight stay on the long and often hazardous trail to Jerusalem. Next to it, you see the remains of the destroyed 1948 convoys—shriveled, repainted skeletons of the siege-breaking vehicles.

Coolish, arid mountain air replaces the stickiness of the coastal plain. Everything around you reminds you of the heroic battles that finally succeeded, in 1949, in linking Jewish Jerusalem to Tel Aviv. The Palmach units, which fought here against overwhelming Arab forces, suffered unbearable casualties: every third soldier died in battle. Now there are new towns and shopping centers where desperate battles ravaged the innocent-looking hills. Now, all of a sudden, Jerusalem appears. Two structures pierce the skyline: on your left, the reputed tomb of the prophet Samuel; on your right, the Crowne-Plaza Hotel tower.

Now you reach Mount Scopus, site of the Hebrew University, established here in 1923 and isolated, by the surrounding Jordanian army, between 1949 and 1967.

Here is the Mount of Olives, and you view the familiar, but always stunning, panorama. Initially you take in the whole composite picture; then you begin to discern the details: a collection of Moslem domes and minarets, Christian spires, Jewish high-rise buildings. Two Muslim mosques dominate the scene: the gold-plated Dome of the Rock and the al-Aqsa, in whose name Arafat unleashed a suicidal wave of terror against all Israelis. Now you can notice other landmarks: the Christian Dormition Church, where Jesus is reputed to have slept before the crucifixion, and the King David Hotel, seat of the British Mandatory government, blown up by Menachem Begin's Irgun in its struggle to force the British out and establish a Jewish homeland.

Here stood legions of pilgrims, explorers, and painters admiring the site of King Solomon's temple. Here Roman commanders of the Tenth Legion watched, in A.D. 70, how the obstinate Jewish city and its holiest of sites went up in flames and its survivors went into captivity. From here, the first of the mountaintop bonfires was lit, signaling all the way to the Diaspora in Babylon the beginning of Jewish holidays. Here stood Herzl and wrote in his diary: "Great moments—a lot can be achieved in this landscape." Here Jerusalem and the desert, the Judean desert, meet.

You descend into this desert and as you go downhill, the crisp mountain air gives way to the hot yellowness of the arid landscape. Here hermits, robbers, seekers, and zealots—as well as King David—found shelter. Here Essenes, early Christians, and Jewish prophets sought salvation. Now you descend below sea level and the heat becomes unbearable. You pass the green oasis of Jericho. The conquest of Canaan by the nomadic children of Israel began here. You reach the Dead Sea. Here is total, unbroken silence. Here along the narrow canyons sloping down to the metallic lake, the Jews of Qumran meticulously wrote down their sacred scrolls, copying old scriptures, composing new ones. Not far from here the Jews of Masada fought a last, hopeless, desperate battle against the Roman Empire—thus combining political zealotry with religious fervor, risking the future existence of Jews in Judea. Here, in unreachable caves, the survivors of the Bar Kochba rebellion wrote their last will and testament. Here it all ended—tragically and recklessly—and here it began afresh.

And in this journey—an incredibly short two-and-a-half-hour journey from Tel Aviv—lies the essence of what Israel means to me.

Douglas Rushkoff

Douglas Rushkoff *is the author of nine books, which have been trans-lated into over twenty-five languages. His most recent work,* Nothing Sacred: The Truth about Judaism, *takes aim at what he sees as the problems with modern Judaism and puts forward solutions that, in his words, are "based on Judaism's core values and teachings."*

The Medium Is the Message: Getting Over Race and Nation

I love religions. I think they're great great things—as long as no one actually believes in them.

As a Jew by choice who also happens to have been born Jewish, what excited me about Judaism was its emphasis on religion as a process, rather than a thing one "believes" in. Judaism, in many ways, is less a religion than a process by which we get over religion. And I don't just mean this facetiously. No, in a world where people's inflexibly absolutist perspectives on our shared reality are colliding with disastrous results, we are in dire need of a way to negotiate an understanding of our world that is not mired in obsolete notions of race, place, and God "himself." Judaism offers just such a negotiation. At least it used to.

Let me explain.

Historically, the Israelite religion was a reaction to land-based reli-gions where different localities worshiped different gods for good for-tune. The ancient world was one where people depended on the grace of their gods for rain, sun, children, and pretty much everything. The calendar was circular, since nothing ever really changed. Each season was differentiated only by how much or how little the gods favored the people.

In such an environment, people did all sorts of things to appease their deities. They enslaved their fellows to build monuments, and even—according to some archeological evidence—sacrificed their firstborn male sons to the god Moloch. There had to be a better way.

The Torah (let's look at the narrative allegorically, for the time being) shows a people desecrating the gods of their civilization in order to build a new one. The "first" civilization, represented by all those firstborn sons who are damned, exiled, or otherwise rejected in Genesis, is replaced with a new civilization—that of Jacob, the man who wrestled with God to become Israel.

Instead of accepting the preexisting conditions of gods who either bestow or withhold their mercy, the Israelites invent a new scheme. First, they rid themselves of the Egyptian gods they worshiped. The plagues—recounted every Pesach—are not mere lists of awful things that the Israelites' God did to the Egyptians. They are each a desecration of an Egyptian god. Blood desecrates the Nile, a god. Locusts desecrate the corn god, and darkness desecrates the sun god. Finally, the slaying of the Paschal lamb is the desecration of the most important of the Egyptian gods, who was to be celebrated and worshiped in the Egyptian new year's month of April. Instead, its blood is put on the doorposts in defiance of local religion and law.

And what does this slaying and sacrifice accomplish in the story? It spares the Israelites from losing their firstborn sons. If we are to understand Torah as allegory, we see how the abandonment of these false local gods—iconoclasm—frees us from the obligation to sacrifice our firstborn male children. We are liberated from this passive and self-destructive relationship to deity.

Once iconoclasm is achieved, the Israelites learn to relate to a more abstract notion of God. No one knows who or what God is, and that's about all that can be said. The boundaries that used to exist between people—their individual races and nations beneath particular gods—no longer count. There's only one. This abstract monotheism gets God out of the way, so that people can get on with the real work of making the world a better place: social justice.

As I experience it, Judaism is the fuel for modernism. The birth of our civilization—or at least a significant strand of it.

But as I approached institutional Judaism for a confirmation of this sensibility, I got something very different. It seemed to me, as a so-called lapsed or unaffiliated Jew, that Judaism had become obsessed with intermarriage and assimilation. We were mistaking ourselves for a race, rather than a set of ideas that intentionally transcend race. Jewish "fidelity" became the reason to be Jewish, instead of the ever more attractive call to make the world a better place. Jews were to ask of themselves what they could do for Judaism, rather than what Judaism could do for the world. Our philanthropies began the counting game, treating Jews like an endangered species, and then wondering why this strategy further disenfranchised people looking for a spiritual path.

Our current disconnection with the lifeblood of this tradition stems, I fear, from three major sources: misperceptions about race, a lack of knowledge about Jewish texts, and an inability to discuss Israel.

It's not surprising that Jews think of themselves as a race. Everybody else does—especially our oppressors. The first person in Torah to mention an "Israeli people" is the pharaoh. He thinks that "Am Yisrael" won't recognize themselves as Egyptians if there's a war. The first people, historically, to talk of a Jewish race were the Inquisitors of Spain. Jews had converted to Catholicism, so a new reason needed to be invented to hate them: their blood. Finally, it was Hitler, bastardizing a bit of Carl Jung, who justified the extermination of fully assimilated German Jews by claiming Jews had a "genetic memory" for their inquisitive nature.

So the Jews, who were originally persecuted for their refusal to submit to the artificial racial and theistic boundaries of their contemporaries, now thought of themselves as a race, too.

In an effort to appear more like their contemporaries, Jews in the Reform movement made the synagogue into something like a church: the rabbis donned robes and stood on a stage, ministering the religion to their congregations. But this distanced Jews from their texts. Jews regressed to a childlike state, and transferred parental authority onto their rabbis. Judaism became more of a religion to be ministered than a negotiation with which to be engaged. The shul—literally "school"—became a "temple." Active study was replaced by monotone responsive reading.

Finally, the establishment of Israel—though perhaps a necessary way of saving Jewish bodies from continued persecution in Europe—has also affected Jews' relationship to their religion. By equating Judaism with Israel or, worse, seeing Israel as a prerequisite for the coming of the Messiah, we concretize an otherwise abstract religion in the realities of State. We turn Torah into proof of a land claim, and sacrifice its more allegorical function. We start to think of ourselves as a people "chosen" by "God" to own a particular stretch of land—rather than as the carriers of a universal truth that transcends nation, race, and even religion.

We end up with our own nation to protect and our own flag to wave, just like everybody else. In a sense, it is the ultimate form of assimilation.

The way out is Judaism, itself. Judaism is a conversation, not a doctrine. Our rules—our laws—are highly procedural in nature. They are the requirements for respectful interaction between people. Even the requirement for a minyan—ten people to open the Torah—conveys a lot about the priorities of this religion. In a sense, the Torah is just the starting place for a living interaction between real people.

Our shared narrative is an excuse for us to interact. A conversation starter. Judaism serves not just as a message, but as a medium through which people can have more profound and intimate relationships with one another. It is a process through which people can get over their racial, religious, and national misperceptions, and relate to one another on a higher level.

The conversation that is Judaism must be opened up. Nothing is too sacred in Judaism that it can't be put up for discussion—not Israel, not our peoplehood, not even God. The last thing a Jewish God would want to do is stand in the way of a good conversation.

So let's not use her that way.

Julie Salamon

Julie Salamon is the author of Rambam's Ladder: A Meditation on Generosity and Why It Is Necessary to Give, *a best-selling book that explores the Jewish approach to doing good deeds. She also writes on culture for the* New York Times.

On June 7, 1967, two news events dominated the front page of the *Portsmouth Times* in southern Ohio, where I was raised: the Six-Day War in Israel and my participation in the National Spelling Bee in Washington, D.C.

That odd juxtaposition epitomized where Israel stood in my family's life. After World War II my parents—concentration camp survivors—had immigration applications pending for entry to Israel (then still Palestine and under British rule) and to the United States. Believers in fate, and eager to escape Communist rule, they decided to go to the country that accepted them first—even though my mother's two older sisters had left Czechoslovakia for Palestine in the 1930s. This strategy eventually led my parents to a tiny rural town in Ohio, and a culture dominated by farming and Christian fundamentalism, marching bands and spelling bees.

I was born and grew up in this curious mid-American haven, our peculiar Promised Land, but always knew my family also belonged someplace else. Almost every week my mother exchanged letters with her sisters, hers typed on thin blue airmail stationery, now made obsolete by e-mail. Israel was ever present at our dinner table. *Exodus*, the popular novel by Leon Uris, was my mother's idea of suitable children's literature.

America was our home; Israel was critical to our identity. It was the place where Jews were strong, in charge of their own destiny, not the Other, not oddities or victims. Our feelings about Israel were not religious, in orthodox terms, but primal and deeply personal. If nothing else, this tiny plot of ground seemed like minimal payback for the destruction of European Jewry.

That was the general idea. The specific relationship was far more complex than this starkly biblical vision.

Visiting Israel the first time at age six and then several more times into adulthood, I confronted a Jewish landscape that seemed glamorous, cosmopolitan, alluring, and frightening. As a devoutly nice Midwestern Jewish American, I was unnerved by the cultish Hasidim with their side curls and suspicious (I thought) glances—unnerved and attracted by the aggressive sexuality of the sabras on the beach, with their Olympian bodies barely concealed.

Every day I found another seductive, intimidating glimpse into the world I would have inhabited if the bureaucratic odds had played out differently. I regarded this alter ego with pride and a kind of wistfulness. Why weren't we brave enough to live there?

But most compelling to me was the chance to uncover more information about our family's past. Over several subsequent visits to Israel—including a summer-long stay in high school, in 1970—the personal dominated. Though I diligently toured and marveled at the history, underwent bouts of spirituality, and agonized over politics, I always returned to the private obsession of my family's fragmented narrative. Aunt Rozsi and her husband, my Uncle Frantisek Winkelsberg, were prime sources.

They had come to Palestine on their honeymoon in 1934, returned to Czechoslovakia after a business setback, and then returned in 1939. After all those years, they retained their Middle European ways. My aunt always dressed well; early photos show her wearing mock Chanel and high heels in the sand. My uncle, an engineer and accomplished cellist, also cooked. No falafel in the Winkelsberg home, but Czech and Hungarian delicacies, elegant sauces, and rich, buttery cakes. In their home I happily examined photo albums containing pictures of my mother when she was a girl, wearing bikinis and a Girl Scout uniform.

Later, I took the man I would marry to Israel, a kind of litmus test. Though he was Jewish, his family had been in the United States for several generations. For him, Israel was an abstraction, another Hebrew school lesson. He fell in love with the country; my relatives fell in love with him. A year later Aunt Rozsi and Uncle Franz danced at our wedding in Manhattan.

It was never that simple, of course. Even in my early diaries, which tended to be travelogues, I scribbled wistful hopes for peace, interspersed like public service announcements. I was generally dismissive of Arabs as either dangerous or picturesque. Yet I also remember the excitement I felt at attending the wedding of an Arab friend of one of my kibbutznik cousins. Despite everything—my family's history, the hatred for Israel that dominated the Arab world, I was determined to feel hopeful.

In 1981 my Aunt Rozsi and Uncle Franz were killed in a car crash while visiting their daughter and her family, who had moved to the United States. I visited Israel a year later and found centuries of tragedy eclipsed by my personal loss. My urge to return vanished. Yet even after years of absence, the bleak political situation, my opposition to various Israeli governments, and my entrenchment in the American Diaspora, the attachment remains. I am here, but part of me is there. It's time to take my children for a visit.

Stephen Schwartz

Stephen Schwartz is executive director of the Center for Islamic Plural-
ism, a member of the board of the Daniel Dajani Albanian Catholic
Institute, and an adjunct fellow at the Western Policy Center. He is the
author of The Two Faces of Islam: Saudi Fundamentalism and Its
Role in Terrorism *and* Sarajevo Rose: A Balkan Jewish Notebook.

Israel, to me, is the historic, sacred land of the Jews. Neither more nor less. It was given to the descendants of Abraham, Isaac, and Jacob by the Almighty as their eternal home.

In making this affirmation, I offer no opinions on the legal or political system that exists within Israel. It is up to the Israelis themselves to define their constitutional and other arrangements. That said, I support the maintenance of halacha as the fundamental law of the land, and of aid to the religious educational institutions and norms supported by the pious. Were I Jewish, I would most likely be *Haredi*.

This latter statement requires some explanation, as does my entire position on this matter. My father was Jewish, but my mother was Christian, and I was brought up without a religious education of any kind. My parents were of the radical left and extremely antireligious. I was never once taken to a religious service or inside a synagogue or church, except during tourist trips to the Spanish missions in California and the American Southwest, where I lived most of my life. I am now fifty-six, and left California at age fifty.

Nevertheless, I have been a believer in the Almighty since childhood. And I have contributed extensively to Jewish periodicals, especially the *Forward* but also including the *Jerusalem Post*.

In religion, I am an American Sufi. I became a formal adherent of the Islamic way of spirituality while working as a journalist and writing on the Balkan wars of the 1990s. From 1999 to 2001 I resided in Sarajevo, Bosnia-Herzegovina. I am closely associated with Balkan Sufi traditions. But I have also worked extensively on interfaith projects with Catholics, and while in the Balkans did extensive research on, and contributed to efforts at preservation of, Jewish sacred sites: synagogues and cemeteries that had often been neglected since the Holocaust.

I argue for the legitimacy of Israel on the basis of Qur'an, the Islamic Holy Book. While Jerusalem is never mentioned as a holy city in Qur'an, therein we read the following unequivocal statements:

"Children of Israel, remember the blessing I have bestowed upon you, and that I [the Almighty] have exalted you above the nations" (Chapter 2, verse 47).

"Bear in mind the words of Moses to his people. He said, 'Remember, my people, the favor which [the Almighty] has bestowed upon you. He has raised up prophets among you, made you kings, and given you that which He has given no other nation. Enter, my people, the holy land which [the Almighty] has given you. Do not turn back, or you shall be ruined'" (Chapter 5, verse 21).

"[The Almighty] said to the Israelites, 'Dwell in this land. When the promise of the hereafter comes to be fulfilled, we shall assemble you all together'" (Chapter 17, verse 104).

I believe it is necessary for traditional Muslims around the world to free their global community, or *ummah*, from the grip of radicalism, fostered above all by Saudi Arabia and its cult of Wahhabism, and to restore pluralism and moderation among Islamic believers. The prophet Muhammad himself said, "I want my *ummah* to be a community of moderation."

A necessary step toward cleansing Islam of the taint of extremism and terrorism, a purification that is inevitable, is represented by recognition of the state of Israel as the home of the Jews, and advocacy of true, lasting peace between the Jewish, Muslim, and Christian faithful, all of whom worship the same Creator, and all of whom are children of Abraham.

Bernie Siegel

Bernie Siegel, M.D., is the author of the best-selling Love, Medicine, and Miracles, *among other books. A pediatric and general surgeon, Dr. Siegel has written, lectured, and taught extensively about the mind-body connection in healing.*

What Israel means to me relates to its role as a demonstration of the problems of mankind. As the Bible tells us, everything that God created God saw as *tov*, but when God created man that statement is not made. A rabbi shared that the word *tov* should not be translated as "good" since the word *good* has lost its meaning. The word *tov* should be interpreted as complete. So to me Israel represents man's incompleteness and inability to see that we are all one family.

A Hasidic tale shares the story of two men fighting over a treasure, which can be land or jewels, which each feels belongs to the other. There is no way to get them to accept what they feel belongs to the other person. A wise elder asks one, "Do you have a daughter?" and the other, "Do you have a son?" When the men answer yes the elder responds, "Then have them get married and let this be their wedding present."

As a surgeon I know we are all the same color inside and share a common origin. And as a surgeon I have learned what I can accomplish with a knife to cure or kill, and that when we lose our identity as children of God and become fundamentalists, our words, words, words become swordswordswords that can kill or cure the problems of the world, depending upon how we use them.

What I hope Israel will come to mean is an example of what

mankind can do when we decide to love and use our free will to show love and compassion for one another no matter the race, religion, nationality, or sex of the individual.

Please understand, God created an imperfect world because a perfect world is a magic trick and not creation. We are here to live and learn. So let us not fight and kill the uneducated but help them to see that we are all here to complete the process of creation by creating a Garden of Eden here on earth of our own making. When we do this, love will have meaning because to love will be a choice we make, and Israel will become a symbol of why God created us, our completeness and what we are capable of.

We need to love our neighbors as ourselves and not define our neighbors by how externally alike we are. When we serve the true Lord and listen to His voice and use our bodies to display the word and be cocreators, the world will know peace and Israel will mean that mankind is capable of love and completeness.

When all the money spent on weapons and security is spent on loving one another, the world will know peace. When the power of love overcomes the love of power, the world will know peace. And as Golda Meir said, "When we love our children more than we hate our enemies the world will know peace."

May we live to see the day when Israel means we are all blinded by love to one another's faults. God teaches us justice and mercy, and so let Israel show us how to live the message. As God's message in the High Holy Days service tells us, "Everything you remember I forget and everything you forget I remember." Let us live the message, stop making excuses, forgive, and heal. Amen.

Ned L. Siegel

Ned L. Siegel is the founder and chairman of the Siegel Group and the vice chairman of the Republican Jewish Coalition, which is active in Israeli issues.

Honor your father and your mother, so that you may live long in the land the Lord your God is giving you" (Exodus 20:12).

America is my father. Israel is my mother. As a Jew born and raised in America, I have the distinct privilege of honoring them both.

America is my homeland. Israel is my spiritual home.

I didn't always know this. It has been a maturing process for me, much as the state of Israel herself has matured as a nation on the international stage since my first visit in 1972.

The state of Israel declared her independence as a nation in May 1948. I declared my independence as a man in Israel in May 1973—some twenty-five years later.

My first visit to Israel was with my parents and brothers in December 1972. It was a family trip, and I was twenty-one years old. We were there for approximately two weeks, and I knew from the moment I had arrived that I was someplace special. However, it wasn't until I returned by myself in the summer of 1973 that I knew Israel would leave such a lasting impression on my life.

Many Jewish families assimilated to life in America and my family was no different. I grew up in a secular home, while my parents had grown up in much more observant homes. My grandfather read the Torah from the *bima* every Shabbat. I thought it was an honor just to be able to read the Torah with my grandfather on the day of my bar mitzvah. I didn't like Hebrew school and, to be quite frank, Hebrew school didn't like me. I was loud, active, and a little too much for the rabbi and teachers to handle, so there was an emotional and psychological disconnect at a young age between my Judaism and me. But visiting Israel that first time made me long for something that had been missing and made me want to reconnect with the spiritual side of my Judaism. Israel brought that back to me in a very real way.

And so following the visit with my family, I made arrangements to return at the end of the school year—the trip when I would claim my independence as a man separate from my parents, discover the importance of my Jewish heritage and the role it would play in my life, and begin to understand the struggle for security that still exists to this day.

When I arrived in Israel that summer of 1973, everyone was preparing for the Yom Kippur War. There was a certain feeling that we were all part of something bigger than ourselves. It was frightening and magical all at the same time. While many of us from America knew that we were cloaked in the security of returning stateside before the war would actually begin, we also felt an obligation to our new Israeli brothers and sisters to gain a better understanding of what life in Israel meant. And so we did.

Life in Israel means to fight, to struggle, to stand on the front lines in order to preserve the land promised to generation after generation for over five thousand years. Life in Israel means working to turn a desert into an economically viable Promised Land. Life in Israel means fighting for acceptance by the world and knowing that in order for the world to accept Israel, it will have to accept Judaism. And if it accepts Judaism, is it accepting it as a religion or as a heritage? This question is difficult to answer not only for the world, but also for those of us within the Jewish community. Is our Judaism more of a religion or a heritage?

I came to understand that in Israel, much like in America, Judaism may be lived as a heritage, a religion, or both. There are many secular Jews in Israel. There are many religious Jews in Israel. I have always seen myself as a secular Jew with a deep spiritual connection to the land of Israel rather than to the religion. I am passionate about the state of Israel. And no matter where one falls on this debate, one thing is certain—Israel is the focus of our Judaism. It is the homeland of our heritage and of our faith.

When I left after that summer of 1973, I didn't return to Israel until many years later, when I had the chance to accompany Florida governor Jeb Bush on a trade mission. I had seen the Israel of my youth go from an agrarian society to a prosperous high-tech show-place for biomedical research and the telecom industry, and become a leader in the antiterrorism and security business.

Since that visit with the governor, I now go to Israel four to six times a year. I have invested money in the state of Israel through business ventures. I have invested time in the people of Israel through friendships that have come to mean so much to me. I have invested my soul in my spiritual home of Israel by going to the Wall and praying to my God and knowing my prayers are heard. I have invested my life in Israel because it is where I wish to be buried when I die.

While I am not an Israeli, I am a Jew. I am both an American Jew and a Jewish American. Only in America could a Jew also be the chairman of the board of an Episcopal school. At Saint Andrew's School in Boca Raton, Florida, our theme for the year is "Growing a Sacred Place" because we want the Saint Andrew's experience to be a special and sacred experience and place that students will carry with them for life. We want it to be a place, a time, and a knowledge that no matter how far they go in life, Saint Andrew's will always hold a "sacred place" in their lives. Israel is my sacred place.

Ultimately, Israel means so much to me because it represents everything that I believe I am as a person—Jewish, prosperous beyond expectations, deeply rooted in family, a fighter when provoked, a peacemaker at heart, a believer that democracy will always prevail however badly outflanked, young enough to still learn and old enough to know to learn from those who have gone before me, and still growing into what I will ultimately become.

R. Emmett Tyrrell Jr.

R. Emmett Tyrrell Jr. is the founder and editor in chief of the American Spectator.

On the Road in Israel

"Travel narrows the mind," my old friend Malcolm Muggeridge used
to cackle. Of course, he was making fun of an old fatuity. Actually, I
have found that travel deepens some of the mind's perceptions. Certainly, travel in Israel has deepened my perceptions of Israel as a nation
deserving America's support and of the Jews as a people responsible
for the creation of many of the values key to Western Civilization, the
civilization that has done most through the centuries to establish the
dignity and liberty of man. I do give the ancient Greeks equal billing.

In the late 1970s I traveled through Israel for the first time on a
tour with American journalists. Midge Decter, my editor at the time
and an American Jew, warned me that the Israelis were not a very
humorous people. Possibly she thought I was anticipating a land full of
George S. Kaufmans and Groucho Marxes. Expect extreme seriousness,
she advised. Well, the Israelis I met were satisfactorily humorous—at
least as compared with my bus full of gloomy, nitpicking, egotistical
American journalists. Yet Israel's condition was, indeed, serious. The
Israelis were and are surrounded by a sea of hostile people.

Returning home, I wrote an article for *Harper's* magazine that has
stood the test of time, though it roused hackles then and still does. My
thesis then was that Israel had no alternative but to stand fast and resist
its enemies. The Arabs have proven through history, I wrote, to be "a

warlike people wedded to a warlike religion." In the 1970s they shot innocent women and children as a matter of military practice. Today they use suicide bombers. Negotiating with such people is not very promising. Diplomacy should always be at the ready, but the Israel Defense Forces will always be the most reliable instrument for peace. Much depends on its strength and prudence.

As a consequence of that article, I found myself immortalized by the late Edward Said, who declared me in one of his books, which I believe became a college textbook, a "typical American Know-Nothing." Inasmuch as the Know-Nothings embraced, among other bigotries, anti-Semitism, Said had provided me with yet another reason for not taking him seriously.

My initial perceptions of Israel were not solely the consequence of travel. I had read extensively on the Arabs, the Jews, and Islam, as I continue to do. Today books on the Great Game, the nineteenth-century competition for Central Asia between the British and the Russians, strike me as particularly useful in understanding America's present role in Iraq and Afghanistan and our relationship to Israel. But travel continues to take me to Israel and to sharpen my insights.

In December 2002, I banged around the country pretty much on my own, carrying Paul Johnson's *History of the Jews* as my reading material. As I walked across the old stones of Jerusalem and was taken through such ancient excavations as Ir David, borne in on me was an aspect of Johnson's book I had not theretofore thought about. The historical documents he cites in his history of the Jews of the ancient world are, in large part, the books of the Old Testament. That is to say, Israel was founded on what many believe is the inspired word of God. Now, many of the regimes of the ancient world claimed to be based on religious documents. There was no division between church and state in those times. Yet only one nation remains from that period, basing its origin on the same documents, scripture. And only one people from that period has remained pretty much intact through all the subsequent years of suffering and peril, the Jews.

The values that they have brought down through the ages are values that make Western Civilization distinct and the best hope of mankind as against the cruelty and nihilism that we still see haunting our headlines. There is no confusion between right and wrong and no confusion about an individual's duty to neighbors in the original scriptures of Judaism that now, in modern times, might even edify many atheists and agnostics. Israel holds to those values. On the other hand, the values exhibited by Israel's enemies are not so wholesome. I feel a debt to Israel.

There are other reasons I feel America must stand by Israel. Starting with President Harry Truman, we gave our word to stand by Israel. Every president since has vowed to defend its existence. In return, Israel has come to be a bulwark of democracy and stability in a stupefyingly tyrannical and unstable region. Not only is Israel an inspiring nation, it is a useful ally. Finally, as Bob Bartley, the longtime editor of the *Wall Street Journal*, pointed out shortly before his death, Israel has shown America and the world how a proper mixture of resolve and boldness can beat back a vast preponderance of hostile forces.

Thus for historical, philosophical, and practical political reasons, I stand with the Israelis. What is more, there is the matter of those hoary scriptures. When I visited Ir David, a young Israeli archaeologist—I believe he grew up in Detroit—took me down an ancient passageway deep into the earth to a set of old stone steps just above what was now an underground waterway. He told me that when archaeologists discovered this spot near King David's home, they were perplexed. What might it have been? Then he read to me a passage from the Book of Kings. Scripture was coming to the aid of archaeology. We were standing where King David had Solomon anointed three thousand years ago. Skeptic that I am, my conclusion is that Israel is a special nation with an ally even more powerful than Washington.

Milton Viorst

Milton Viorst *has reported on the Middle East for decades, his articles appearing in the* New Yorker, Foreign Affairs, *the* New York Review of Books, *and many other publications. He is the author of over a dozen books, including* What Shall I Do with This People?: Jews and the Fractious Politics of Judaism *and* In the Shadow of the Prophet: The Struggle for the Soul of Islam.

Before taking on the subject of what Israel means to me, I think it's important that I examine what being Jewish means to me, since the two are inextricably linked. Being Jewish, as I see it, doesn't mean attending the synagogue regularly. It doesn't mean keeping a kosher house, or observing the dietary laws in restaurants. It doesn't mean wearing a yarmulke at work during the day. I respect those who feel otherwise about their Jewishness, but I don't do any of those things. Yet I have no doubt that I am Jewish, because that's what my heart tells me.

Forgive me if my explanation sounds a shade mystical; be assured that I am not a mystic. On the contrary, as a product of my century, I am a rational man, and I recognize that mystical feelings are the opposite of rational. Yet within the mind of even a rational man, there can be room for some mystical sentiments and, from wherever they derive, I don't doubt that they are real. It is such feelings, I believe, that explain the bonds that humans have with loved ones—that a man or a woman has with a spouse and family, or that Jews have with other Jews or with Israel as a nation. However irrational, these mystical feelings largely account, I believe, for the survival of the Jews as an identifiable community since we were driven from our homeland nearly two millennia ago.

Ordinary language, drawing on objective evidence, probably can't do justice to defining mystical feelings. It's likely that only metaphor will do. And the most persuasive metaphor that I know comes from the pen of Ahad Ha'am, the pseudonym of an esteemed Ukrainian-born thinker who lived at the turn of the last century. He wrote:

Why are we Jews? How strange the very question! Ask the fire why it burns! Ask the tree why it grows! . . . So, too, the Jew may be asked why he is a Jew. It is not within our capacity not to be what we are. It is within us; it is one of our laws of nature. It has an existence and a constancy of its own, like a mother's love for her children, like a man's love of his homeland! It rises and bursts forth from the depth of our souls, it is part of our hearts! . . . It would be easier to uproot a star from the heavens than to uproot from our hearts that certain mysterious something, beyond the grasp of reason, that makes us Jews.

And so, in addressing the question of what Israel means to me, I answer as a Jew who lives within the boundaries that Ahad Ha'am sketches. The thought never occurred to me *not* to have a bond with Israel. Since childhood, Israel has been as much a part of me as are the leaves on the trees. My attachment did not come from the rational sector of my mind, where decisions are reached by the ebb and flow of intellectual calculation. It came from the mystical part, which produces loyalties on its own initiative, without many questions, with little or no intellectual output. I know that some Jews do not share this reflex; Israel is not important to them. But in my own case, if I am asked why it is important to me, my response is like Ahad Ha'am's: "How strange the very question!"

So why, one might go on to ask, am I so often critical of Israel, or at least of the political course it has adopted in recent years? My response again: "How strange the very question!" Just as my bond to my children carries with it the obligation to counsel them on their best interests, so I see it as my duty to convey my criticism when I believe that Israel is making mistakes, especially grievous mistakes, placing its survival in jeopardy. Being adults, my children have no obligation to follow my advice; similarly Israel, as a sovereign state, makes its own decisions. But, as a Jew, I nonetheless have a duty to say that I am deeply troubled by the course Israel has taken since its intoxicating military victory in 1967. If occasionally it has tried to make course corrections, in each case it turned away from them toward rising danger. If I did not argue for what I believe would be a safer course, I would be abdicating my responsibility to my people.

Let me explain further. I said earlier that, as a rational man, I am a product of my century. The century in which I spent most of my life was not very good for the Jews. Though anti-Semitism had imperiled Jews for thousands of years, it rose to an unprecedented pitch in my century, until it finally placed every Jewish life in jeopardy. Zionism, the movement to establish a Jewish state, was a rational response to the danger. It envisaged creating a refuge in our ancestral homeland for the Jewish people. I emphasize "refuge" because the concept is secular, without religious overtones, and many Orthodox Jews dismissed it as not Jewish enough. But in fact, theology had little to offer. In 1948, a Jewish state emerged, rooted in Jewish history and geography, but it was also the practical, sensible answer to a palpable threat to the Jews.

Let's be realistic, however. Though Israel was created by Jews for Jews, as a people we are rather few in number. Only with the support of dozens of nations, great and small, did Israel become a reality. Never without its enemies, it owes not just its establishment but its survival to the friends who look with sympathy on the Zionist vision of a homeland in which Jews can find refuge when they need it. The notion which some Jews entertain that Israel, proudly sovereign, can now forgo these friends is pure bravado.

Having taken its place among the world's sovereign states, Israel has been remarkable in meeting the obligations of refuge. After World War II, it welcomed the survivors of Holocaust Europe. In the ensuing decades, it embraced nearly all the Jews living within the borders of Islam. In more recent decades, it offered a home to the beleaguered Jews of the Soviet Union, Ethiopia, and Argentina. Moreover, it accepted in its mandate the provision to make available to Jews, wherever they lived, the opportunity to join other Jews in a Jewish society. From around the world, many Jews have chosen to do so.

It is an achievement that Israel has grown from a few hundred thousand at independence to more than five million Jews today. Absorbing these newcomers was not easy, and the work of the state was not perfect, but it provided the conditions for most migrants to build a decent life. Meanwhile, it erected the framework for a renaissance of Jewish creativity in literature and the arts, science and technology, commerce and even sports. Though the newcomers proved to be socially contentious as well as culturally heterogeneous, Israel managed to forge them into a real nation. As a body, we Jews have every interest in not putting that achievement at risk.

But the exhilaration of the Six-Day War produced a turnabout in the vision of refuge. Many Israelis—indeed, many Jews worldwide, including in America—replaced the earlier image of the Jewish state with something far grander. A major segment suddenly burned with the dreams of an ardent nationalism. Another segment adopted Israel as a religious calling. Hubris replaced restraint, and territory became an object of Jewish worship.

The transformation was rife with irony. Judaic orthodoxy had traditionally barred the Jews' return to the Holy Land except as part of the process of redemption, led by the Messiah. After decades of hostility to Jewish statehood, much of orthodoxy adopted the tenet that Israel's military victory was a divine command that Jews must possess every acre of the Holy Land. This vision coincided with the long-standing aspiration of a Zionist minority which held that the Jews' destiny was to rule over all of biblical Israel. After 1967, a territorial ideology superseded the practicality that had been present at Israel's founding. No longer was it enough to have a state that provided refuge in two-thirds of historic Palestine. Now much of the Jewish people insisted on having it all.

As a Jew who exulted in the outcome of the Six-Day War, I was not quick to perceive the vulnerabilities created by the newborn doctrine. I understood the risks of living next to hostile neighbors. These risks were obvious. But after many visits to the Middle East, I reluctantly reached the conclusion that Israel's unwillingness to relinquish land exposed it to far wider risks. The most dramatic example was the Yom Kippur War of 1973, the direct consequence of Israel's rejection of Egypt's overtures to trade the Sinai for a peace agreement; three thousand young soldiers died before the Israeli government accepted the deal. In 1987, I published a book titled *Sands of Sorrow*, in which I registered my concerns.

"The difficulty," I wrote, "lies not with the neighbors alone. The lesson of the years since 1967 is that Israel must achieve a sense of proportion that is appropriate to its place in the Middle East. As Harkabi (an Israeli historian and retired general) suggests, Israel's security requires the acquisition by Israelis of the recognition of its limitations as a nation. After that, Israel can join its neighbors in search of a stability with which they can all live. That is Israel's best hope for a secure future."

Since I wrote those lines nearly twenty years ago, the conflict in which Israel is embroiled has grown increasingly deadly. The practical notion of refuge has been forced into a corner by the aggressive ideology of territorial enlargement. The result has been disastrous. Instead of the shelter that Zionism envisaged, Israel has become a place where Jewish life is in daily peril. It is ironic that no country is more dangerous for Jews than Israel. It is indisputable that a Jewish state does not require all the land between the Jordan River and the Mediterranean Sea to provide security and prosperity to six million Jews. The loss of countless lives has told us that Israel is less in need of land than of a harmonious relationship with its neighbors and friends.

So, to return to the initial question, what does Israel mean to me? Yitzhak Rabin, whom a religious zealot murdered for seeking to trade land for peace, noted that in our day no people can live alone, least of all the Jews. Rabin proposed a return to the concept of a Jewish state where Jews can realize themselves freely as individuals and as a society, where the well-being of a people has a higher priority than the possession of acreage. Instead, in opting for what I see as territorial over human values, Israel has alienated not just its neighbors but much of international society. Israel to me means being a respected member of the community of nations. Without that respect, I believe it may not survive, and it matters to me that Israel be there if ever my progeny need it for a refuge.

Rabbi Noah Weinberg

Rabbi Noah Weinberg is the dean and founder of Aish HaTorah International and the recipient of the Treasured of Jerusalem Award. He is the author of several books and educational materials on the practice of Judaism, including ABCs of Judaism and What the Angel Taught You: Seven Keys to Life Fulfillment.

TO RESTORE OUR DESTINY

For two thousand years, the Jewish people were wanderers. Exiled to every corner of the world, we were oppressed, beaten, and gassed. Yet in the process, something incredible happened: we defined the moral makeup of humanity. Values that the civilized world takes for granted—monotheism, love your neighbor, peace on earth, justice for all, universal education, all men are created equal, dignity of the individual, the sanctity of life—are all from the Torah. This is an enormous impact and we accomplished it under the most adverse conditions.

When the state of Israel was proclaimed, the world watched with great anticipation. Everyone knew that the Jewish state had the potential to change the course of human history. If the Jews had such an awesome impact despite the great difficulties of exile, then reunited in their ancient homeland, they would surely transform the world!

Indeed, the first fifty-plus years have been miraculous. The first generations of immigrants knew this was a historic opportunity and they were infused with a tremendous sense of idealism. Jews were willing to dig ditches in return for peanuts! The result? We've succeeded in building the finest hospitals, roads, schools, and industry—even amid hardship, terror, and wars.

But along the way something got lost. We got so caught up in building an infrastructure that in the process we forgot what we really came home to accomplish. The Jewish dream of a utopian society somehow became muddled in a hodgepodge of Western ideals. For example:

The Jewish system of jurisprudence is the basis for every great legal system in the world. The Romans derived their judicial system from the Torah, as did those who wrote the Magna Carta and the U.S. Constitution. So you would think that in setting up the modern Israeli legal system, we would look directly to the Torah for guidance, framework, and principles. But instead—we adopted Ottoman law!

The result is devastating. Not only do we have a less effective legal system, but on a much deeper level, we have communicated a message to Israeli youth that the "Jewish way" is arcane, to be replaced by a more progressive "non-Jewish" approach.

This is just one example of how, in the process of building a state, we have too often made tactical decisions that have devalued fundamental principles of Jewish life.

In Israel today, much of the idealism is gone because we're not really sure we want to be Jewish. What respect is there for the words of the prophets, the Talmudic sages, or the rabbinic giants of today? One million Israelis are now living in the Diaspora, because if life is all about McDonald's and MTV, then frankly there's a better version available in Los Angeles.

So what do we do now?

We have to recapture our destiny, our sense of purpose. And that begins with a recognition that *tikkun olam* is the basis of what drives the Jewish people to greatness. It all started back with Abraham. His business was to go out and teach what it means to be "created in the image of God." He demonstrated how a human being has to take responsibility for the world. Abraham's undertaking was the first progressive, liberal movement the world had ever seen. And look how it succeeded!

In looking back at the first three thousand years of Jewish history, we don't recall the names of great entertainers or athletes or corporate executives. Rather, we recall the great teachers of the Jewish message: Moses, King David, Maimonides, the Vilna Gaon. That is the essential Jewish legacy. The message was ingrained in our souls at Mount Sinai and it is the single defining characteristic of our people. To ignore it is to commit national spiritual suicide.

Whether you say our message is God-given or whether you say it was written by man is a separate issue. The fact is that humanity is thirsting for Jewish ideals.

And the world needs that message now more than ever. Consider, for example, the institution of marriage. In Western society, the divorce rate is over 50 percent. That's a crisis of immense proportion. Family structure is crumbling, and dysfunction in relationships is at an all-time high. It seems that nobody has a clue how to stem the tide.

Not long ago, "morality" was a dirty word. It implied an imposition of conscience and a curtailment of personal freedom. But today, the leaders of Western society realize that morality is the key to human survival. The great civilizations of Greece and Rome fell due to moral decay. That's why the great universities—Columbia, Harvard, Hebrew University—are investing hundreds of millions of dollars to develop curricula for teaching "morality" to primary and high school students. They're scouring centuries of philosophical texts to try to find an effective approach.

Yet the answer is right before our eyes! Our very own Torah has time-tested tools for personal and communal success: how to give and how to receive, when to be strict and when to be compassionate, individual rights versus communal responsibility, how to show appreciation and respect, when to lead and when to follow, balancing family and career, the boundaries of modesty in actions and in dress, how to listen and converse effectively . . .

Torah methodology is universal—for Jews and non-Jews, religious and secular, Israel and the Diaspora, left and right. The Torah is alive and relevant for today. And for the Jewish people, the ability to effectively communicate this message is our single most important undertaking.

Now as our globe becomes increasingly complex, we need solid moral direction to navigate the maze. The world needs to know . . . and we need to teach.

. . .

In its essence, morality is a "Jewish" movement. It's the natural self-expression of a Jew. I've seen it time and time again: when a Jew is turned on to Torah, it sparks enthusiasm, energy, and unbridled passion. Imagine an entire nation of Jews empowered to carry forth the Jewish message!

The Jewish people are experts in this field and we have an obligation to share, not by yelling, not by condemning, but by offering rational, relevant wisdom for living. This is precisely Isaiah's vision of "Light Unto the Nations."

With technology, the world is far more reachable today than ever before. The message can go forth rapidly and effectively. As Isaiah said, "*Ki Mitzion Tetzei Torah*"—"For out of Zion shall come Torah, and the word of God from Jerusalem." How beautiful this would be.

Ultimately, the solution may come in some far different form. But one thing is certain: we must do something to turn this ship around. The state of Israel is hemorrhaging in terms of enthusiasm, idealism, and commitment. Our challenge is to instill in each Jew a pride in our heritage, a confidence in our future, and an appreciation of how precious his involvement with the Jewish people can be for himself, his children, grandchildren, and all humanity.

Otherwise, the state of Israel will have squandered its single greatest opportunity: to fulfill our destiny of *tikkun olam.*

We've succeeded before. And with the Almighty's help, we can do it again.

Rabbi Sherwin Wine

Rabbi Sherwin Wine is the founder and former president of the Society for Humanistic Judaism and the author of several books on the secular humanistic Jewish movement.

The greatest achievement of the Jewish people in modern times was the creation of the Jewish state. Of all the movements in Jewish life that mobilized the passions of the Jews, Zionism was among the most powerful. Nothing in the world of religion could arouse the intensity of feeling that Jewish nationalism did. Zionism was the liberation movement of the Jewish nation and Israel was its child. Even today the safety and security of the Jewish state is an obsession—not only in Israel, but especially in the Diaspora. In the lives of most contemporary Jews today, the Torah takes a second place to their sometimes unexplainable bond to this small political entity.

When Zionism began, it was deemed by most Jews to be hopeless. Most of the leaders of Orthodoxy condemned it as blasphemous chutzpah, a pathetic human attempt to replace the divine mission of the coming Messiah. Reform Jews overwhelmingly denounced it as a threat to the safety of Jews in emancipated lands because it maintained that Jews were a nation, not a religious denomination. Yiddishist nationalists found fault with it because Eastern Europe, with its masses of Yiddish-speaking Jews, was the only reasonable setting for the revival of the Jewish people. Radical socialists believed that it was necessary because the international solidarity of the working class had superseded nationalism as the correct passion of progressive humanity. As for the land, it was in the hands of the Turks. As for the money, the Jewish money aristocracy was disinterested. As for the immigrants, most of the potential settlers were already on their way to America.

But surprising events undermined the hopelessness. America closed the doors to immigrants in 1924. The Great Depression brought Adolf Hitler to power in Germany and violent anti-Semitism into the very heart of German nationalism. The success of the Nazi armies and the fury of the Holocaust eliminated most of the Yiddish-speaking Jews of Eastern Europe. And the idealism of the socialist revolution turned into the anti-Semitic repression of Stalinist Russia. By the end of the Second World War, most Reform Jews embraced Zionism. By the conclusion of the Six-Day War, most Orthodox Jews were enthusiastic supporters of the Jewish state. In between, most Jewish socialists had become bourgeois liberals who loved Israel.

For many Jews, the significance of the state of Israel arises out of its role as a place of refuge for the persecuted Jews of the world. For other Jews, its importance lies in the fact that the Jews, for the first time in two thousand years, can enjoy the experience of being a majority in their own land. For still others, its meaning is captured by the new image of the Jew that Israel presented to the world—strong, "cool," and adept at military power. For Herzl, the purpose of the Jewish state was to "normalize" the Jewish people and to cure anti-Semitism with the return of the Jews to Israel and the disappearance of the Diaspora. This expectation that Jew-hatred would end with the establishment of a Jewish state was naive. The Zionist enterprise provoked the Arab and Muslim world into a furious anti-Semitism. Israel is now surrounded on three sides by a wall of Jew-hatred.

Today Israel remains the center of a great controversy. Almost all of the Arab and Muslim world deny the legitimacy of the Jewish state. The grievance against Israel serves as the major mobilizing component of Arab nationalism. Millions of people press against its borders in a determination to eliminate it. With the exception of America, Israel has no powerful allies. Isolation and war have become its major political anxieties. Security, not peace, has become its obsessive concern. The Herzl vision has proved faulty. The Diaspora is safer than the homeland.

Realistically, Israel as a refuge from hostility is a fantasy. In the minds of Jewish and Christian fundamentalists, this insecurity may be viewed as an asset, the beginning of the final war in which God will redeem both the Jews and humanity. But for rational people, there must be some other compelling reason to give meaning to Israel's existence.

For me, the importance of Israel does not lie in safety from persecution. It lies in the fact that the Jews are a historic nation, entitled, like the Arabs, to a national existence. Throughout its history, the Jewish nation has featured a wide variety of ideologies, ranging from polytheism and monotheism to atheistic socialism. Throughout its history, the Jewish nation has embraced diverse political systems, including authoritarian theocracy and liberal democracy. None of these options defines the Jew because Jewish identity is neither religious nor philosophic. It is ethnic and national.

Israel is significant because it has provided the Jewish nation with territory, language, and independence. Religious denominations need none of these three assets. Nations do—even small nations. The greatest achievement of the state of Israel is not the defense of its borders. It is the revival of the Hebrew language and the creation of a new vital culture that flows from it. Yiddish culture in the Ashkenazic Diaspora was vital, but it was compromised by having neither territory nor independence. In the end, the Holocaust and the assimilative power of both America and Russia destroyed it. Zionism has provided the only successful attempt in two thousand years to secure the survival and dignity of Jewish national existence. It has provided a dynamic center of Jewish culture for the Diaspora, and it has strengthened Jewish self-esteem throughout the world by allowing Jews to proclaim what they have always been—an international family united by ethnicity and history.

Whether the Jews should have chosen another territory in the South Pacific or in central Africa is purely academic. The only destination that could have motivated millions of Jews to choose an independent national existence was the historic Jewish homeland. Over five million Jews now reside in Israel. Most of them were born there. They are as native as the Anglo-Saxons in North America.

Whether the future of a globalist planet will render all nationalism obsolete is also purely academic. When that messianic millennium arrives, Jews will be happy together with all other nations to surrender their national identity. But until that time, they insist on equal rights.

Whether the Jewish state is able to survive against the overwhelming hostility of the Muslim world is still problematic. Whether it can negotiate with the Arabs a border that works is equally problematic. But none of these difficulties diminishes the significance of Zionism to the cause of Jewish self-awareness and Jewish dignity.

Rabbi Eric Yoffie

Rabbi Eric H. Yoffie is the president of the Union for Reform Judaism, the congregational arm of the Reform Jewish Movement in North America.

Whenever I am in Israel, for whatever reason, what do I find myself thinking?

That the Jewish state is cause for rejoicing and thanksgiving.

That Israel has done what it was intended to do—it has restored the Jewish people to national sovereignty after two thousand years, and has returned us to history.

That there must be an Israel, because without Israel we are a truncated, incomplete people; and that our love for Israel is eternal, proclaimed in unconditional and unmistakable tones.

That Jewish life cannot be sustained without Israel at its core; that the Torah that spells out for us a way of life and a religious destiny also binds us to a land; and that any distancing from Israel for any reason whatsoever is Jewishly unacceptable; it flies in the face of everything we know about Jewish commitment, Jewish thought, Jewish history.

And this too: that Zionism means controlling your destiny; it means achieving power, mastering the gun, and sometimes, tragically, misusing power. But this is far better than being powerless in a dangerous world, because in the absence of power, all other Jewish values can be turned to dust.

And this above all: that now and always we are lovers of Zion in the old-fashioned way, in sickness and in health, for better or for worse, until death do us part.

But like every lover of Zion, I also worry incessantly about Israel, with my fears focused on the two major crises that Israel is facing: the political one and the religious one.

The political crisis may or may not be open to resolution. The best solution by far would be a negotiated peace between Israel and the Palestinians that would create a Palestinian state and provide security and stability for both sides. Even the mainstream Israeli right has come to understand that the occupation must be ended and that Israel must withdraw from much of the territory it now holds. However, we simply do not know if there exists a Palestinian leadership that is prepared, in establishing its own state, to abandon the so-called right of return and to accept unequivocally the existence of a Jewish state as its neighbor. We hope and pray that there is, but if not, Israel will be obligated to take unilateral measures to minimize terror and protect its citizens. Such steps will include carrying out a substantial but partial withdrawal from the territories, building a security fence, and responding with appropriate military force to attacks on its civilian centers. This process has already begun, of course; Israel has withdrawn from the Gaza Strip and from four West Bank settlements, and will soon complete the security fence.

Unilateral steps by Israel create a situation that is far from ideal; they will not bring peace and will not put a complete end to terror, but such action might be the best that Israel can do until there is a return to sanity on the Palestinian side. If Israel is forced to move in this direction because the Palestinians are not ready for serious negotiations, it becomes my task and the task of all American Jews to urge the U.S. government to be supportive of Israel's course of action.

But Israel's religious crisis is no less important than the political one. Given that there will probably be no quick solution to the political conflict with the Palestinians, a prolonged period of instability, uncertainty, and terror is likely. Therefore, Israel will need a strong army and political backing from the United States to assure her security. But security alone will not be enough. Security—which will be imperfect under the best of circumstances—is not a philosophy of life and is not an answer to the question, Why should I be here? To answer this question, Israelis will need to have a firm belief in the justice of their cause, a love for the Jewish people, an identification with Jewish religious tradition, and an understanding of what it is that ties the Jewish people to the land of Israel. Absent these beliefs, Israelis will ultimately be drawn—as many, tragically, already have been—to Melbourne or Toronto, or to other places that offer more security than Jerusalem or Tel Aviv can ever offer.

But if the commitment of Israelis to the justice of their cause is to be strengthened, this will only happen through the revival of Judaism in the Jewish state. In the absence of Judaism, Israel's cause makes no sense whatever. The concept of the Jews being one people with a deep connection to the land of Israel is a religious idea—and not an ethnic or political one. It is an idea rooted in covenant, in Torah, and in religious commitment and faith. If we are to talk about the rightness of Israel's cause and the totality and interdependence of the Jewish people, then we must revive the religious ideas on which these notions are based.

Just as the absence of Jewish values and religious commitment threatens Jewish survival and continuity everywhere in the world, so too is it a threat in the Jewish state. Without such commitment, it will be difficult if not impossible to mobilize the Jewish people on behalf of Israel's cause. There are those who say that Israel "is a state of all its citizens," and this is true in the limited sense that all Israeli citizens must be guaranteed full civil and human rights. But it is equally true that Israel was created to promote the religion, civilization, and culture of the Jewish people and its dominant Jewish majority, and doing so now is as important as it was at any time in Israel's history.

And how will Israel do this? By striving to develop and encourage a form of Judaism appropriate to its well-educated citizenry—a Judaism that is modern, moderate, and pluralistic. This has not happened to date, because two related phenomena have emerged in Israel that are largely unknown in the Diaspora: first, an assertive Jewish secularism that attempts to construct a model of Jewish identity built entirely on culture, language, and ethnicity; and second, a deep and profound hostility to all forms of Jewish religious practice and belief.

These phenomena have developed for many reasons, the first being the influence of socialist Zionism that prided itself on its secular principles. Even more important, however, has been the disastrous impact of Israel's monopolistic religious establishment on the religious attitudes of average Israelis. Throughout the Diaspora, Jews voluntarily take upon themselves both the joys and burdens of Jewish religious practice. But in Israel, and in Israel alone, religion is imposed upon them from without. In Israel alone, there is a preferred, government-sponsored version of Judaism. In Israel alone, representatives of the various religious streams are not permitted to compete openly in the free marketplace of ideas. The result is that Torah, the spiritual legacy of the entire Jewish people, has been turned into an instrument of religious coercion.

The establishment of the state of Israel offered the most significant opportunity in modern Jewish history to win support and sympathy for Jewish religion and to disseminate the message of Torah. The decision to place religious affairs in the hands of a politicized religious establishment represented an extraordinary failure of imagination and of intellect. By choosing coercion over persuasion, the religious authorities sent the message that Jewish religion is primarily about the exercise of force. Under the circumstances, it is hardly a surprise that for a substantial number of Israelis, Jewish religion is anathema—a club used by corrupt religious parties to diminish the autonomy and freedom of everyone else. It is hardly a surprise that so many Israelis reject religion in all forms and attempt to construct a Jewish identity that relies entirely on elements of secular culture.

But this effort will not succeed, no matter how sincere the advocates of Jewish secularism and no matter how understandable their response. Surely it is absurd to assume that the Jews of Israel are the first Jews in all of Jewish history who have no need for God, prayer, and the sacredness of Jewish texts and traditions. If we know anything at all from Jewish history it is this: Torah-free Jewish civilizations have no staying power, and it is silly to think that the state of Israel will constitute an exception to this rule.

In the state of Israel, the radical proponents of de-Judaization—whether they be post-Zionist historians, well-meaning secularists, angry Orthodox haters, or assimilated yuppies—are likely to fail, and if by some miracle they were to succeed, their "victory" would mean the end of Israel as a Jewish state. Jewish religion, in some appropriate form, is the key to Jewish survival and continuity.

And how is Jewish religion to be strengthened and Jewish identity to be revived in Israel? By separating religion and state, ending religious coercion and monopoly, creating a single school system for religious and secular children, and permitting the creative religious genius of the Jewish people to thrive in a religious "free market." If this is not done, the possibility exists that Israelis might separate themselves from the covenantal promise to become a holy nation. But if this is done, soon and in our day, Israel will foster among its Jewish citizens a vibrant Jewish identity that will strengthen her security and boost her morale. At the same time, Israel will offer a meaningful Jewish response to the boredom and emptiness of modern life, will become a classroom to world Jewry in matters of Jewish identity, and will join in partnership with Diaspora Jews in strengthening Jewish religious civilization wherever Jews are found.

Fred S. Zeidman

Fred S. Zeidman is the chairman of the United States Holocaust Memorial Museum.

My relationship with Israel began in what may seem an unlikely place: Wharton, Texas. It was my hometown, a rural community sixty miles south of Houston with a Jewish population of about a hundred. It was where my family settled more than a century ago.

There was one synagogue, yet there was lots of organized community activity. Looking back now, I can see that it took real determination and a deep commitment to your beliefs to keep tradition. That had a great impact on me. My upbringing was as close to Orthodox as my parents could manage. With there being only one synagogue, those who were Orthodox and those who were Reform worked together and compromised to be sure they had a functioning, harmonious community. Kosher meat came to us packed in ice by bus from San Antonio. People would drive thirty to forty miles to bring their children to the Jewish school. Parents had to drive hundreds of miles with their kids to bring them together with other Jewish children.

As I look back, I see how the sacrifices and efforts people made in order to practice Judaism were enormous, and their dedication is something I have never forgotten.

When I was growing up, Israel was an important part of my life. My parents were active Zionists. Since they owned the clothing store in Wharton, they would pack up all of the out-of-season clothing twice a year into crates and send them off to Israel. I asked my father, why are we doing this? He replied that if Israel is going to survive, we must all do our part. In the early 1950s, when Israel was still so new, they contributed all they could and set an example for me that has lasted and deepened throughout my life.

Jewish education was a passion of my mother's and she would regularly send contributions to many Israeli charities and Jewish ones in the United States. Growing up around those strong beliefs and dedication, attending Jewish summer camps, regularly studying with our synagogue's rabbi, who was a Holocaust survivor—I was profoundly affected by all of this. It imbued me with an enormous sense of responsibility for Judaism, for continuity, and for Israel.

While the direction I chose for my career has been business, I have also followed a path of Jewish activism and quickly found how involvement in the political system can be a highly effective way of working on Israel's behalf. As my political work deepened in Texas, I did whatever I could to educate our political leaders about matters relating to Israel and to Jews, and to sensitize them to the issues at stake.

Over the years in Houston, I followed my parents' example of getting involved in the community—for Israel and for America. I became more active in the pro-Israel community.

My work and political efforts culminated in 2001 with my appointment by President George W. Bush as chairman of the United States Holocaust Memorial Museum. It was an opportunity I wanted above all others. Through this role, my dedication to Holocaust remembrance and to Israel has been given its greatest opportunity to flourish and be transformed into tangible, positive results.

In my life, Holocaust remembrance and commitment to Israel are bound together. They are about exertion and action. They are about fighting against complacency. They are about energetically working for the future of Israel and assuring the integrity and truth of the Jewish history at its foundation. And they are about what we have endured, and what we have created and must work to protect.

Anyone who has read the headlines of the past few years knows that in some places of the world, the lessons of the Holocaust and the security of Israel can be too easily overlooked or taken for granted. They cannot. There hasn't been such widespread anti-Semitism in the world since 1945. And in Europe, the very place of the Holocaust, synagogues have been torched, Jews beaten, cemeteries vandalized. There is no justification for it. We may prefer to believe that the world is now enlightened, holds Israel in deep respect, has learned the lessons contained in the Holocaust, has matured. Clearly, these are dangerous assumptions to make. We must be more vigilant, protective, and active than ever before. Israel and the United States are strong democracies— in partnership with each other. Through my political work, I have tried to strengthen the bonds of this enduring friendship. I believe that the stronger these ties grow, the more secure the world will become.

As the head of an institution whose central mission is about the dangerous potential of hatred, I have become involved in the renewed emphasis on educating the public about the evils of unchecked anti-Semitism that has been undertaken by the museum both in the United States and internationally. These initiatives are a part of the action and dedication to history that underlies my passion for Israel and all it stands for.

The Holocaust represents all that was brutally taken from us. The rebirth of Jewish life that followed, especially with Israel's creation, represents the humanity and faith survivors miraculously reclaimed from its ashes. And for their involvement in the creation of Israel and of this museum, I am honored to be working with them. Words cannot express my admiration for how Holocaust survivors have entrusted us with their history, demonstrated mankind's capacity to create life and renewal in the wake of overwhelming loss, and stirred us with their dignity so future generations might live in a more humane world. Being in their presence, especially as they are so rapidly diminishing in number, and simultaneously playing an active role to strengthen the life of Israel, are blessings I will cherish forever.

Stephen Zunes

Stephen Zunes is a professor of politics and the chair of the Peace and
Justice Studies Program at the University of San Francisco. He is the
author of Tinderbox: U.S. Middle East Policy and the Roots of
Terrorism.

DEFENDING ISRAEL WHILE CHALLENGING ITS POLICIES

Some may find it surprising that I, as someone who has emerged in
recent years as one of the American academic community's more
prominent critics of Israeli policies and U.S support for the Israeli
government, would want to contribute to a volume filled with testi-
monies on behalf of the modern state of Israel.

Yet just as my critical view of U.S. foreign policy makes me no less
an American patriot, I firmly believe that one can be critical of Israeli
policies and be no less a Zionist. Indeed, it is that very right to dissent
from government policies without fear of persecution—a right that is
unusual in that part of the world—that is one of Israel's greatest
strengths.

Just as the establishment of a national homeland for the Jews and
Israel's development of exemplary democratic and social institutions
for its Jewish citizens is to be celebrated and defended, the displace-
ment and the ongoing repression of the Palestinians by the Israeli
government must be challenged. There is no contradiction between
these two positions.

The recognition of modern Israel by the international community
has constituted a kind of restorative justice, where every Jew knows—
for the first time in nearly two thousand years—that there is a place to
go where he or she will be welcome.

The noted Argentine Jewish dissident Jacobo Timerman was an outspoken opponent of Israel's 1982 invasion of Lebanon while living in Israel. He noted, however, that despite having to endure enormous hostility for his position, at least he was no longer being persecuted as a Jew, and for that he was grateful and proud to be considered a Zionist.

Given the pervasive insecurity Jews have suffered as a minority in virtually every society, I see Zionism as a kind of global affirmative action. Just as the slogan "I'll be post-feminist in the post-patriarchy" attests to the ongoing need for women's liberation, I'll be anti-Zionist when there is no more anti-Semitism.

Like any nationalist movement, Zionism consists of elements ranging from the reactionary to the progressive, and while the former have tended to dominate the Zionist movement in recent decades, this does not mean that Zionism is in itself illegitimate. Few nations have been created without displacing and subjugating large numbers of indigenous inhabitants, including Britain, France, Japan, and most of today's "Arab" states. Most of the English-speaking world—the United States, Canada, Australia, and New Zealand—was far more brutal and thorough than the Israelis in coming to dominance over the territories they now occupy. This does not make Israeli repression any more legitimate, its ongoing policies more acceptable, or the need for a viable Palestinian state less urgent; but the tendency of many to use Israeli policies as the rationale for failing to recognize the legitimacy of Zionism is no more justifiable or practical than using the crimes of terrorists as the rationale for failing to recognize the legitimacy of Palestinian nationalism.

In seeking a nationalistic solution to anti-Jewish persecution, Zionism was inherently exclusionary of non-Jews in some important areas. Virtually every movement by an oppressed group to reclaim its identity from the majority culture, however, has found a need for a degree of separatism, as demonstrated in Western societies by black nationalists, radical feminists, and others. While such efforts have often brought charges of "reverse discrimination" and "reactionary segregation," they are generally seen by the left to have merit to the degree that they allow for autonomous development in a space relatively free from the oppressive institutions of the broader society. Unfortunately, much of the left fails to give Zionism the same degree of understanding.

Given the growth of such a nationalist movement, and its culmination into a nation-state on already inhabited land, the support of outside forces became necessary from the outset. The British prime minister Lloyd George had wanted to annex Turkish-occupied Palestine since the beginning of World War I, and an alliance with the Zionists seemed a good pretext, so the British government opened up negotiations that led to the Balfour Declaration. European diplomatic support led to the 1947 United Nations partition that legitimized the creation of Israel, while virtually every African and Asian state in the General Assembly voted in opposition. The massive influx of Czech arms to Jewish forces played a crucial role militarily in the subsequent war. British and French arms flowed to Israel during the country's first two decades, and when these European colonial powers sought to block the nationalization of the Suez Canal Company and overthrow Egyptian leader Gamal Abdel Nasser, they called on the Israelis to seize Egypt's Sinai Peninsula as the pretext for their own invasion.

Subsequent to the 1967 war, the United States has played the role of Israel's primary backer. Israel has successfully prevented victories by radical nationalist movements in Lebanon and Jordan, as well as in Palestine. They have kept nationalist governments such as Syria in check. Their air force is predominant throughout the region. Israel's frequent wars have provided battlefield testing for U.S. arms. They have been a conduit for U.S. arms to regimes and movements too unpopular in the United States for openly granting direct military assistance, such as apartheid South Africa, Iran's mullahs, Guatemala's juntas, and the Nicaraguan Contras. Israeli military advisers have assisted pro-Western governments and insurgencies. The Mossad and the CIA have cooperated in intelligence gathering and covert operations. The military-industrial complexes of the two countries are tightly intertwined, especially as the United States increases its military presence in the Middle East.

As a result, the United States has been encouraging some of the more chauvinistic and militaristic elements in the Israeli government, and undermining the last vestiges of Labor Zionism's commitment to socialism, nonalignment, and cooperation with the third world. As

Israel's military strength and repression of the Palestinians has increased, so has U.S. aid, contradicting the widespread belief that U.S. military assistance is used to defend a threatened and democratic Israel.

One of the more unsettling aspects of U.S. policy is how closely it corresponds with historic anti-Semitism. Throughout Europe in past centuries, the ruling class of a given country would, in return for granting limited religious and cultural autonomy, set up certain individuals in the Jewish community as its visible agents, such as tax collectors and money lenders. When the population would threaten to rise up against the ruling class, the rulers could then blame the Jews, sending the wrath of an exploited people against convenient scapegoats, resulting in the pogroms and other notorious waves of repression that have taken place throughout the Jewish Diaspora.

The idea behind Zionism was to break this cycle through the creation of a Jewish nation-state, where Jews would no longer be dependent on the ruling class of a given country. The tragic irony is that, as a result of Israel's inability or unwillingness to make peace with its Arab neighbors, the creation of Israel has perpetuated this cycle on a global scale, with Israel being used by Western imperialist powers to maintain their interests in the Middle East. Therefore, one finds autocratic Arab governments and other third world regimes blaming "Zionism" for their problems rather than the broader exploitative global economic system and their own elites, who benefit from and help perpetuate such a system.

It is important to note that most of the actions of the Israeli government that have brought the most criticism from the world community would not have been possible without the acquiescence and, at times, encouragement, of the United States and other Western powers. This has placed the Zionist movement in a serious dilemma. Through a combination of historical circumstances—however legitimate the goals of national self-determination for the Jewish people may have been—it has inexorably been linked in the eyes of most of the world as a neocolonial movement backed by Western imperialism, and a major obstacle to the national liberation of Arab peoples.

Anti-Semitism has been called "a fool's socialism," in that it often takes on populist rhetoric in support of economic justice against capitalist exploitation, yet focuses on an exaggerated view of the power and influence of a tiny subsegment of the ruling class.

In a similar way, anti-Zionism may be a "fool's anti-imperialism," where Jewish nationalism itself is erroneously seen as the problem rather than the alliance its leaders have made with exploitative Western interests.

This is why it is often hard to distinguish between legitimate and illegitimate criticism of Israel. For example, when I overhear a conversation about oppressive policies of the Israeli government, I am initially concerned—even if I agree with everything they are saying—about what is actually motivating their opposition. Is it part of a universal commitment for human rights, international law, self-determination, and justice? Or are Israeli policies being used simply as an excuse to bash the world's only Jewish state?

If there were only one black state in the world, certainly most African Americans and many white liberals would be similarly sensitive to criticism of that government's policies, even if justified, out of a fear that the criticism was an excuse for racism.

This has led many Jews and other supporters of Israel sensitive to the pervasiveness of anti-Semitism to be reluctant to publicly criticize Israeli policies for fear it would encourage such bigotry. The effect, however, could be just the opposite. If those of us who do care about Israel's security do not criticize Israeli actions for the right reasons, it will be left to the Pat Buchanans and David Dukes to criticize Israel for the wrong reasons. And the more universal Jewish support is for what are clearly illegal and unethical policies by the Israeli government, the more Jews as a whole will be blamed.

I oppose the occupation and colonization of Palestinian lands on the West Bank not just for what it is doing to the Palestinians, but for what it is doing to Israel. Because I care deeply about Israel, I have long advocated a policy of "tough love": unconditional support for Israel's right to exist in peace and security, but ending support for a policy of occupation and colonization that not only brings great suffering to the Palestinians, but ultimately harms Israel as well.

Unfortunately, certain right-wing Jewish leaders, both in Israel and in the United States, have played on the fears, mistrust, and insecurities of their constituencies and have given the false impression that increasing militarism and repression by the state of Israel enhances the security of Jews everywhere. The reality, of course, is just the opposite: Israeli security and Palestinian rights are not mutually exclusive but mutually dependent. Israel will be far more secure with a viable demilitarized Palestinian state on its borders than in trying to suppress nearly two million people in the occupied territories engaged in open rebellion.

Only when Israel sees its future with the third world—made necessary by its geography, its Semitic language and culture, its sizable Sephardic population, and the Jews' history of exploitation by the Europeans—will Israel end its isolation and find the real security that it has been missing. Many of the so-called supporters of Israel in American politics are actually making Israel vulnerable by tying its future to an imperial agenda, and blocking its more natural alliance with the world's Afro-Asian majority. The combination of Israeli technology, Palestinian industriousness and entrepreneurship, and Arabian oil wealth could result in an economic, political, and social transformation of the Middle East that would be highly beneficial to the region's inhabitants, but not necessarily to certain elites in the United States and other Western nations who profit enormously from the continued divisions between these Semitic peoples. Meanwhile, Israeli leaders and their counterparts in many American Zionist organizations are repeating the historic error of trading short-term benefits for their people at the risk of long-term security.

This cycle can only be broken when current American policy is effectively challenged, and Israelis and Palestinians will finally be able to settle their differences among themselves and join together in liberating the Middle East from both Western imperialism and their own short-sighted rulers.